Friend to Friend · Families A

MW01169698

¿Amazing English!™

AN INTEGRATED ESL CURRICULUM

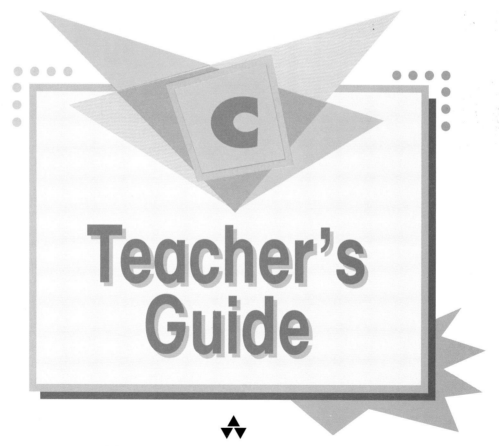

C

Teacher's
Guide

▲

Addison-Wesley Publishing Company

ISBN 0-201-85375-2
3 4 5 6 7 8 9 10-WC-99 98 97 96

Across the USA · Adventures in Space · Around the World · Adventures in Space · Across the USA · Animals Wild and Tame · Changing Seasons · Friend to Friend · Families

Amazing English!

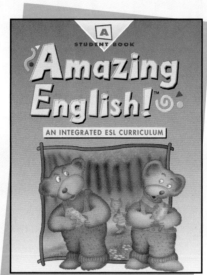

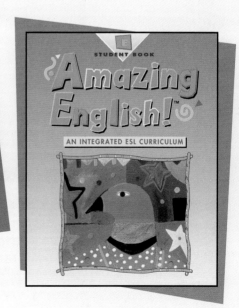

Amazing is **THEMATIC,** promoting *Meaningful Communication* across all levels of language proficiency • **Amazing** is **CHILD-CENTERED** and designed for **JOYFUL LEARNING** in a nurturing environment • **Amazing** is **LITERATURE-BASED,** moving learners from **EMERGENT LITERACY** to a *LOVE OF READING* that is the cornerstone of school success • **Amazing** is **CONTENT-BASED,** focused on the **LEARNING STRATEGIES** and language competence needed to compete in school and in a literate culture • **Amazing** is **MULTICULTURAL,** with objectives and perspectives that reflect and *VALIDATE DIVERSITY* • **Amazing** is eclectic, reflecting proven language acquisition and reading principles...the *Natural Approach*...**TPR** ...**whole language**...PHONICS... **collaborative learning...**

AND ABOVE ALL, Amazing IS FUN!

UNIFYING THEMES and SUPERB CONTENT tie the integrated curriculum together.

THEMES

		K	A	B	C	D	E
1	WORKING AND PLAYING TOGETHER	Making Friends at School	School Days	New Friends	Friend to Friend	We Work and Play	Friends Near and Far
2	FAMILY & COMMUNITY	Home and Family	At Home	Family Times	Families Around the World	Family Memories	Me and My World
3	IMAGINE THAT!	All About Me	More About Me	Yes, I Can!	Adventures in Space	That's Amazing!	Would You Believe?
4	PEOPLE & PLACES	Exploring the Neighborhood	Everybody Eats!	Busy Days	Across the U.S.A	Stories Across Time	Special People, Special Places
5	ANIMALS	Animal Tales	Farm and Forest	Around the Pond	Animals Wild and Tame	Animals Around Us	Animal Life
6	NATURE & DISCOVERY	The World Outside	Outside My Window	Nature Walk	Changing Seasons	Outdoor Adventures	Planet Earth

(Please refer to the AMAZING HOW-TO HANDBOOK for a complete discussion of language acquisition, application of general principles, methods and strategies, setting up an integrated curriculum, and more.)

"...The activities were meaningful and easy to do—factors that I really appreciate as a busy teacher!"

TAMARA CONSTAN,
Spanish Bilingual Program Teacher

"...appropriate, enjoyable, and encouraging for my students and myself."

KAREN RUDGIS, ESL Pull Out Teacher

Teachers are already applauding AMAZING.

"...interesting, meaningful and fun lessons that I would certainly like to repeat."

DENISE B. HENDRIGAN,
Korean Bilingual Program Teacher

"...delightful. I liked it and the children liked it; they take to it naturally."

MYRIAM IONESCU, ESL Pull Out Teacher

"The children were very motivated and attentive. The activities were very easy to set up and not time-consuming."

LINDA O'BRIEN, ESL Teacher

"Wonderful! I could see the program's solid roots in current research... I like the way this program integrates literacy skills... there is a terrific emphasis on a variety of effective learning strategies and approaches."

AUDREY A. FONG,
Staff Developer/Teacher Trainer

v

THE Early Childhood
LEVELS K • A • B

TLLC
Integrated Kindergarten level

- MULTICULTURAL AND ACTIVITY-CENTERED
- HOME-SCHOOL CONNECTIONS
- LITERATURE-BASED FOR EARLY LITERACY

STUDENT BOOKS

- THEMATIC UNITS
- CROSS-CURRICULAR CONTENT
- MULTICULTURAL LITERATURE AND MUSIC

LANGUAGE ACTIVITIES BIG BOOKS

- BASIC SOCIAL AND SCHOOL SURVIVAL SKILLS
- COMMUNICATION ACROSS THEMES
- FLUENCY, ACCURACY, PERSONAL EXPRESSION

LITERATURE BIG BOOKS AND LITTLE BOOKS

- EARLY LITERACY AND SHARED READING
- MULTICULTURAL, TRADITIONAL AND SING-ALONG TALES
- SIX DAZZLING, THEMATIC TITLES PER LEVEL

LEVEL

K

It's Pink, I Think (Sing-along story)

I Love My Family (Sing-along story)

The Little Red Hen (Traditional)

Early in the Morning (Sing-along story)

Run, Run, Run (Kutenai Indian tale)

The Farmer and the Beet (Traditional)

LEVEL

A

On the First Day of School (Sing-along story)

Goldilocks and the Three Bears (Traditional)

I Like You (Sing-along story)

The Gingerbread Man (Traditional)

The Very Fine Rooster (Cuban folktale)

The Most Wonderful One in the World (Mexican folktale)

LEVEL

B

The Rabbit and the Turnip (Chinese folktale)

How the Moon Got In the Sky (African folktale)

The Little Ant (Mexican folktale)

Only a Nickel (Eastern Europe folktale)

Why the Coquí Sings (Puerto Rican folktale)

Here It's Winter (Sing-along story)

- **ASSESSMENT PACKAGES**
- **PLACEMENT TEST**

TEACHER'S GUIDES
- EASY PLANNING
- EASY TEACHING
- PROFESSIONAL GROWTH

SKILLS JOURNALS
- EARLY LITERACY
- OPEN-ENDED WRITING ACTIVITIES
- HOME-SCHOOL CONNECTIONS

AUDIO CASSETTES
- RICH, COMPLETE LISTENING EXPERIENCES
- STORIES, POEMS, CHANTS, MUSIC
- HOLISTIC ASSESSMENT

THE AMAZING HOW-TO HANDBOOK
- LANGUAGE ACQUISITION PRINCIPLES, METHODS, STRATEGIES
- LITERACY DEVELOPMENT
- MULTICULTURAL CLASSROOMS
- CONTENT-BASED INSTRUCTION

VIDEO LIBRARIES
- STUNNING VIDEOS OF TRADE BOOK FAVORITES
- SIX THEMATIC TITLES PER LEVEL (ENGLISH OR SPANISH)
- PROCESS WRITING, SHARED READING, CONTENT CONNECTIONS

LEVEL K

Changes, Changes (Pat Hutchins)

Noisy Nora (Rosemary Wells)

Musical Max (Robert Kraus)

The Snowy Day (Ezra Jack Keats)

Rosie's Walk (Pat Hutchins)

Here Comes the Cat
(Vladimir Vagin & Frank Asch)

LEVEL A

Monty (James Stevenson)

Joey Runs Away (Jack Kent)

Whistle for Willie (Ezra Jack Keats)

The Little Red Hen (Paul Galdone)

Why Mosquitos Buzz in People's Ears
(Verna Aardema)

Charlie Needs a Cloak
(Tomie de Paola)

LEVEL B

The Day Jimmy's Boa Ate
the Wash
 (Trinka Hakes Noble)

Picnic (Emily Arnold McCully)

Amazing Grace (Mary Hoffman)

Doctor De Soto (William Steig)

The Caterpillar and the Polliwog
(Jack Kent)

Hot Hippo (Mwenye Hadithi)

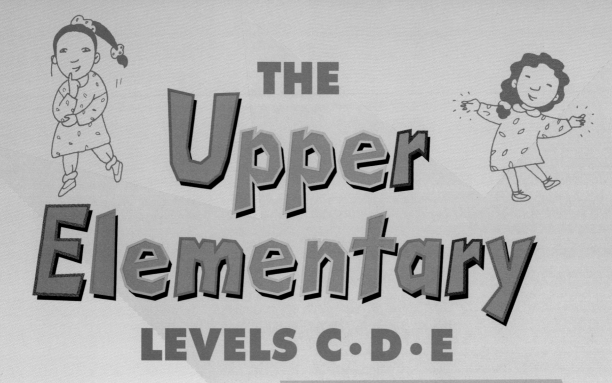

THE Upper Elementary
LEVELS C·D·E

STUDENT BOOKS
- THEMATIC UNITS
- CROSS-CURRICULAR CONTENT
- MULTICULTURAL LITERATURE AND MUSIC

SKILLS JOURNALS
- FOCUSED LANGUAGE PRACTICE
- OPEN-ENDED WRITING ACTIVITIES
- HOME-SCHOOL CONNECTIONS

AUDIO CASSETTES
- RICH, COMPLETE LISTENING EXPERIENCES
- STORIES, POEMS, CHANTS, MUSIC
- HOLISTIC ASSESSMENT

TEACHER'S GUIDES
- EASY PLANNING
- EASY TEACHING
- PROFESSIONAL GROWTH

BOOKBYTES CD ROM

- MOTIVATIONAL TOOL FOR READING AND RESPONDING TO LITERATURE
- GUIDED WRITING OF BOOK REVIEWS, REPORTS, AND RELATED ACTIVITIES FOR EACH AMAZING THEME
- BOOKLISTS COVERING A WIDE VARIETY OF FICTION AND NON-FICTION TO ENCOURAGE READING FOR PLEASURE AND INFORMATION

WORD ATTACK SOFTWARE

- FIVE INTERACTIVE VOCABULARY GAMES
- BEGINNER TO CHALLENGE LEVELS OF PLAY
- USER-FRIENDLY DATA BASE FOR CUSTOMIZED GAMES

PROCESS WRITING PORTFOLIO

- STEP-BY-STEP GUIDED WRITING IN STUDENT PORTFOLIO AND TEACHER HANDBOOK
- HUNDREDS OF IDEAS AND TOPICS TIED TO EACH AMAZING THEME
- PERFECT COMPANION TO BOOKBYTES

- **ASSESSMENT PACKAGES**
- **PLACEMENT TEST**

THE AMAZING HOW-TO HANDBOOK

- LANGUAGE ACQUISITION PRINCIPLES, METHODS, STRATEGIES
- LITERACY DEVELOPMENT
- MULTICULTURAL CLASSROOMS
- CONTENT-BASED INSTRUCTION

THE NEWCOMER KIT

- THE BASICS FOR BEGINNERS AGED 8-10
- BUDDY STUDY/PEER TUTORING
- LITERACY AND SURVIVAL SKILLS

Multicultural Literature

ESTABLISHES EARLY LITERACY AND A LIFE-LONG LOVE OF READING

A compelling collection of reading and related writing activities captivates children's imaginations as they share their own ideas and feelings.

TORTILLAS

Tortillas, tortillas
Tortillas para mamá.
Tortillas, tortillas
Tortillas para papá.
Tortillas, tortillas
Tortillas para mí!

Tortillas, tortillas
Tortillas for my mother.
Tortillas, tortillas
Tortillas for my father.
Tortillas, tortillas
Tortillas for me!

22   LANGUAGE ARTS   Theme 2

Poems and chants

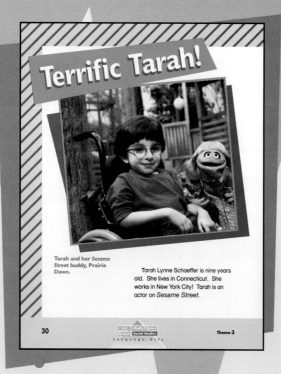

Terrific Tarah!

Tarah and her *Sesame Street* buddy, Prairie Dawn.

Tarah Lynne Schaeffer is nine years old. She lives in Connecticut. She works in New York City! Tarah is an actor on *Sesame Street.*

30   Language Arts   Theme 3

Photo Essays

Plays

SEE FOR YOURSELF

A FOLKTALE FROM ASIA

CHARACTERS:

Storyteller   Rabbit   Fox   Monkey   Elephant   Lion

Storyteller A long time ago a rabbit lived by a lake. One day a piece of fruit fell from a tree. It landed in the lake. KERPLUNK!

Rabbit was scared.

Rabbit I must go and tell Fox.

Run, run, run for your life. KERPLUNK is coming after us!

68   LANGUAGE ARTS   Theme 6

Family Pictures

EXCERPTED FROM THE BOOK BY CARMEN LOMAS GARZA

The pictures in this book are all painted from my memories of growing up in Kingsville, Texas, near the border with Mexico.

Carmen Lomas Garza

36

Social Studies
LANGUAGE ARTS

Theme 2

Personal Recollection

Music

May There Always Be Sunshine

May there always be sunshine
May there always be blue sky
May there always be Mama
May there always be me.

© 1990 Addison-Wesley Publishing Company, Inc. Illustrator: Paul Moschell

Balto the Brave

A TRUE STORY FROM ALASKA

Balto was the lead dog on a team of sled dogs. His owner's name was Gunnar. Gunnar thought that Balto was the smartest and bravest dog in Alaska.

In January 1925, Nome, Alaska, was buried in snow. People were sick with diphtheria. They needed medicine from the hospital in Anchorage. Doctors in Anchorage put the medicine on a train, but the train derailed in a terrible snow storm. The medicine was still 700 frozen miles from Nome.

120

Art Math Music
Music Social Studies
LANGUAGE ARTS

Theme 6

True life stories

Folktales and fables

Hot, Hot, Really Hot, Red Hot Peppers

A FOLKTALE FROM KOREA

One day an old woman was in her garden. She was picking carrots and onions and cabbages and some hot, hot, really hot, RED HOT PEPPERS. Suddenly, a huge, hungry tiger came out of the forest.

"Grrrrr-ah! I'm going to eat you for lunch!" the tiger said.

"Dear me, dear me," cried the old woman. "I am too thin to make a good lunch for you. Let me eat some of my vegetables. Then I'll make a better dinner for you."

"I'll give you until midnight," the tiger said. "Then I'll be back to eat you up."

The old woman ran into her house. She cooked up a big pot of vegetables and thought about how to escape from the tiger. She sat down to eat her carrots and onions and cabbages and the hot, hot, really hot, RED HOT PEPPERS. Huge tears rolled down her cheeks. She couldn't think of a way to escape from the tiger.

58

Art Math Music
Music Social Studies
LANGUAGE ARTS

Theme 3

Extensive Literature Links Bibliographies in the Appendix of this Guide build thematic and linguistic bridges to independent reading. These lists feature books in English and in other languages for every AMAZING theme.

xi

An Integrated Curriculum

PREPARES STUDENTS FOR MAINSTREAM SUCCESS

Hands-On Content

Photo Essays

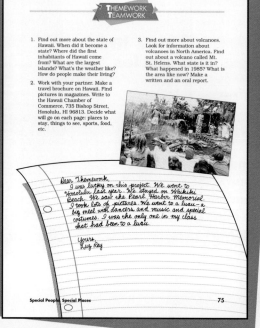

Themework/Teamwork
**Independent and
Collaborative Learning**

Problem Solving
CALLA strategies

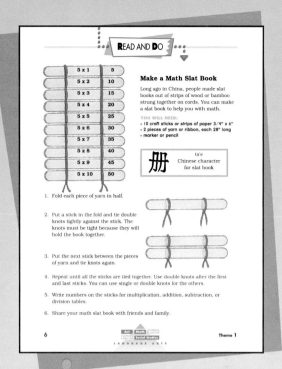

Read and Do
Understanding and responding to written directions

Language Power
Grammar in context and mechanics essential to mainstream success

Check This Out!
Reading for information and fun

xiii

Outstanding Teacher's Guides

PROMOTE PROFESSIONAL DEVELOPMENT AND CREATIVE CLASSROOMS

Everybody Eats — THEME 4 — PREVIEW

Theme 4, "Everybody Eats," introduces students to common foods and food-related activities, such as shopping and cooking. The children will share their favorite foods and learn about the foods and traditions of different cultures. They will begin to learn the words for food items and for life-skill situations, such as ordering from a menu.

Learning language through literature is a cornerstone of the *Amazing English!* program. In Theme 4, students participate in Shared Reading with the **Big Book** *The Gingerbread Man*. They explore the poems, songs, and non-fiction selections featured in their **Student Books** and enjoy a **Video Library** selection, *The Little Red Hen*. Role-playing activities presented in the **Language Activities Big Book** provide still other opportunities for practicing and personalizing language.

Multi-Level Teaching Strategies integrated into each lesson plan insure that all students can participate in these class activities, each at his or her own language level. **Home-School Connection** activities provide enjoyable extension activities for students and family members to do together.

The **Ongoing Assessment** suggestions in the lesson plans will help you keep track of your students' progress. On **Student Book** pages 50-51, the "Listen, Speak, Read, Write, Think" selection offers an opportunity for **holistic assessment**. The end-of-theme **Wrap-Up** page includes guidelines for implementing the full range of assessment tools and interpreting the results.

PLANNING TIPS

The **At-a-Glance Lesson Planner** on the next two pages provides an overview of the Key Experiences and Key Language presented in each lesson of the theme. Quickly scan the lesson plan Materials lists to see if there are materials to gather or prepare. Check the **Wrap-Up** page in case you want to plan ahead for the Theme Celebration.

The following recommended **Read-Aloud Books** are referenced in lesson plans and on the **Wrap-Up** page. Gather these titles and your own theme-related favorites. We recommend that you read aloud to your students every day. If possible, record the stories on tape and let students reread the books as they listen to the tapes.

- *More Spaghetti, I Say!* by Rita Golden Gelman (Lesson 3)
- *Feast for Ten* by Cathryn Falwell (Lesson 4)
- *If You Give a Mouse a Cookie* by Laura Joffe Numeroff (Lesson 8)
- *Pancakes for Breakfast* by Tomie de Paola (Lesson 12)
- *The Doorbell Rang* by Pat Hutchins (Lesson 10 and Wrap Up)

> Addison-Wesley has a variety of **Related Resources** that offer further exploration of the "Everybody Eats" theme. Look for references to selected materials in the margin notes of each lesson plan.

Wrap Up — THEME 2 — AT HOME

ASSESSMENT

You will find background information on the latest thinking in assessment as well as the assessment instruments for this theme in the *Amazing Assessment Package*.

You have been collecting assessment data through the ongoing and holistic assessment options (Oral Language Checklists, Reading Checklist, Writing Checklist, Anecdotal Record form) in this theme. The following are specific end-of-theme assessment strategies that will help you evaluate your students' progress as well as adapt your instruction to meet their needs.

Key Vocabulary. Observe your students as they play the Amazing Word Game provided on page 91 of the Skills Journal. Record their familiarity with the oral vocabulary and their ability to communicate with their game partner on their Anecdotal Record forms.

Student Self-Assessment. Self-assessment surveys are a means for students to have input into their own learning process. Students can use them to **reflect** on the work they have done and the learning strategies they have used during this theme.

Interpreting and Applying Assessment Data. As teachers, you collect assessment data in order to inform your instruction. Assessment information is a tool that helps you tailor your program to better meet the needs and interests of your students.

Evaluate the checklists, anecdotal records, portfolio collections, and test results from this theme as a means of informing your instruction.

- In which areas are students showing confidence and enthusiasm?
- In which areas are they hesitant or confused?
- Should you provide more classroom opportunities for oral language or writing?
- Would certain students (or the whole class) benefit from a focused mini-lesson on a certain area or skill?
- Remember to recycle skills as you teach the next theme and provide students with many opportunities to gain competence.

Review the results of the **Student Self-Assessment** survey and incorporate students' interests as you plan your instruction for the next theme. What do they want to learn next? Which Big Book learning activities did they enjoy most? If your students particularly enjoyed learning language through music or drama, be sure to emphasize those kinds of activities in the next theme.

THEME CELEBRATION

The end of a theme study is a good time for students to share some of their accomplishments with others. Suggest to students that you hold a celebration to spotlight the work they have done with the Student Book selection, "Good night, Juma" by Eloise Greenfield. (Lesson 6). This celebration can be an excellent opportunity to build stronger connections with other students and teachers. If possible invite another first grade class, school staff people, and/or family members.

Together write and deliver invitations and plan the event. Try to include audience participation as well as "show and tell." For example, your students can perform a Readers' Theatre presentation of "Good night Juma." If possible, use an opaque projector so all students can see the enlarged pages of the selection. Half of your class will read the lines of Juma. Half will read "Dad's" lines. Invite the audience to join in a second Reader's Theater reading of the selection.

Then introduce the class-made Big Book, *This Is the Way We Go to Sleep*. Have your students and the audience participate in a shared singing of the text. Afterwards, you may want to share refreshments that the students have prepared or selected.

END-OF-THEME READ-ALOUD BOOK

Make a tape of yourself reading this book so children can hear it again in the listening center.

Coco Can't Wait!
by Taro Gomi
New York: William Morrow and Company, 1984

Charming artwork presents Coco and her grandmother, who live on opposite sides of town, setting out to visit each other at the same time. Coco takes the bus while Grandma takes the train. Their paths cross again and again. Finally, the two meet in the middle.

74

Theme Previews

Theme At-A-Glance Lesson Planners

Theme Wrap Ups

THEME 1 — AT-A-GLANCE LESSON PLANNER

LESSON PLAN	KEY EXPERIENCES	KEY LANGUAGE	CONTENT AREAS
1 LABB Activity 1 / Theme Page	Greeting classmates • Identifying classroom objects • Making a comparison chart	What's your/his/her name? • My/His/Her name is.... • What's this? • Point to...	Art • Math • Music • Language Arts
2 LABB Activity 2	Greeting classmates (R) • Role-play: Asking someone to play • Counting 1-5 • TPR chant	What's your/his/her name? (R) • My/His/Her name is...(R) • Let's ... play. • Show me ... numbers 1-5	Math • Music • Language Arts
3 Student Book p.3 / Theme Page	Discussing playground activities • Learning a song; creating new verses • Learning and personalizing a fingerplay	What can we do? • I/We can ..play .. (on the swings). • How many ... can you see? • His/Her name is .... (R) • numbers 1-5 (R)	Art • Math • Music • Language Arts
4 Student Book pp. 4–6 / Let's Build a Playground	Guided reading, photo essay • Designing a playground • Dictating a Language Experience Story	We (talk, draw, etc.) • Johnny works with ... • Let's ... (R) • How many ... can you see? (R) • Point to/Show me...(R)	Art • Math • Music • Social Studies • Language Arts
5 LABB Activity 3	Identifying classroom objects • Identifying colors • Learning a TPR chant and song • Mixing colors	What's this? • This is a .... • What color is ...? • Point to/Show me... (R) • left, right	Art • Math • Music • Science • Language Arts
6 Big Book / On the First Day of School	Shared reading • Dramatizing a story • Comparing reality and fantasy • Counting/graphing	How many ... can you see? (R) • names of animals • classroom objects and activities	Art • Math • Music • Language Arts
7 LABB Activity 4:	Counting 1-10 • Singing counting songs • Reading and writing numerals • Identifying colors • Making color sequence patterns	How many .... are there? • What color are the ...? • word order: seven black boots	Art • Math • Music • Language Arts
8 Student Book p. 7 / Alphabet Cheer	Reciting the alphabet • Reading and writing letters • Alphabetizing • Making a class bar graph	Letters A-Z • Give me a/an ...(G/H) • Whose name starts with ...	Music • Science • Language Arts
9 Student Book pp. 8-9 / What are kids like?	Guided reading: poem • Identifying rhyming words • Playing pantomime games • Writing own story • Matching words	Kids are... • Kids have ... • descriptive adjectives • some/both	Art • Language Arts
10 LABB Activity 5	Singing a song; creating new verses • Following directions (TPR) • Understanding sequence	I can.... (write, read, sing, draw) (R) • first, next, then • daily routines and tasks	Art • Music • Social Studies • Language Arts
11 LABB Activity 6	Exploring the school • Asking directions • Role-play: Making a school map • Practicing polite language	Where is the ...? • Here /There it is. • Thank you. You're welcome. • school locations	Math • Social Studies • Language Arts
12 Big Book / On the First Day of School	Shared reading • Learning days of the week • Making a class Big Book	days of the week • first, second, third, fourth, fifth • word order: three hopping hippos	Art • Math • Music • Language Arts
13 Student Book pp.10-11 / I Spy School Supplies	Exploring a hidden objects photo • Identifying and counting objects, letters and numbers • Making "I Spy" photo collages	How many ... can you see? (R) • word order: two green bears (R) • I spy ... • preposition: on	Art • Math • Science• Language Arts
14 Student Book pp. 12-13 / Holistic Assessment	Listening to a new story • Demonstrating comprehension • Retelling the story • Playing a board game • Reading numbers 1-5	Show me/Point to ...(R) • How many ... ? (R) • What's this? (R) • What color is ...? (R) • I brought	Assessment
15 Student Book p. 14 / Hands-On-Math	Making self-portraits • Making and interpreting class graphs • Appreciating diversity	What color is your hair? • How many ...? • What is your favorite...?	Art• Math • Language Arts
16 Video Library / Monty	Enjoying and listening to a story • Comparing cartoon and narrative stories • Drawing a cartoon story sequence	How do you come to school? • first, next, last (R)	Art • Science • Language Arts

2   3

✓ CLEAR

✓ CREATIVE

✓ COMPLETE

Lesson Plans

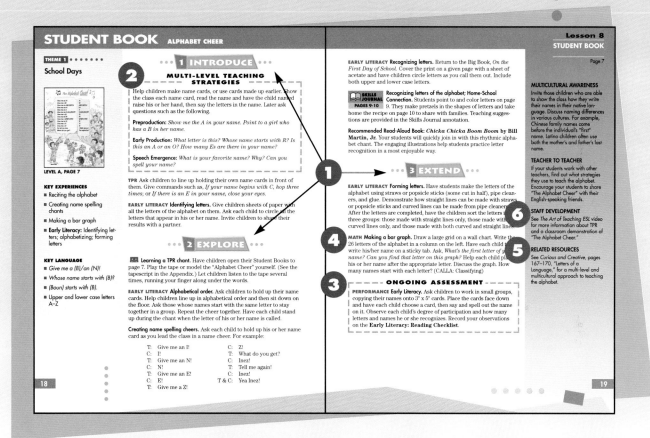

STUDENT BOOK ALPHABET CHEER

THEME 1 • • • • • • •

School Days

LEVEL A, PAGE 7

KEY EXPERIENCES
- Reciting the alphabet
- Creating name spelling chants
- Making a bar graph
- Early Literacy: Identifying letters; alphabetizing; forming letters

KEY LANGUAGE
- *Give me a (B)/an (N)!*
- *Whose name starts with (B)?*
- *(Boun) starts with (B).*
- Upper and lower case letters A–Z

18

1 INTRODUCE

MULTI-LEVEL TEACHING STRATEGIES

Help children make name cards, or use cards made up earlier. Show the class each name card, read the name and have the child named raise his or her hand, then say the letters in the name. Later ask questions such as the following.

Preproduction: *Show me the A in your name. Point to a girl who has a B in her name.*

Early Production: *What letter is this? Whose name starts with R? Is this an A or an O? How many Es are there in your name?*

Speech Emergence: *What is your favorite name? Why? Can you spell your name?*

TPR Ask children to line up holding their own name cards in front of them. Give commands such as, *If your name begins with C, hop three times;* or *If there is an E in your name, close your eyes.*

EARLY LITERACY Identifying letters. Give children sheets of paper with all the letters of the alphabet on them. Ask each child to circle all the letters that appear in his or her name. Invite children to share their results with a partner.

2 EXPLORE

Learning a TPR chant. Have children open their Student Books to page 7. Play the tape or model the "Alphabet Cheer" yourself. (See the tapescript in the Appendix.) Let children listen to the tape several times, running your finger along under the words.

EARLY LITERACY Alphabetical order. Ask children to hold up their name cards. Help children line up in alphabetical order and then sit down on the floor. Ask those whose names start with the same letter to stay together in a group. Repeat the cheer together. Have each child stand up during the chant when the letter of his or her name is called.

Creating name spelling cheers. Ask each child to hold up his or her name card as you lead the class in a name cheer. For example:

T:	Give me an I!	C:	Z!
C:	I!	T:	What do you get?
T:	Give me an N!	C:	Inez!
C:	N!	T:	Tell me again!
T:	Give me an E!	C:	Inez!
C:	E!	T & C:	Yea Inez!
T:	Give me a Z!		

EARLY LITERACY Recognizing letters. Return to the Big Book, *On the First Day of School.* Cover the print on a given page with a sheet of acetate and have children circle letters as you call them out. Include both upper and lower case letters.

SKILLS JOURNAL PAGES 9-10 **Recognizing letters of the alphabet; Home-School Connection.** Students point to and color letters on page 9. They make pretzels in the shapes of letters and take home the recipe on page 10 to share with families. Teaching suggestions are provided in the Skills Journal annotation.

Recommended Read-Aloud Book: *Chicka Chicka Boom Boom* by Bill Martin, Jr. Your students will quickly join in with this rhythmic alphabet chant. The engaging illustrations help students practice letter recognition in a most enjoyable way.

3 EXTEND

EARLY LITERACY Forming letters. Have students make the letters of the alphabet using straws or popsicle sticks (some cut in half), pipe cleaners, and glue. Demonstrate how straight lines can be made with straws or popsicle sticks and curved lines can be made from pipe cleaners. After the letters are completed, have the children sort the letters into three groups: those made with straight lines only, those made with curved lines only, and those made with both curved and straight lines.

MATH Making a bar graph. Draw a large grid on a wall chart. Write the 26 letters of the alphabet in a column on the left. Have each child write his/her name on a sticky tab. Ask, *What's the first letter of your name? Can you find that letter on this graph?* Help each child place his or her name after the appropriate letter. Discuss the graph. How many names start with each letter? (CALLA: Classifying)

ONGOING ASSESSMENT

PERFORMANCE Early Literacy. Ask children to work in small groups, copying their names onto 3" x 5" cards. Place the cards face down and have each child choose a card, then say and spell out the name on it. Observe each child's degree of participation and how many letters and names he or she recognizes. Record your observations on the **Early Literacy: Reading Checklist.**

Lesson 8
STUDENT BOOK

Page 7

MULTICULTURAL AWARENESS
Invite those children who are able to show the class how they write their names in their native language. Discuss naming differences in various cultures. For example, Chinese family names come before the individual's "first" name. Latino children often use both the mother's and father's last name.

TEACHER TO TEACHER
If your students work with other teachers, find out what strategies they use to teach the alphabet. Encourage your students to share "The Alphabet Cheer" with their English-speaking friends.

STAFF DEVELOPMENT
See *The Art of Teaching ESL* video for more information about TPR and a classroom demonstration of "The Alphabet Cheer."

RELATED RESOURCES
See *Curious and Creative*, pages 167–170, "Letters of a Language," for a multi-level and multicultural approach to teaching the alphabet.

19

1 Consistent, three-step lesson plans

2 Applications of the Natural Approach reach learners at different levels of proficiency

3 Ongoing assessment

4 Innovative ideas for teaching across the curriculum

5 Related Resources

6 Staff Development

MANAGEMENT AND Assessment TOOLS MAKE YOUR JOB EASIER

HOLISTIC ASSESSMENT PAGES

"Five-skill" assessment in every Student Book Theme

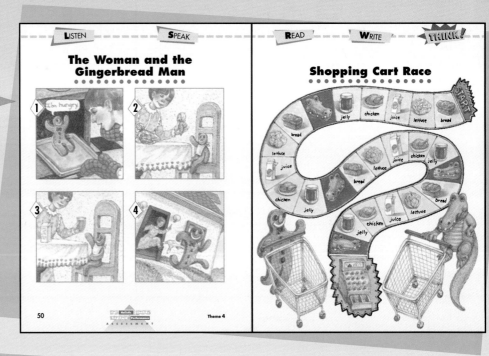

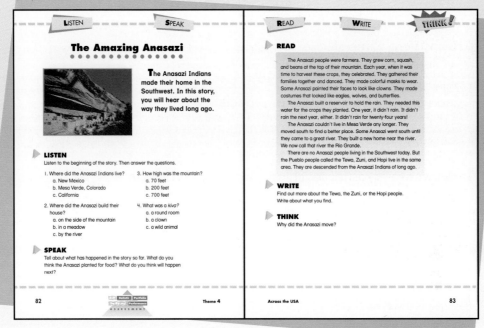

WORD BANK

| crayon | scissors | marker | paste |

(Supports Language Activities Big Book A, Activity 3) **Figure-ground discrimination.** Students use small pictures as clues to find and circle hidden objects in big picture. Give directions for coloring hidden pictures. *Color the crayon red. Color the scissors yellow. Color the marker blue. Color the paste green.* The Word Bank strip will be cut out after students complete this theme.

6

Spin and Draw

(Supports Student Book A, pages 12-13) **Following directions; recognizing numerals.** Students play the game "Spin and Draw" with a partner using the game board on Student Book page 13. At the end of each turn, they will add a certain number of objects to the classroom map on this page, following the game board directions.

17

PORTFOLIO PAGES

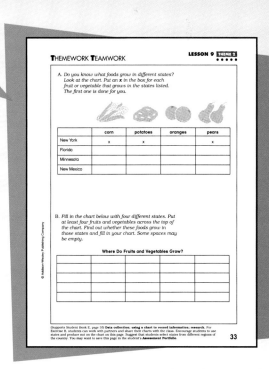

THEMEWORK TEAMWORK

A. Do you know what foods grow in different states? Look at the chart. Put an **x** in the box for each fruit or vegetable that grows in the states listed. The first one is done for you.

	corn	potatoes	oranges	pears
New York	x	x		x
Florida				
Minnesota				
New Mexico				

B. Fill in the chart below with four different states. Put at least four fruits and vegetables across the top of the chart. Find out whether these foods grow in those states and fill in your chart. Some spaces may be empty.

Where Do Fruits and Vegetables Grow?

(Supports Student Book E, page 35) **Data collection; using a chart to record information; research.** For Exercise B, students can work with partners and share their charts with the class. Encourage students to use states and produce not on the chart on this page. Suggest that students select states from different regions of the country. You may want to save this page in the student's **Assessment Portfolio.**

33

ASSESSMENT PACKAGES

(one for each level) include observation checklists, student self-surveys, anecdotal records and charts. Interpreting and applying assessment data is easier and less time-consuming than ever before.

The AMAZING ENGLISH Team of Educators

Michael Walker is the author of more than sixty language textbooks for English language learners. AMAZING ENGLISH marks his fifth major and most innovative program, developed in collaboration with many creative and caring educators.

Carolyn Grigsby is a Mentor Teacher in the Jefferson School District, Daly City, CA. She is the author of THE BUDDY BOOK, and the AMAZING NEWCOMER KIT.

Susan Hooper is a teacher in the Newton Public Schools, Newton, MA. She is one of the authors of TLLC and a key contributor to other levels of the program.

Caroline Linse is an elementary ESL staff developer who is currently Associate Director of the EEC schools in Korea. She is one of the authors of TLLC and a contributor to other components of the program.

Mary Lou McCloskey is an early childhood educator and curriculum developer. She is one of the authors of TLLC and an advisor to the other levels of the program.

Elly Schottman is a curriculum developer and early childhood educator. She is a key contributor to TLLC and Levels A and B of the program.

Teresa Walter is a Resource Teacher for San Diego Unified School District, San Diego, CA. She is the author of the Teacher's Guides for the Video Libraries and the How-To Handbook, and a key contributor to all levels of the program.

REVIEWERS/ADVISORS/ FIELD TEST TEACHERS

Linda Arnold, Dingle Elementary School, Woodland, CA

Armando Ayala, Multicultural Consultant, Sacramento, CA

Mary Cazabon, Head of Bilingual Services, Cambridge Public Schools, Cambridge, MA

Tamara Constan, Sutton Elementary School, Phoenix, AZ

Victoria Delgado, Supervisor of Bilingual Education, CSD #32, Brooklyn, NY

Sandra Fradd, University of Miami, Miami, FL

Audrey A. Fong, Franklin School, San Jose, CA

Delia Garza, Hidalgo ISD, Hidalgo, TX

Angie M. Ginty, ESL Coordinator CSD #15, Brooklyn, NY

Denise B. Hendrigan, Morse Public School, Cambridge, MA

Ana Hernandez, Patrick Henry School, Long Beach Unified School District, Long Beach, CA

Doris Hernandez, Donna ISD, Donna, TX

Myriam Ionescu, Harrington School, Cambridge, MA

Polly Morales, Donna ISD, Donna, TX

Linda O'Brien, Maynard School, Cambridge, MA

Doris Partan, Longfellow School, Cambridge, MA

Jean Pender, British Council, Mexico

Karen Rudgis, Maynard School, Cambridge, MA

John Travers, Supervisor of ESL, Rochester Public Schools, Rochester, NY

Julie Wood, Curriculum specialist and literature consultant, Cambridge, MA

Phyllis I. Ziegler, ESL/Bilingual Consultant, New York, NY

We are also grateful to thousands of teachers and students across the country who participated in customer interviews, surveys, focus groups, classroom pilots, and workshops. Their counsel and creative ideas are central to the Amazing English curriculum.

RELATED RESOURCES

These fine products, correlated throughout AMAZING ENGLISH, further enrich and extend the integrated curriculum.

LANGUAGE ARTS

The Addison-Wesley Picture Dictionary

Alligator at the Airport
(A Language Activities Dictionary)

Curious and Creative
(Critical Thinking and Language Development)

Exploring Literature Theme Kits 1-6

The Global Classroom
(Volumes 1 and 2)

Over and Over Again:
(Whole Language through Music)

Sharing a Song Music Videos
(Whole Language through Music)

Story Club:
(Multicultural Folktales from Around the World)

MATH

Addison-Wesley Quest 2000:
Exploring Mathematics

DataWonder! (Software)

SCIENCE

Addison-Wesley Destinations in Science
    Board Games
    Science Theater
    Videos
Eureka! Science Demonstrations for ESL Classes

CD ROM

    The Cat Came Back
    Sitting on the Farm
    WordStuff

STAFF DEVELOPMENT

The Amazing How-To Handbook
The Art of Teaching ESL (Video-based)
The Art of Teaching the Natural Approach
(Video-based)
Authentic Assessment for
    English Language Learners
The CALLA Handbook

WELCOME TO LEVEL

C

Amazing English! recognizes that ESL is taught in a wide variety of circumstances. This course is complete, yet flexible, inviting teachers to customize the program to suit the needs and interests of their own classes.

• •

Literature-based lessons allow students to enjoy a wide variety of selections from around the world. The rest of the integrated curriculum makes great use of CALLA. The Cognitive Academic Language Learning Approach is designed to help students make a successful transition into the mainstream academic curriculum. Each content-area CALLA lesson has three parts:

Content: academic content lessons in science, math, social studies, language arts, reading, or health.

Language: the academic listening, speaking, reading, and writing skills students need to handle the content of a lesson successfully.

Strategy: the technique students are taught to be consciously aware of applying to understand and remember the academic content of a lesson.

See the *Amazing How-To Handbook* for a complete discussion of CALLA.

THE STUDENT BOOK
Six thematic units offer a rich array of traditional and contemporary literature. Music and mainstream content are also featured. An annotated "content pyramid" at the bottom of each student page provides a quick reference to the richness of each lesson. This book and the SKILLS JOURNAL form the core of the level.

THE SKILLS JOURNAL
The Skills Journal reinforces and expands upon the language concepts and skills introduced through the Student Book. Teaching suggestions are given at the bottom of each page.

THE TEACHER'S GUIDE

This Guide is devoted to making your job easier, less time-consuming, and more fun. Each theme has a **Theme Preview Page** and an **At-A-Glance-Planner** that will help you choose the activities and the pace appropriate for your students. The **three-step Lesson Plans** are clear, easy to follow, and creative. Ongoing Assessment opportunities are cited in every lesson. Recommended **Read-Aloud Books** are referenced in every lesson; gather these and your own favorites for each theme. **Theme Wrap-Ups** feature a **Theme Celebration Assessment Strategies,** and a special end-of-theme **Read-Aloud Book.**

THE AUDIO CASSETTES

The audio tapes feature professional adults and children performing all the songs, chants, poems, plays, conversations, and story-telling. The Holistic Assessment pages for each theme are also key parts of the audio cassettes.

WORD ATTACK SOFTWARE

Five interactive vocabulary games are irresistible fun for students and a great way to build vocabulary. All the key words from Levels C, D and E are included in this software. See the manual that supports WORD ATTACK for complete information.

ASSESSMENT PACKAGE

This package is an essential part of the program to help you evaluate and track student progress. The latest research and practical applications of theory, along with a variety of checklists, survey sheets, anecdotal records and scoring rubrics make interpreting and applying assessment data easier than ever before.

PROCESS WRITING PORTFOLIO PROGRAM

Student-centered portfolio with specific writing projects linked to each of them for this level. Projects feature collaborative brainstorming, peer editing, game studies, and practice in specific writing skills. Separate Teacher's Handbook includes Lesson Plans, Reproducible checklists, and Scope and Sequence charts for Levels C, D, and E.

BOOKBYTES CD-ROM

This innovative software motivates students to read and respond to their reading. Students choose from a variety of activities to create personalized book reviews they can play back in class or print, to share at home. Extensive bibliographies help students choose a new book to read.

A FINAL WORD

AMAZING is an unusually rich and deep curriculum that provides you with an "Instant Classroom" of unparalleled beauty and strength. As you explore the program, add your own favorite ideas and proven activities to create an even more "Amazing" classroom in which you and your students prosper and grow.

CONTENTS

		PREVIEW	WRAP UP
Theme 1	**Friend to Friend**	1	34
Theme 2	**Families Around the World**	35	66
Theme 3	**Adventures in Space**	67	98
Theme 4	**Across the USA**	99	130
Theme 5	**Animals Wild and Tame** . .	131	162
Theme 6	**Changing Seasons**	163	194

Appendix 195
   Home School Connection: Family Involvement Letters (English and Spanish)
   Reading Corner: Literature Links Bibliographies
   Tapescript
   Student Book Index
   Process Writing Portfolio Program: Level C Scope and Sequence
   Language Activities Big Book Index
   Scope and Sequence

Friend to Friend

Theme 1 welcomes your students to a new school year. Through literature, articles, poetry, and language activity pages in the **Student Book**, the students will explore friendship and sharing. They will talk about their favorite weekend activities, write secret codes to each other, and learn about the game of soccer. The **Skills Journal** offers opportunities for further language practice, reading, writing, and research on a variety of theme-related topics.

Multi-Level Teaching Strategies integrated into each lesson plan insure that all students can participate in these class activities, each at his or her own level of language proficiency. **Home-School Connection** activities provide enjoyable extension activities for students and family members to do together.

The **Ongoing Assessment** suggestions in the lesson plans will help you keep track of your students' progress. On **Student Book** pages 20–21, the "Listen, Speak, Read, Write, Think" selection offers an opportunity for **holistic assessment**. The end-of-theme **Wrap-Up** page includes guidelines for implementing the full range of assessment tools and interpreting the results.

PLANNING TIPS

The **At-a-Glance Lesson Planner** on the next two pages provides an overview of the Key Experiences and Key Language presented in each lesson of the theme. Quickly scan the lesson plan Materials lists to see if there are materials to gather or prepare. Check the **Wrap-Up** page in case you want to plan ahead for the Theme Celebration.

The following **Read-Aloud Books** are recommended with this theme. Gather these titles and your own theme-related favorites. We encourage you to read aloud to your students every day. If possible, record the stories on tape and let students reread the books as they listen to the tapes.

- *Friends* by Helme Heine

- *Birthday Presents* (poetry) by Cynthia Rylant

- *Arnie and the New Kid* by Nancy Carlson

- *Masai and I* by Virginia Kroll

- *The Wizard of Oz* by L. Frank Baum

- *A Weekend with Wendell* by Kevin Henkes (Wrap-Up page)

READING CORNER

Encourage independent reading for information and pleasure. If possible, set up a reading corner—a quiet, comfortable place that is just for reading (and perhaps listening to any books on tape you've collected). Make a bulletin board on which you can post book covers, students' BookBytes reviews and the Literature Links Bibliographies that support each theme. See the Appendix for the complete Literature Links Bibliography for this theme. It offers a variety of fiction and non-fiction choices **in English and in other languages.**

LESSON PLAN

KEY EXPERIENCES

1 **Student Book p. 3**
Theme Opener

Making introductions • Talking about friendship • Singing a song • Predicting theme content • Sharing personal experiences

2 **Student Book p. 4**
Communication 1A

Roleplaying conversations • Talking about favorite pastimes • Asking for and giving information • comparing ages

3 **Student Book p. 5**
Communication 1B

Asking for and giving directions • Identifying places in school • Reading a map of the school • Building sight vocabulary

4 **Student Book p. 6**
Read and Do

Discussing secret codes • Following directions • Using the secret code • Making new secret codes

5 **Student Book p. 7**
The Weekend

Identifying days of the week • Talking about favorite weekend activities • Creating new song verses • Making a personal calendar

6 **Student Book p. 8**
Communication 2A

Identifying days of the week (R) • Identifying months of the year • Talking about birthdays • Roleplaying conversations

7 **Student Book p. 9**
Communication 2B

Describing/classifying objects • Creating new conversations • Roleplaying offering/accepting gifts • Comparing birthday celebrations

8 **Student Book pp. 10-11**
Check This Out!

Discussing friendship • Guided reading of a poem • Reading "Amazing Facts" • Reading quotes about friendship • Enjoying humor

9 **Student Book p. 12**
Language Power A

Talking about preferences • Sharing interests • Roleplaying an interview • Creating "Things I Like" stories • Making take-home books

10 **Student Book p. 13**
Language Power B

Telling time • Roleplaying making plans • Making a schedule • Making sand clocks • Finding out about schedules/times

11 **Student Book pp. 14-15**
Hands-On Math

Using a ruler/a scale • Measuring/describing size and weight • Following directions • Making a simple scale

12 **Student Book pp. 16-17**
A New Friend Named Charlie

Discussing ways to communicate • Reading letters • Identifying main ideas • Writing a letter to a friend or relative

13 **Student Book pp. 18-19**
Let's Play Soccer

Reading about soccer • Explaining rules of a game • Making up a game • Writing rules for a game

14 **Student Book pp. 20-21**
Holistic Assessment

Listening to a new story • Describing story events • Retelling the story • Thinking critically • Guided reading • Writing a soup recipe

15 **Student Book p. 22**
Amazing Facts Game

Recalling details • Playing a game • Finding other facts • Making up new questions in groups

KEY LANGUAGE

Hi, I'm . . . What's your name? • My name is . . . Nice to meet you. • I have a friend. • His/her name is . . . • We like to . . .	Art • Music • Language Arts
Is your best friend a boy or a girl? • What's his/her first/last name? dance, first /last name, play soccer, older/younger, together	Math • Language Arts
Where's the (library)? • What's this? • This is (the library). • Places in a school	Art • Music • Language Arts
What is this message? • Crack these codes! • Make a new secret code. • letters, message, numbers, secret, symbols, system	Math • Language Arts
It's the weekend. • Days of the week • playing, weekend	Music • Social Studies • Language Arts
Is your birthday in (July)? • No, it isn't. It's in (August). What day of the week is it on? • It's on (Saturday). • Days of the week (R)	Art • Social Studies • Language Arts
Happy birthday! • Here's a present for you. • Open it and find out. • baseball cap, book, bracelet, pin, ring, scarf, sweater	Art • Social Studies • Language Arts
A friend is someone . . . • born, cry, friend, hug, lend, share • Names of animals	Math • Science • Language Arts
Do you like (animals)? • Do you like to (sing)? • Yes, I do./No, I don't. • animals, sing, games, vegetables, dance, draw, like, swim	Art • Language Arts
It's (a quarter after one). • Let's (go to the movies) on (Saturday). • What time do you want to go? • half past, quarter to, quarter after	Music • Science • Language Arts
How long is (your pencil)? • How wide is (your desk)? • Which is longer/heavier? • inches, foot, heavy, measure, ruler, scale	Math • Language Arts
Dear . . ., • Your nephew, • I was so happy to hear . . . • Please write again soon. • envelope, letter, mail, stamp	Art • Language Arts
soccer, dribble, goal, goalie, opponent, score, tackle, pass, mark, foul, fake	Art • Music • Social Studies • Language Arts
brains, brick, cyclone, fence, scarecrow, wicked	Assessment
Review	Assessment

CONTENT AREAS

THEME OPENER

Friend to Friend

LEVEL C, PAGE 3

KEY EXPERIENCES

- Making introductions
- Talking about friendship
- Singing a song
- Predicting theme content
- Sharing personal experiences

KEY LANGUAGE

- *Hi. I'm ... What's your name?*
- *My name is ... Nice to meet you.*
- *I have a friend.*
- *His/her name is ...*
- *We like to ...*

---

1 INTRODUCE

MULTI-LEVEL TEACHING STRATEGIES

Building background: Greetings and introductions. Greet the class. Use two puppets. Have them greet each other.

> 1: *Hi. I'm... What's your name?*
> 2: *My name is ... Nice to meet you.*
> 1: *Nice to meet you, too.*

Write the introduction on the board. Model it with several students, using one of the puppets.

MUSIC Playing musical names. Have students practice introducing themselves to the students sitting near them. Then ask the students to stand up. Tell them you will play some music (choose any music you like) as students move around the room. Whenever the music stops, they stop and greet the student closest to them. Model first.

> S1 to S2: *Hi. I'm (Anna). What's your name?*
> S2: *My name's (Joseph).*

Ask the two students to return to their seats. Review all the student's names. Then include all the students by asking questions appropriate to each student's language stage. Here are some sample questions:

Speech Emergence: (Using the puppet, ask yes/no questions or choice questions.) *Is your name Robert? Nice to meet you, Robert. Is your name Luisa or Beatriz?*

Developing Fluency: (Using the puppet, ask choice or information questions.) *Hi, what is your name?* Encourage students to respond *My name is (Tran).*

ART Creating a class chart. Make a class name chart. Invite students to add photographs or small drawings of themselves and their favorite activities next to their names.

---

2 EXPLORE

Activating prior knowledge. Open to Theme Opener page 3 of the Student Book. Read the unit title, "Friend to Friend," aloud. Then read the unit titles. Encourage students to comment on the photograph. To prompt discussion, ask **multi-level questions,** such as *How many boys do you see? Do you think these two boys are friends? What do they like to play together?*

♪♫

🎵 MUSIC "I Know Everyone's Name" Play the tape or sing the song with students. (See the Tapescript in the Appendix.) Encourage students to sing along and then to make up their own verses.

Talking about the weekend. Use a calendar to review days of the week. Ask students which days are weekend days. Then ask students what they like to do on the weekend. List their ideas on the board. Prompt individual students if necessary, *Do you like to ride your bike? Do you play with friends?* etc.

Talking about friendship. Talk about a friend. Say, *I have a friend. (Her) name is (Mary). We like to (play tennis).* Ask the students to each think of a friend. Ask them to think of something they like to do together. *What is your friend's name? What do you like to do?* On the board, write: *I have a friend. His/Her name is ... We like to ...* Model the conversation with several students. In pairs, have student tell each other about their friends.

Predicting unit content. Ask students to tell you what a story titled "A New Friend Named Charlie" might be about. Encourage students to use their imaginations. On the board, write the title "Let's Play Soccer". Ask students what they think this story will be about. Encourage students to share their ideas freely. (CALLA: Predicting)

SKILLS JOURNAL PAGE 3

Free writing. Students do free writing on the unit theme of friendship. Teaching suggestions are provided in the Skills Journal annotation.

3 EXTEND

Language experience writing. On the board, print, *On the weekend I like to ...* Have students copy the words on a separate piece of paper and complete the sentence. Encourage students to write other sentences about what they like to do. Have students illustrate their sentences.

ONGOING ASSESSMENT

PERFORMANCE Oral language. Ask the students to tell you about their friends. Observe different students' levels of participation. Does the student use single words or phrases? Complete sentences? Does the student have difficulty with pronunciation? Use the **Oral Language Checklist** in the *Amazing Assessment Package*.

PORTFOLIO Writing. Save **Skills Journal** page 3 as an example of independent writing.

STAFF DEVELOPMENT

See the video *The Art of Teaching the Natural Approach* by Jane Zion Brauer for more on Speech Emergence and Developing Fluency stages. By asking multi-level questions and using whatever you have at hand to help ensure comprehension, you are providing students with comprehensible input.

TEACHER TO TEACHER

If your students work with other teachers, you may want to suggest to them that providing opportunities to discuss old friends is beneficial to students transitioning into a new culture and new social environment. Acknowledging the difficulties many students face will help to alleviate the isolation some students experience.

COMMUNICATION 1A

Friend to Friend

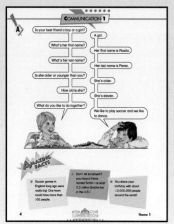

LEVEL C, PAGE 4

KEY EXPERIENCES

- Roleplaying conversations
- Talking about favorite pastimes
- Asking for and giving information
- Comparing ages

KEY LANGUAGE

- *Is your best friend a boy or a girl?*
- *What's his/her first/last name?*
- *Is he/she older or younger than you?*
- *What do you like to do together?*
- *We like to (dance).*
- dance, first name/last name, play soccer, older/younger, together

• • • 1 INTRODUCE • • •

MULTI-LEVEL TEACHING STRATEGIES

Building background. Use a puppet to greet the students. Puppet to Class: *Hello, my name is Anna. What is your name?* Circulate, stopping to ask students one or more questions about their names and preferences. Include all the students by asking questions appropriate to each student's language stage. Here are some sample questions:

Speech Emergence: *What is your first name? What is your last name? Is your favorite color red? Do you like to play on the weekend?*

Developing Fluency: *What do you like to do on the weekend? What is your best friend's name?*

Learning classmates' names. Print the first and last names of all the students on the board, or have students print their own names. Remind everyone that both names begin with a capital letter. Say the students' names in random order. Have each student stand up when his or her name is called.

Playing a name chain. Ask students to stand in groups of six. Have the first student in the group introduce himself/herself. Each student then introduces himself/herself and says the names of all the students who have already introduced themselves. Remind students to listen carefully and to help one another as needed. S1 to S2: *I'm (Theresa). What's your name?* S2: *My name's (Elizabeth).* S2 to S3: *She is (Theresa). My name's (Elizabeth). What's your name?* S3: *My name's (Sam).* S3 to S4: *Her name is (Theresa). Her name is (Elizabeth). I'm (Sam). What's your name?*, etc. As a summary, ask each student to say his or her name for the class.

• • • 2 EXPLORE • • •

Activating prior knowledge. Open to page 4 of the Student Book. Ask students to comment about the picture. How do they know that this is a conversation?

Look, listen, and talk. Point to each of the dialogue bubbles as you read the text or play the tape for the conversation. Then as you replay the tape, have students point to the appropriate questions and answers and say them **chorally.** Divide the class into two groups. One group asks the questions, the other answers. Have students switch roles and repeat. Practice question-asking inflection as needed.

LIFE SKILLS Talking about best friends. Explain that not everyone has a best friend and that it is all right not to have a best friend. Ask students about their best friends. Ask **multi-level questions** appropriate to the level of each student. *Do you have a best friend? Is your best friend a boy? Is your best friend a girl? What does your best friend like to do?*

 **Reading for information: Amazing Facts.** Direct students' attention to the text and title at the bottom of the page. Read the title, "Amazing Facts," aloud. Elicit that "Amazing" means surprising. Read or play the tape. Then have students reread independently. Ask **multi-level questions,** such as *Did they play soccer in England? How many people could be on a team? Where are there a lot of people named Smith?* Invite the class to talk about the most common names in their own languages.

SKILLS JOURNAL PAGE 4 **Data collection.** Students collect and record information and use it for paired conversation practice. Teaching suggestions are provided in the Skills Journal annotation.

MATH Doing a class survey. In small groups, have students interview their classmates about their favorite pastimes. Before students begin, help them brainstorm a list on the board of questions they can ask. For example, *What do you like to do? What do you like to do the most? Do you have a best friend? What do you like to do together?* Show students how to write down what their partners say. As a class, compile the information: *Who likes to go swimming? How many like to play soccer?* (CALLA: Grouping)

Comparing ages. Ask each student to write down the names of three friends. Next to each name, have students write down an age, real or make-believe. In pairs, have students ask each other questions about their friends. *Is your friend a boy or a girl? / A (girl). / What's (her) first name? / (Lisa). / What is (her) last name? / (Schmidt). / Is (she) older or younger than you? / (She)'s older. / How old is (she)?*

ONGOING ASSESSMENT

PERFORMANCE Oral language. Have partners roleplay the conversation in the book. One student asks the questions, the other answers, using information about his or her best friend or about a make-believe friend. Observe students' levels of participation. Use the **Oral Language Checklist** in the *Amazing Assessment Package.*

PORTFOLIO Oral/aural abilities. Save **Skills Journal** page 4 as an example of oral/aural abilities and completing a crossword puzzle.

MULTICULTURAL AWARENESS

Invite volunteers to teach the class a fact from their home cultures. It can be a simple fact, for example, *Many people eat fried bananas for breakfast.* Ask each volunteer to write his or her fact on a small piece of paper or dictate it for you to write. Read the facts aloud in random order. Have the students identify whose fact it is.

STAFF DEVELOPMENT

See the *Amazing How-To Handbook* for more information about paired practice in conversation.

Friend to Friend

LEVEL C, PAGE 5

KEY EXPERIENCES

- Asking for and giving directions
- Identifying places in school
- Reading a map of a school
- Building sight vocabulary
- Drawing/labeling a map of the school

KEY LANGUAGE

- *Where's (the library)?*
- *What's this?*
- *This is (the library).*
- Places in a school

••• 1 INTRODUCE •••

MULTI-LEVEL TEACHING STRATEGIES

Building background: Identifying places in the school. Take students on a tour of the school. Point out the *classrooms, office, girl's room, boy's room, library, cafeteria, gym, playground.* Say, *This is the (office).* Point out and read aloud any signs that are posted for the rooms. Model and have students repeat *This is the office,* etc.

When you return to the classroom, have students draw pictures of different school locations. Also have them make a set of word cards for *classroom, office, girls' room, boys' room, library, cafeteria, gym,* and *playground.* Spread out the drawings and ask, *Where's the (classroom)?* Encourage students to respond, *Here it is.* One student then picks out the word card and puts it on the correct picture. Continue asking questions appropriate to each student's language stage. Here are some sample questions:

Speech Emergence: *Where's the library? Is this the cafeteria or the gym?*

Developing Fluency: *Which is bigger, the cafeteria or the gym? How many girls' rooms are in the school?*

••• 2 EXPLORE •••

Activating prior knowledge. Open to page 5 of the Student Book. Ask students to say something about the picture. Ask, *Where's the ... ?* questions and let students point to the answer. Let them name any places and objects they know.

Look, listen, and talk. Point to each part of the school map and say the location; have students repeat **chorally.** Next, have students look and listen as you describe the scene, *Where's the library? Here it is. This is the first grade classroom,* etc. Check understanding with **TPR.** Have students put their fingers on the picture of the *office.* Ask, *Where's the boys' room? Show me how to get to the boys' room.* Have the students trace the route from the office to the boys' room with their fingers. (CALLA: Imagery)

Play the tape or read the dialogue. Ask half the class to repeat the first part of the conversation and the other half to repeat the second part **chorally.** Help students continue to repeat the dialogue, substituting students' names, the other locations in the picture, and appropriate *-ing* verbs: *Where's **Michael**? He's in the **music room.** What's he doing? He's **playing** the piano. Where's the music room? It's next to* *the art room.* (Use the phrases *next to, across from, between.*) Work **Teacher-Class** and **Teacher-Student.**

Playing *Where Am I?* Have students play a guessing game in pairs. One student describes what he or she is doing. The other guesses his or her location S1: *I am reading a book. Where am I?* S2: *Are you in the library?* S1: *I am eating lunch. Where am I?* S2: *Are you in the cafeteria?* etc. Students answer *Yes, I am* or *No, I'm not.* Have students switch roles and continue. (CALLA: Guessing)

 **Comparing written language with pictures.** Students answer true/false questions and rewrite false statements. Teaching suggestions are provided in the Skills Journal annotation.

ART Drawing a school map. In pairs, have students draw a map of one or more floors of your school. Have students label the different locations: *library, cafeteria,* etc. Next, have students play a guessing game. One partner chooses a location. S1: *I am next to the library.* The other partner guesses S1's location. *Are you in the computer lab?* Students take turns.

LIFE SKILLS Asking for and giving directions. In pairs, have students use their maps of the school to take turns giving each other directions from your classroom to other parts of the school. Review *left, right, next to, across from,* and *between* as needed. Encourage students to combine known and new language. For example, *Where's the library? / Go straight. Turn left. It's next to the office.*

 MUSIC "Bingo." Play the tape or sing the song. (See the Tapescript in the Appendix.) Encourage students to sing along.

ONGOING ASSESSMENT

PORTFOLIO Self-introduction. Ask students to write self-introductions. Have them include *name, age, where they live,* and *favorite colors/foods/activities.* Observe different students' levels of participation. Does the student use phrases and single words? Complete sentences? Are ideas easy to follow? Use the **Anecdotal Record Form** in the *Amazing Assessment Package.*

MULTICULTURAL AWARENESS
Invite students from other countries to tell the class about the layout of their schools in their home cultures. Ask students to make simple drawings on the board. Ask them to describe any differences between their former school and the school they now attend.

TEACHER TO TEACHER
If your students work with other teachers, you may want to mention to them that learning how to give and follow directions, both inside and outside of the classroom, is valuable for ESL learners. Controlled practice with a map makes the new words, phrases, and question patterns easier to learn.

READ AND DO

Friend to Friend

LEVEL C, PAGE 6

KEY EXPERIENCES
- Discussing secret codes
- Following directions
- Using the secret code
- Making new secret codes

KEY LANGUAGE
- *What is this message?*
- *Crack these codes!*
- *Make a new secret code.*
- code, letters, message, numbers, secret, symbols, system

MULTI-LEVEL TEACHING STRATEGIES

Building background: Discussing secret codes. Show students the code at the top of page 6 of the Student Book. Explain that a code is a secret way of sending a message. Ask students if they ever send codes in their own languages. Ask who else might use codes. Then ask students questions at appropriate levels. Here are some sample questions:

Speech Emergence: *Does the code use letters? How many numbers does the code use? What does 2 mean?*

Developing Fluency: *How many letters are there in English? So how many letters are in this code? What does 2-15-25 mean?*

Following directions. Continue asking students about the code. Elicit answers **Teacher-Class, Teacher-Student,** for example, *What does 4 mean? / Four is D (or 4 means D). / What is K? / 11 is K.* Divide the class into two teams. Write a simple word on the board using the code. Have students raise their hands when they know the word. A correct answer earns a point for the team. Possible words: *girl* (7-9-18-12), *is* (9-19), *go* (7-15), *play* (16-12-1-25), *toy* (20-15-25). (CALLA: Sequencing)

TPR code words. Have students sit in a circle. Assign one or more letters to each student, depending on the number in your class. Call out a number. The appropriate student stands and says the corresponding letter in the code. T: *3,* S1: *C,* T: *7,* S2: *G.* Next, say the numbers for a simple word, for example, *3-1-18 (car).* The appropriate students stand up and say the letters *C-A-R.* The rest of the class repeats the word *car.*

2 EXPLORE

Activating prior knowledge. Direct students' attention to the first message on page 6. Ask, *What is this message?* Ask students to work on their own to figure out the message. Circulate, helping as needed. Then have students tell their neighbors what the message is. Check the message with the class. (Message: *Meet me after school.*)

Following directions. Ask students to read the next two directions. Check understanding by asking **multi-level questions,** such as *How can you make the code harder? What is another way to make the code harder? What happens if you do the code backwards? If 9 is "A," what does 10-9-20-20 mean? (ball)*

Using the code. In pairs, have students figure out the two messages in Exercise B. Remind students to pay attention to the punctuation in the codes. Circulate, helping as needed. Check the messages with the class by asking two volunteers to write the messages on the board. (Messages: *Learning English with friends is fun! You are my best friend!*) Invite partners to continue using the codes to write simple messages.

••• **3 EXTEND** •••

MATH Adding and subtracting in code. Ask each student to write one math problem in code on a small piece of paper. Provide two examples on the board: *20-11= what letter?* (I) and *5 + 8= what letter?* (M). Gather all the problems in a pile. Have students draw one problem at a time from the pile and read it to the class. Pause for students to write their answers. After five problems, pause to check answers, then continue.

Making a geometric code. Together with the students, make a code using shapes. Review geometric shapes as needed (*triangle, square, circle, rectangle*). Then have pairs or small groups each write a message and give it to you on a separate piece of paper. Write the messages on the board in code. Have each student write down the messages. Then check answers. (CALLA: Guessing)

Challenge: Making new secret codes. As a challenge, invite students to create new secret codes in pairs or small groups. When students have finished the code, have them write a message. Ask pairs or groups to exchange messages and try to crack the new codes. Have students present their codes to the class, explaining how the codes work.

Conducting a coded scavenger hunt. Explain that a scavenger hunt is a game in which players must follow clues to find various things. Use the code in the book to write clues for a scavenger hunt in the classroom or on the playground. You may want to send each group on a different quest. Present an example clue on the board: *7-15, 20-15, 20-8-5, 4-15-15-18 (Go to the door)*. Have small groups work cooperatively to figure out the clues. (CALLA: Cooperation)

STAFF DEVELOPMENT
See the *Amazing How-To Handbook* for more on developing critical thinking skills.

MULTICULTURAL AWARENESS
You may want to mention that secret codes have been used around the world for thousands of years. During World War II, the U.S. used the Navajo language as a secret code. This Native American language proved so complex that the code was never broken.

TEACHER TO TEACHER
If your students work with other teachers, you may want to suggest that they encourage ESL students to write messages to their classmates using the code.

THE WEEKEND

Friend to Friend

LEVEL C, PAGE 7

KEY EXPERIENCES

- Identifying days of the week
- Talking about favorite weekend activities
- Creating new song verses
- Making a personal calendar
- Writing poems about weekend activities

KEY LANGUAGE

- *Monday, it is gone.*
- *It's the weekend.*
- days of the week
- playing, weekend

●●● **1 INTRODUCE** ●●●

MULTI-LEVEL TEACHING STRATEGIES

Building background. Open to the song, "The Weekend," on page 7 of the Student Book. Engage students in a discussion of the scene. Introduce and practice the names of the activities: *jump rope, play ball, fly a kite, play soccer, ride a bike.* Include all the students by asking questions appropriate to each student's language stage. Here are some sample questions:

Speech Emergence: (Point to the girl jumping rope.) *Do you like to jump rope? Is there a boy playing soccer? How many girls do you see?*

Developing Fluency: *Why is the weekend fun? Who can you play with?*

Days of the week. Explain to the students that Saturday and Sunday are weekend days. Ask students what they like to do on the weekend. Write the days of the week on the board. Model each word, pausing for students to repeat. Have students print each day of the week on a separate card. Have students shuffle the cards, then put the words in correct order. In pairs, have students take turns turning over a card and saying the name of the week. *Monday. Tuesday*, etc., then talking about what they do each day. *On Monday I go to swimming class*, etc.

●●● **2 EXPLORE** ●●●

♫♪

📼 **MUSIC "The Weekend."** Play the tape or sing the song. Have students place their cards of the days of the week face up in a row. Encourage students to point to each day of the week as it is sung. Then sing the song again as students sing along. Have students point to each line as they sing.

Talking about favorite weekend activities. Point to the students playing in the pictures. Say, *They're having fun.* Ask students to say what they're doing. Have students read the questions at the bottom of the page: *Do you love the weekend? Why? What do you do on the weekend?* Ask students to talk with partners about their favorite weekend activities. Children can then take turns pantomiming what they like to do. Print the names of the activities on chart paper.

Creating new song verses. Help students create new verses to the song. The art on page 7 can serve as cues for additional song verses. You can also refer to the list of the students' favorite activities. Write the words on chart paper to the new verses created by the class. Later, students can illustrate the chart.

GUIDED READING Comparing a song and a poem. Tell students that this time you are going to read "The Weekend" as a poem. Have students read along with you **chorally.** Do they like "The Weekend" better as a song or as a poem? Why?

SKILLS JOURNAL PAGE 6

Home-School Connection. Students write about their weekend activities. Teaching suggestions are provided in the Skills Journal annotation.

Home-School Connection: Making a personal calendar. Have students make personal calendars for the current month. Make sure there is enough space for students to write down activities. Encourage students to illustrate the calendar with themes related to the current month. Have students take the calendars home and ask for help from parents filling in information about games, classes, and special events such as weddings, family birthdays, etc.

Writing poems about weekend activities. In small groups, have students write poems about weekend activities. First, brainstorm a list of possible activities to include. Ask several groups to write their poems on the board. Set the poems to a popular melody, such as "Old MacDonald."

SOCIAL STUDIES Special events in the community. Have students make a bulletin board of events and activities in your community that are of special interest to students. Show students how to look for information in your local newspaper. Students may want to contact libraries, museums, and recreation departments. Encourage students to request posters and brochures. Display the information in the classroom. (CALLA: Resourcing)

ONGOING ASSESSMENT

PORTFOLIO Creative writing. Save a copy of **Skills Journal** page 6. You may also want to use the **Writing Checklist** in the *Amazing Assessment Package.*

MULTICULTURAL AWARENESS

Invite volunteers to teach the class the days of the week in their native languages. First, have the volunteers write the words on the board. Then have the class repeat the words.

TEACHER TO TEACHER

If your students work with other teachers, you may want to remind them that lyrics can help ESL learners learn new language. Often lyrics are both predictable and repeated, and they provide a natural context for new language items. The rhythm and stress patterns also help make the words easier to learn.

STAFF DEVELOPMENT

See the *Amazing How-To Handbook* for more information about creative writing strategies.

WRITING PROJECT

Writing Project 1A, *What a Day!* is directly linked to this lesson. See the Process Writing Portfolio Program Teacher's Handbook, pages 8-9, for the Lesson Plan.

Students will find instructions and a Prewriting Sheet in the Writing Projects booklet inside the Portfolio.

COMMUNICATION 2A

Friend to Friend

LEVEL C, PAGE 8

KEY EXPERIENCES

- Identifying days of the week (R)
- Identifying months of the year
- Talking about birthdays
- Roleplaying conversations

KEY LANGUAGE

- *Is your birthday in (July)?*
- *No, it isn't. It's in (August).*
- *What day of the week is it on?*
- *It's on (Saturday).*
- days of the week (R)
- months of the year
- birthday

1 INTRODUCE

MULTI-LEVEL TEACHING STRATEGIES

Building background. Open to page 8 of the Student Book. Engage students in a discussion of the calendar. Encourage students to comment on the page. Ask questions with one-word or yes/no answers, such as *Do you like rain?* as you point to the pictures. Introduce and practice the months of the year: *January, February, March,* etc. Include all the students by asking questions appropriate to each student's language stage. Here are some sample questions:

Speech Emergence: (Point to the calendar.) *This is a calendar. How many months do you see?* (Point to a month.) *What month is this? Is this January or February? Is this July?*

Developing Fluency: *This is a calendar.* (Point to a month.) *What month is this? What month is before (March)? What month is after (October)?* Encourage students to respond in full sentences: *(November) is after (October).*

Learning a TPR chant. Teach students a months of the year chant. Clap before saying each month: (clap) *January,* (clap) *February,* (clap) *March,* (clap) *April,* etc. Assign each student a month of the year (more than one student may be assigned to each month, depending on class size). Do the chant again. As you say each month, the students who are assigned to that month stand up, clap, and then sit back down.

Learning the months of the year. Make a word card for each month. Show students the word cards. Help them read the months by syllables: *Jan-u-a-ry.* Then, place the word cards on the chalk rail in random order. Ask two students to come to the front and put the cards in correct order. Say the months in correct order, pausing after each month for students to repeat **chorally.** Follow the same procedure to review days of the week.

Using a calendar. Point to the word on the calendar for the present month. Ask students, *What month is this?* Encourage students to respond, *This is (October).* Ask about other months. Work **T-C; T-S.** Next, point to the days of the week. Ask students, *What day is this?* Encourage students to respond, *This is (Friday).* Work **T-C; T-S.**

2 EXPLORE

 **Look, listen, and talk.** Play the tape or read the conversation at the top of page 8 as students follow along in their books. Then divide the class into two groups to practice the conversation. One group asks the questions, the other answers. Have groups switch roles and repeat.

Talking about the calendar. Read the month words on the page **chorally.** With the students talk about the pictures that illustrate the calendar. Adapt the discussion to the experiences of your students and ask **multi-level questions,** such as *Does it snow here in December? Is it sunny in June or rainy? When do we go back to school? What other things could you use to illustrate a calendar?*

Vocabulary development. Students practice ordinal numbers and reading a calendar. **Data collection.** Students collect information about which day they were born and graph it. Teaching suggestions are provided in the Skills Journal annotations.

ART Making a birthday chart. Cut twelve large birthday cakes out of construction paper. Write the months on the birthday cakes or have student volunteers write the months. Invite partners or groups to decorate the cakes with glitter and confetti. Have students write their birth dates on the birthday cakes: *Alexander- March 16.* Display the chart in the classroom.

SOCIAL STUDIES Marking birthdays of famous people. As a class, brainstorm a list of possible famous people's birthdays to mark on a class calendar. Assign one famous person's birthday to a pair of students. Have students use their textbooks or resource materials to find out the birth dates. Have students write the birth dates on the chart, for example, *Martin Luther King, January 16, 1929.* (CALLA: Resourcing)

SOCIAL STUDIES Celebrating birthdays. Discuss typical birthday celebrations in the U.S. Mention that at birthday parties young students often sing "Happy Birthday," play traditional games like "Pin the Tail on the Donkey," and eat birthday cake and ice cream. Some students have an extra candle on the cake "to grow on."

ONGOING ASSESSMENT

PERFORMANCE Oral language. Display the month word cards and the day word cards. Point to the word cards at random. Can the students say the months of the year? The days of the week? Cue two students to do the conversation in the book by pointing to two month cards and a day card. Observe different students' levels of accuracy and fluency. Record your observations on the **Oral Language Checklist** in the *Amazing Assessment Package.*

MULTICULTURAL AWARENESS

Invite volunteers to teach the class birthday games from their home cultures. First have the volunteers demonstrate, using the primary language as needed. Then have groups or pairs play one of the games.

Be aware that in some parts of the world, specific birth dates are not always recorded and not all culture groups or religions celebrate birthdays.

Friend to Friend

LEVEL C, PAGE 9

KEY EXPERIENCES

■ Describing/classifying objects

■ Creating new conversations using the Data Bank

■ Roleplaying offering/accepting gifts

■ Comparing birthday celebrations

■ Making a birthday card

KEY LANGUAGE

■ *Happy Birthday!*

■ *Here's a present for you.*

■ *Open it and find out.*

■ *I hope you like it.*

■ *Thank you!/You're welcome.*

■ baseball cap, book, bracelet, pin, ring, scarf, sweater, tape, tee-shirt

MULTI-LEVEL TEACHING STRATEGIES

Building background: Describing and classifying objects. Bring to class a variety of things used to help celebrate birthdays, such as party favors and hats, balloons, candles and streamers, and a wrapped birthday present. You might also bring empty containers of the following: ice cream, cake mix, ice cream cones, and soft drink mix. Later have the students describe the objects and sort them by function, color, and size. Have students guess why you brought these objects to class. Also ask students to predict what the wrapped birthday present is. List their ideas on the board. (CALLA: Grouping)

Include all the students by asking questions appropriate to each student's language stage. Here are some sample questions:

Speech Emergence: (Hold up a birthday hat.) *Is this a candle or a balloon? What is the candle for? What color is this balloon?*

Developing Fluency: *What do you think this is for?* (Hold up the ice cream cone.) *What do you put in this?*

Roleplaying with puppets. Hold up two puppets. Explain that one of them is having a birthday. Set up some of the birthday objects and put party hats on the puppets. Model a conversation with the puppets:

P1: *Happy birthday! How old are you today?*
P2: *I'm nine.*
P1: *Here's a present for you.*
P2: *Thank you. What is it?*

Practice **Teacher-Class; Teacher-Student; Student-Student.**

Activating prior knowledge. Open to page 9 of the Student Book. Encourage students to comment on the page. Have students describe the girls and what they are wearing.

📺 Look, listen, and talk. Say, *Today is Sue Lin's birthday.* Students listen as you read the text or play the tape. Read or play the tape again. Have students follow along. Then ask **multi-level questions,** such as *What does she have? Which girl is having a birthday? How old is the girl? Is the present something to wear or to eat?*

Personalizing the conversation. Have students use the Data Bank as they roleplay the conversation in the book. Then have them switch roles. Encourage students to personalize the conversation in any way they choose.

Vocabulary development. Students learn names of common items. Teaching suggestions are provided in the Skills Journal annotation.

ART Drawing a gift. Have students choose the name of another classmate at random and draw what they would give that person as a gift. Ask several pairs to roleplay the conversation in the book, substituting their own information and the gifts they have drawn. Label the drawings as picture/vocabulary cards and display in the classroom.

Making a birthday banner. Have students use crayons and long sheets of paper to make birthday banners for a friend's birthday. Have students start by printing HAPPY BIRTHDAY (+ name of student) in big letters. Help students add other things about their friend, *You're nice. You're my friend.*

SOCIAL STUDIES Comparing birthdays. With students talk about different birthday customs throughout the world, such as piñatas in Mexico. Encourage students to bring different birthday songs to class and teach them to other class members. In addition, encourage students to bring to class examples or descriptions of traditional birthday foods from their home cultures. (CALLA: Comparing)

Home-School Connection: Making a birthday card. Bring in some examples of birthday cards for students to look at and discuss. Then invite students to make their own cards for a family member's next birthday.

ONGOING ASSESSMENT

PORTFOLIO Vocabulary. Save **Skills Journal** page 9 as an example of vocabulary mastery.

MULTICULTURAL AWARENESS
Set aside a special day for students to share birthday food and games from their home cultures.

Friend to Friend

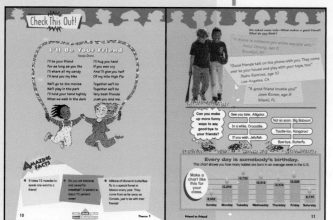

LEVEL C, PAGES 10–11

KEY EXPERIENCES

- Discussing friendship
- Guided reading of a poem
- Reading "Amazing Facts"
- Reading quotes about friendship
- Enjoying humor
- Using a chart to get information

KEY LANGUAGE

- *A friend is someone ...*
- born, cry, friend, hug, lend, share
- names of animals

1 INTRODUCE

MULTI-LEVEL TEACHING STRATEGIES

Building background: Discussing friendship. Engage students in a discussion of friendship. Talk about what makes someone a good friend. List the students' ideas in a **word web.**

Include all the students by asking questions appropriate to each student's language stage. Here are some sample questions:

Speech Emergence: *Do friends share? Is a friend someone you have fun with?*

Developing Fluency: *What makes a good friend? Think of a special friend. Why do you like him or her?*

Sharing friendship. Ask students to stand up one at a time and mime something that shows what friendship is to them or that shows an activity they can do with a friend. Have the rest of the class guess what the activity is, for example, *a hug, swimming, playing catch.* (CALLA: Guessing)

2 EXPLORE

Activating prior knowledge. Open to pages 10 and 11 of the Student Book. Read the title of the section aloud, "Check This Out!" Indicate that the title means "look at this" and that these are all short, interesting pieces. Encourage students to comment about the pages.

GUIDED READING Poem. Have students listen as you play the tape or read the poem aloud. Read or play again as students follow along in their texts. Divide the class into two groups. Have groups read the poem **chorally,** alternating verses. Ask students to identify the rhyming words in each stanza. Then have partners read the poem, alternating verses.

Reading for information: Amazing Facts. Direct students' attention to the bottom of page. Read or play the tape. Then give students time to reread information **independently.** Ask **multi-level questions,** such as *How many muscles do you need to speak? Does a banana have a lot of water in it?*

Quotes about friendship. Read or play the tape as students read what other students have said about friends at the top of page 11. Point out the use of quotation marks indicating that these are the student's exact words. Find out if the students agree with what is written, *Do you share secrets with your good friends? Do you talk to your good friends on the phone?*

Funny ways to say good-bye. Have students listen as you read the expressions for saying good-bye. Model each expression, pausing for students to repeat. Work **T-C; T-S.** In pairs, have the students work to make up their own expressions. Next, list them on the board.

Using a chart to get information. Play the tape or read and then discuss the chart about birthdays. Check understanding with **multi-level questions:** *How many babies were born on Sunday? Thursday?* etc. *When were the most babies born? The least?* Practice comparatives: *Were more babies born on Monday or Wednesday? Monday or Friday?*

SKILLS JOURNAL PAGES 10–11

Cloze poetry; interviewing. Students complete the poem, using free choice of words and interview classmates about friendship. **Reading for a purpose; research.** Students read about animals, then answer questions. Teaching suggestions are provided in the Skills Journal annotations.

... **3 EXTEND** ...

MATH Creating a class birthday chart. Together, make a chart like the one in the book showing on which day of the week students were born. If any students don't know on which day they were born, have them choose a day. Ask, *How many of you were born on Sunday? Thursday?* etc.

Writing a friendship poem. Have students write their own poems, modeled after the one in the book. Circulate and help as needed. Allowing students to use the first and/or last stanzas from the book will make the activity easier. Ask students to illustrate their poems as well.

SCIENCE Learning about animals. Help students find out about the animals mentioned on page 11. Brainstorm possible questions to explore: *What kind of animal is it?* (amphibian, mammal, etc.) *Where does it live? How does it move?* (swim, jump, fly, etc.) *What does it eat?* Together, make a class chart. Display it in the classroom. (CALLA: Resourcing)

- - - - - ONGOING ASSESSMENT - - - - -

PORTFOLIO Language experience writing. Have students write their own quotes about what makes a good friend. Later you can display student quotes in the classroom. Save **Skills Journal** page 11.

STAFF DEVELOPMENT
See the *Amazing How-to Handbook* for notes on word webs.

LANGUAGE POWER A

Friend to Friend

LEVEL C, PAGE 12

KEY EXPERIENCES

- Talking about preferences
- Sharing interests
- Roleplaying an interview
- Creating "Things I Like" stories
- Making take-home books

KEY LANGUAGE

- *Do you like (animals)?*
- *Do you like to (sing)?*
- *Yes, I do./No, I don't.*
- animals, sing, games, vegetables
- dance, draw, like, swim, soccer, pizza, read

1 INTRODUCE

MULTI-LEVEL TEACHING STRATEGIES

TPR Pantomime various activities the students are familiar with, such as *hop, jump, sleep, eat,* or the activities on page 12 of the Student Book. Ask students to name each action. Model in the pattern, *I like to (hop).* Have students repeat **chorally.** Then have individual students pantomime activities as the other students guess the activity being pantomimed. Then ask the student who pantomimed the activity, *Do you like to ...?* Prompt the student to answer, *Yes, I do./No, I don't.* (CALLA: Guessing)

Building background: Talking about preferences. Hold up pictures or drawings of activities and of various objects the students are familiar with, such as food, animals, toys. As you do, ask, *Do you like (pizza)?* Elicit an answer, *Yes, I do/No, I don't.* Work **T-C; T-S.** Include all the students by asking questions appropriate to each student's language stage. Here are some sample questions:

Speech Emergence: *Do you like to dance? Do you like milk? What do you like to eat?*

Developing Fluency: *Do you like to eat, dance, or play soccer? What fruit do you like to eat best?*

Home-School Connection: Sharing interests. Ask the students to bring to school something from home that they especially like. Encourage them to say, *I like this book.* With students of greater fluency ask, *Why do you like it?*

ART Creating word cards. Have students cut out pictures of things they like and mount them on index cards. Help them label the cards. Partners take turns showing each other the cards they made: S1: *I like (games). Do you like (games)?* S2 responds: *Yes, I do./No, I don't.*

2 EXPLORE

Activating prior knowledge. Open to page 12 of the Student Book. Encourage students to talk about the page. Remind them that the bubbles show that people are talking and that the bold-face (heavy) type signals a substitution word.

 **Look, listen, and talk.** Play the tape or model the page yourself. Students listen and point to each picture and word. Work **T-C; T-S** with the substitution words. Do the top half and the bottom half separately. Then have students work in pairs, taking turns asking and answering all of the possible exchanges.

Roleplaying an interview. Invite students to interview each other. First have students make microphones out of empty paper towel rolls and aluminum foil; they can use a heavy string or yarn as a cord. Next, have the class brainstorm some interview questions: *What's your name? Do you like to sing? Do you like the color red? Do you like soccer?* Then have students continue on their own. (CALLA: Brainstorming)

Building sight vocabulary. Have students "read" the pictures on the page, with the type covered. Then have them cover up the page and read the type. Skip around the page asking, *What's number one at the top? What's number 2 at the bottom?* After the student answers with the noun *(vegetables)*, ask, *Do you like ...?*

Expressing likes and dislikes; art. Students express opinions of various items and give oral presentations of art work. Teaching suggestions are provided in the Skills Journal annotation.

Creating "Things I Like" stories. Have each child make 3 x 5 cards with *Yes, I do* and *No, I don't* labels. Make up a "Things I Like" story about things you really do like. Whenever you say *I like*, have students agree or disagree by holding up their *Yes, I do* or *No, I don't* cards. Then encourage students to make up their own stories, collaboratively or individually. (CALLA: Cooperation)

Home-School Connection: Making take-home books. Have students make their own illustrated take-home books listing things they like to do. Help each student make the book appropriate to his/her level; for example, from drawings + simple labels *(swim)*, to complete sentences *(I like to swim.)*, to longer sentences *(I like to swim, but I don't like to dance.)*.

Building vocabulary. Use *Amazing English!* Word Attack 3 Interactive Vocabulary Games for practice with vocabulary.

ONGOING ASSESSMENT

PERFORMANCE Oral language. Have partners roleplay the conversation in the book. One student asks the questions, the other answers *Yes, I do./No. I don't.* Observe students' levels of participation. Record your observations on the **Oral Language Checklist** in the *Amazing Assessment Package.*

MULTICULTURAL AWARENESS
Encourage students to talk about activities and sports popular in their home cultures. Ask students to plan demonstrations for the class or to bring in photographs or objects related to the activities.

LANGUAGE POWER B

THEME 1 • • • • • • • •

Friend to Friend

LEVEL C, PAGE 13

KEY EXPERIENCES

- Telling time
- Roleplaying making plans
- Making a schedule
- Making sand clocks
- Finding out about schedules/times

KEY LANGUAGE

- *It's (a quarter after one).*
- *Let's (go to the movies) on (Saturday).*
- *What time do you want to go?*
- *How about two-thirty?*
- half past, quarter to, quarter after

MATERIALS

- a funnel, sand, coffee filter paper, a clear plastic jar

1 INTRODUCE

MULTI-LEVEL TEACHING STRATEGIES

Building background: Telling time. Use a large practice analog clock to teach students how to tell time to the quarter hour. Model the language, *It's a quarter past (three).* Have volunteers practice setting the large analog clock. Continue with other times. Ask, *What time is it?* Include all the students by asking questions appropriate to each student's language stage. Here are some sample questions:

Speech Emergence: *Is it two fifteen? Is it a quarter to three or a quarter after three?*

Developing Fluency: (Set the clock.) *What time is it?* (Set the clock again.) *What time is it now? Which time is later?*

Roleplaying. Use puppets to roleplay a conversation about meeting at a specific time. For example:

> P1: *Let's go to the library on Monday?*
> P2: *What time do you want to go?*
> P1: *How about two-thirty?*
> P2: *Okay. I can go then.*

Divide the class into two groups. Have one group repeat puppet 1's lines; the other group repeat puppet 2's lines. Switch roles and repeat.

2 EXPLORE

Activating prior knowledge. Open to page 13 of the Student Book. Encourage students to comment about the page and to describe any clocks or watches they see in your classroom. Make sure students understand the difference between a clock and a watch.

Look, listen, and talk. Review vocabulary, *clock, watches, movies.* Students listen as you read the text or play the tape. Read or play the tape again. Check comprehension by saying, *Look at number 1. What time is it?* Encourage students to respond, *It's a quarter after one,* or *It's one-fifteen.* Continue with number 2 and number 3. Divide the class into two groups to practice the conversation. Then have partners practice, using the information at the bottom of the page and their own ideas for activities, days, and times.

Discussing time. Point to the analog and digital clocks on the page and ask students what the difference is. Involve each child in the discussion by asking **multi-level questions:** *Do you have a watch or a clock?*

How many clocks do you have? What does the clock in (your room) look like? Why do you use an alarm clock? (CALLA: Deduction)

 **MUSIC "Roll Over"** Play the tape or sing the song for students. (See the Tapescript in the Appendix.) Then invite them to sing along.

SKILLS JOURNAL PAGE 13 **Telling time; writing.** Students practice writing various times and writing simple conversations from prompts. Teaching suggestions are provided in the Skills Journal annotation.

 ••• **3 EXTEND** •••

LIFE SKILLS Making a schedule. Ask students to think about every activity they do on a typical school day and on the weekends, and the times when they do them. Then have each students make two charts: one for the school day, the other for the weekend. Ask students to present their schedules in small groups or to the whole class. (CALLA: Organizational Planning)

SCIENCE Making sand clocks. Tape the filter paper spout closed and punch a small hole in it with a thumbtack. Line the funnel with the paper spout. Place the funnel in the jar, with the bottom of the funnel at least three inches above the bottom of the jar. Fill the funnel with sand. At regular intervals, have students measure how much sand has flowed through. Have students record their measurements. Can they discover a flow rate?

LIFE SKILLS Finding out about schedules/times. Teach students how to use the telephone to get information, such as movie times and bus schedules. Help students understand that they often will get a recorded message that they must listen to carefully to get the information they need. Use a tape recorder to make your own messages for practice.

ONGOING ASSESSMENT

PERFORMANCE Oral language Show students the analog clock set at various times. Ask students to tell you what time it is. Choose the setting according to each student's level of ability. Observe different students' levels of accuracy. Record your observations on the **Oral Language Checklist** in the *Amazing Assessment Package*.

PORTFOLIO Save **Skills Journal** page 13 as an example of mastery of telling time and ability to write conversations from prompts.

TEACHER TO TEACHER
If your students work with other teachers, you may want to encourage them to find opportunities to ask students about the time of day, their schedules, and activity plans. Knowing how to tell time and obtain schedule information is an important survival skill for ESL students, and ample practice will greatly benefit them.

HANDS-ON MATH

Friend to Friend

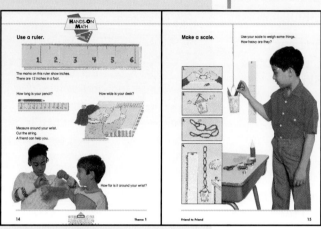

LEVEL C, PAGES 14–15

KEY EXPERIENCES

- Using a ruler/a scale
- Measuring/describing size and weight
- Following directions
- Making a simple scale
- Comparing sizes/weights

KEY LANGUAGE

- *How long is (your pencil)?*
- *How wide is (your desk)?*
- *Which is longer/heavier?*
- inches, foot, heavy, measure, ruler, scale, weigh

MATERIALS

- several rulers, a balance scale, paper cups, string, rubber bands, paper clips, pushpins, strips of paper, pencils

••• **1 INTRODUCE** •••

MULTI-LEVEL TEACHING STRATEGIES

Building background: Using a ruler. Hold up a ruler. Say, *This is a ruler. The marks on the ruler show inches.* Write *ruler* and *inches* on the board. Have students repeat. Continue, *What do we use a ruler for? We use a ruler to measure things.* Invite students to examine rulers: *Find the number 3. That is three inches*, etc. Measure a few objects to the nearest inch. For example, say, *How long is this pencil? It's seven inches long.* Point out how to use *wide* and *long.* Work **T-C.** Then have partners measure objects. Ask questions appropriate to each student's language stage. Here are some sample questions:

Speech Emergence: *How wide is your notebook? How wide is your book? Is your notebook wider?*

Developing Fluency: *Which is wider, your notebook or your book? What is the longest thing at your table? How long is it?*

Building background: Using a scale. To introduce weighing, ask volunteers to hold cups containing small objects, such as paper clips, rubber bands, and push tacks. Ask them which cup feels heavier. Show a balance scale and say, *This is a scale.* Place the cup with the paper clips on the scale. Next, place the cup with rubber bands. Ask, *Which weigh more?* Repeat with various combinations of small classroom objects. Ask students to write down what each cup weighs and make comparisons: *The paper clips weigh more than the stickers. The stickers weigh less than the tacks.* (CALLA: Comparing)

••• **2 EXPLORE** •••

Activating prior knowledge. Open to pages 14 and 15 of the Student Book. Ask students to look at the ruler, pencil, desk, and scale. Next, ask students to hold up their left arms and point to their wrists.

Following directions. Ask the students to read page 14 in sections. Pause and ask **multi-level questions** to check understanding of each section. First section: *What do the marks on this ruler show? How many inches are there in a foot?* Second section: *How long is the pencil in the book? How long is your own pencil?* Repeat with *desk.* Third section: *What are you going to measure? What can you use? Who can help you?* Model *How far is it around your wrist?* Show how to measure using a string, *It's 5 inches.* Students repeat the question and answer **chorally.**

Making comparisons. Ask various students *How far is it around your wrist?* Ask the rest of the class to listen carefully and write down the answer. Model on the board first: *Thomas - 4 1/2 inches.* After eliciting answers from several students, check understanding of the data: *Anna, how far is it around Thomas's wrist?* Encourage complete answers, *It is 4 1/2 inches.* Make comparisons: *Whose wrist is bigger, Theresa's or Tony's?* Work, **T-C** and **T-S.**

Making the scale. Direct students' attention to page 15. Point to the pictures as you demonstrate the steps: *This is a paper clip. You open the paper clip. This is a paper cup. The paper clip is attached to the paper cup,* etc. Encourage students to ask questions about each step. (CALLA: Questioning for Clarification)

Calibrating the scale. Attach the scale to a wall with a push pin. Next to the scale attach a strip of paper. Write the number 0 so that it is parallel to the rim of the cup. Put a nickel in and write the number 1 parallel to the rim of the cup. Explain that each number represents a unit. *It weighs 1 unit.* Continue until there are ten nickels in the cup.

Measuring and weighing. Students work independently or in pairs to complete measuring and weighing activities. Teaching suggestions are provided in the Skills Journal annotation.

MATH Making a height chart. In pairs, have students take turns measuring each other. As students measure, ask them to say their partner's height, *You're 3 feet 10 inches tall.* Have students mark their heights with masking tape and print their names underneath. When the chart is completed, have each child say his or her height: *I'm 3 feet 9 inches tall.* Ask students to listen and make comparisons: *Tina is taller than Gerald.* (CALLA: Comparing)

MATH Estimating weight. Put different objects, such as cotton balls, dimes, and buttons, in paper cups. Next to each cup, place a piece of paper. Have students guess how much each item weighs and write down their guesses. Weigh all of the items to determine whose guess was closest. (CALLA: Guessing)

Home-School Connection. Ask students to measure five objects at home and write down the information. Later, have students tell each other what they measured and the results: *My toothbrush is 10 inches long.*

STAFF DEVELOPMENT
See *The CALLA Handbook* , chapters 9 and 10, for more about teaching math and science in the ESL classroom.

A NEW FRIEND NAMED CHARLIE

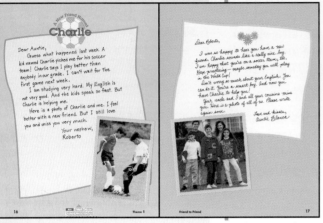

LEVEL C, PAGES 16–17

KEY EXPERIENCES

- Discussing ways to communicate
- Reading letters
- Identifying main idea
- Relating reading to own experience
- Writing a letter to a friend or relative
- Sharing news about a project or activity

KEY LANGUAGE

- *Dear ...,*
- *Your nephew,*
- *I was so happy to hear ...*
- *Please write again soon.*
- *envelope, letter, mail, stamp*

• • • 1 INTRODUCE • • •

MULTI-LEVEL TEACHING STRATEGIES

Building background: Discussing ways to communicate. Engage students in a discussion of how they communicate with friends or family members who live far away. Do they write letters? Do they call on the telephone? What do they talk about? Have they ever sent an audio or video tape? Have students look at the letters from students on pages 16 and 17 in the Student Book. Together, make a list on the board of the advantages and disadvantages of communicating by telephone and by letters. Include all the students by asking questions appropriate to each student's language stage. Here are some sample questions:

Speech Emergence: *Do you write letters? Do you call? Who do you write? Who do you call? What do you tell them?*

Developing Fluency: *Why do you like to write letters? Why do you like to call? Which is better? Why?*

Describing personal experiences. Ask students to think about something nice that happened at school. After several minutes, have students **quick write** for five minutes. As needed, guide students with the following questions: *What happened? When did it happen? Where did it happen? Who else was there? How did you feel? Did you feel happy?* Emphasize that complete sentences are not necessary. Also have students draw pictures. Then have partners take turns telling each other about their experiences, using their drawings to present what happened. (CALLA: Cooperation)

• • • 2 EXPLORE • • •

Activating prior knowledge. Open to pages 16 and 17 of the Student Book. Read aloud the title at the top of the page, "A New Friend Named Charlie." Then ask students to tell you the person each letter is for and the person each is from. Point out the greetings *Dear ...* and the closings *Your nephew* and *Love and kisses.*

📺 **GUIDED READING Recalling details.** Play the tape or read the first letter as the students follow along in their books. Ask students to reread the letter, one paragraph at a time. Pause to ask **multi-level questions.** Paragraph 1: *What happened last week? Who thinks he is a good player? How do you know?* Paragraph 2: *Is he studying hard?*

Does he understand his teachers? Who speaks so fast? Who is helping him? Paragraph 3: *Who is in the photo? Who does he miss?*

Then play the tape or read the second letter. Ask students to reread the second letter, one paragraph at a time **independently.** Again, pause to ask questions.

Identifying main idea. Check general understanding of each letter. Roberto's letter: *Is Roberto happy? Why?* Auntie Blanca's letter: *Does she think Roberto is doing fine?*

Relating reading to own experience. Ask students to reread the second paragraph of Roberto's letter again. Ask them to compare his experience of learning English with their own. (CALLA: Comparing)

Home–School Connection. Students write letters about their activities in class, at home, and in sports to share with the class. **Reading for a purpose; writing.** Students read a paragraph about soccer and write answers to questions. Teaching suggestions are provided in the Skills Journal annotations.

ART Making an activity mural. Ask students to cut out magazine photos or make drawings of activities they enjoy. Have students mount the pictures on a large piece of paper. Ask students to label the activities. Assist with vocabulary as needed. Display in the classroom.

Home-School Connection: Writing a letter. Ask each student to write a letter to a friend or relative about a recent project or activity. Suggest that students use the letters in the book as models, but brainstorm other closings students might use. Circulate and help as needed. Then provide examples and show students how to address envelopes. Encourage students to ask parents for help getting addresses so that they can mail the letters.

ONGOING ASSESSMENT

PERFORMANCE Letter writing. Check the letters the students wrote to a friend or relative. Did they express their ideas clearly? Consider spelling, phrasing, and grammar. Do you have a general understanding of what students want to communicate? Use the **Writing Checklist** in the *Amazing Assessment Package.*

PORTFOLIO Save a copy of **Skills Journal** page 15 as an example of free writing and knowledge of basic spelling and basic structures.

STAFF DEVELOPMENT
See the *Amazing How-To Handbook* for more on reading strategies and teaching writing.

TEACHER TO TEACHER
Students may enjoy writing letters to students in another school in your town or in a nearby community. Contact a colleague to arrange such an exchange. Students may feel most comfortable writing to other ESL students who can most readily relate to their own experiences.

WRITING PROJECT
Writing Project 1B, *A Friendly Letter,* is directly linked to this lesson. See the Project Writing Portfolio Program Teachers' Handbook, pages 10-11, for the Lesson Plan.

Students will find instructions and a Prewriting Sheet in the Writing Projects booklet inside the Portfolio.

LET'S PLAY SOCCER

THEME 1 •••••••

Friend to Friend

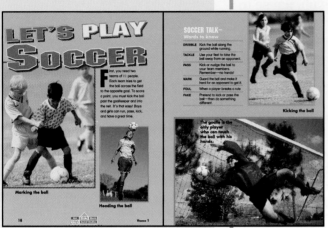

LEVEL C, PAGES 18–19

KEY EXPERIENCES

- Reading about soccer
- Explaining rules of a game
- Making up a game
- Writing rules for a game

KEY LANGUAGE

- soccer
- dribble, goal, goalie, opponent, score, tackle, pass, mark, foul, fake

1 INTRODUCE

MULTI-LEVEL TEACHING STRATEGIES

Building background. Open to pages 18 and 19 of the Student Book. Ask students to cover the text and look at the photographs. Engage students in a discussion of the scene. Find out who likes soccer, who plays it, who watches it on TV, etc. Include all students in the discussion by asking questions appropriate to each student's language stage. Here are some sample questions:

Speech Emergence: *Do you like soccer? Do you play soccer? Is it a difficult game? Do you have to be a fast runner to play soccer?*

Developing Fluency: *Why do you like soccer? Who is your favorite soccer player? Why is soccer popular?*

Explaining rules of a game. Ask students to share with the class what they know about soccer. Write the ideas on the board, rewording as needed. Prompt students, if necessary, by asking the following questions: *Is it a team sport? How many people are on a team? What equipment do you need? How do you move the ball? How do you get a point?*

2 EXPLORE

Activating prior knowledge. Ask students to look at the text on pages 18 and 19. Read the title aloud, "Let's Play Soccer," or call on a volunteer to do so. Have students count and point out the sections of the reading.

GUIDED READING Direct students' attention to the first section. Play the tape or read the paragraph aloud as the students follow along in their books. Read again as a **choral reading.** Then continue with the other sections.

Read or play the tape for "Soccer Talk." Ask how many words are explained. To check understanding, read the definitions aloud in random order, for example, *Pretend to kick or pass the ball.* Students say the word: *Fake.* Then ask students to read **independently** about the goalie. Ask, *What can the goalie use? How do the other players hit the ball?*

♪♪

🎵 **MUSIC "All Day Long."** Play the tape or sing the song for students. (See the Tapescript in the Appendix.) Then invite them to sing along.

📖 **SKILLS JOURNAL PAGES 17–18** **Vocabulary development; cloze exercise.** Students complete a cloze paragraph about soccer. **Reading for a purpose.** Students read a paragraph and write answers to questions. Teaching suggestions are provided in the Skills Journal annotations.

3 EXTEND

SOCIAL STUDIES **Making up a game.** Work together as a class or in small groups to make up a game. It can be a game similar to soccer or another field sport. For small group work, include students of varying abilities. Ask students to consider: *How many players are on a team? Do you use a ball? How do you hit it? How do you score a point? How do you win a game?* Encourage students to draw a picture of the game. (CALLA: Cooperation)

Writing rules. Ask students to write out rules to go with the game they created. Model an example on the board: *You can't touch the ball with your hands.* Circulate and help as needed. Ask students to present their rules to the class. Alternatively, have students write out the rules and display them with their pictures of the games.

ART **Drawing soccer pictures.** Ask students to draw pictures of a soccer game. First, ask students to summarize what they have read (there are eleven players on a team; no hands on the ball except for the goalie, etc.). Display in the classroom. (CALLA: Summarizing)

ONGOING ASSESSMENT

PERFORMANCE **Oral language.** Ask students to explain what they know about soccer. Prompt as needed by asking **multi-level questions:** *How many people are on a team? How do you score a point? Can you touch the ball with your hands?*, etc. Observe different levels of performance. What can students explain easily? What do they have difficulty with? Do they respond using single words? Using sentences? Record your observations on the **Oral Language Checklist** in the *Amazing Assessment Package.*

PORTFOLIO Save **Skills Journal** page 17 as an example of recalling details and using context.

STAFF DEVELOPMENT
See the *Amazing How-To Handbook* for more on ways to use music in the ESL classroom.

HOLISTIC ASSESSMENT

Friend to Friend

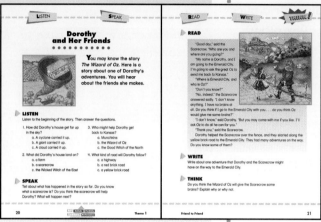

LEVEL C, PAGES 20–21

KEY EXPERIENCES

- Listening to a new story
- Describing story events
- Retelling the story
- Thinking critically
- Guided reading
- Writing a soup recipe

KEY LANGUAGE

- brains, brick, cyclone, fence, scarecrow, wicked

1 INTRODUCE

MULTI-LEVEL TEACHING STRATEGIES

These two pages offer a variety of assessment opportunities. The left-hand page consists of listening and speaking activities that follow a taped presentation. In the speaking activity, students are asked to summarize the story and make predictions based on what they have heard. The right-hand page consists of writing and critical thinking activities. These follow a reading passage that completes the listening component. You can use the activities to assess listening, speaking, reading, writing, and critical thinking skills. Have children work as a class or in small groups. Record your observations on the **Anecdotal Record Form,** the **Reading Checklist,** and the **Writing Checklist** in the *Amazing Assessment Package.*

Building background: Introducing the setting and characters. Begin by asking students if anyone knows where Kansas is. Have volunteers point out the state on a map. Then ask if anyone has ever heard the story *The Wizard of Oz.* Discuss with students that they are going to read and listen to a fantasy story about a girl named Dorothy from Kansas. Ask questions appropriate to each student's language stage. Here are some sample questions:

Speech Emergence: *Is there a real place named Kansas? Where is it? Have you ever seen the movie "The Wizard of Oz"? Is the movie real or fantasy?*

Developing Fluency: *Who knows the story of the Wizard of Oz? What can you tell the class about it? Who are the friends Dorothy makes?*

2 EXPLORE

Previewing the story. Open to pages 20 and 21 of the Student Book and let the students comment on the picture. Say, *You may know the story of the Wizard of Oz. Today we are going to learn about one of Dorothy's adventures. Remember that Dorothy is from Kansas. You will hear about the friend she makes.* If no one has heard of the story, ask them to use their imaginations and guess who the friends she makes might be. Write their ideas on the board. (CALLA: Guessing)

Preparing to listen. Tell the students they are going to hear the beginning of the story. Do **choral reading** of the listening questions before playing the tape. Give students time to do **independent reading** of the questions.

 **Listening to the story.** Read or play the tape for the first part of "Dorothy and Her Friends." You will find the tapescript in the Appendix. Have students work independently to answer the listening questions. Read or play the tape again in segments; pause for students to check their work and make corrections.

Speaking. Elicit that a cyclone is a tornado. Point out the picture of Dorothy's house being pulled in by a tornado. What do students think a wizard might look like? Help students **summarize** what has happened in the story so far. (CALLA: Summarizing)

GUIDED READING Read the story on page 21 as the students listen and follow along in their books. Do a **choral reading;** read the story again as the students read quietly in unison. (CALLA: Predicting)

Paired reading. Have students work in pairs to read the story out loud to each other. Use the **Reading Checklist** in the *Amazing Assessment Package.*

Observing the students. As you discuss the story, notice the level of participation and the particular abilities of each student. What new words have they learned? What language structures do they use? You may want to add progress notes to students' **portfolios** at this time. Use the **Anecdotal Record Form** in the *Amazing Assessment Package.*

SKILLS JOURNAL PAGE 19 **Reading comprehension; cloze exercise.** Students work independently to finish cloze paragraphs. Teaching suggestions are provided in the Skills Journal annotation. Save this page in the student's **Assessment Portfolio.**

Writing a new adventure. Ask the students to write about a new adventure that Dorothy and the scarecrow might have along the way. Use the **Writing Checklist** in the *Amazing Assessment Package.*

SOCIAL STUDIES Discussing Kansas. Have students locate Kansas on a map. Discuss the type of land around Kansas. Ask students to discuss different types of transportation and different routes that Dorothy could use to get back to Kansas. *Could she get home by boat? Why not?* Have students write a letter to Dorothy, giving her instructions on how to get back to Kansas. (CALLA: Imagery)

STAFF DEVELOPMENT

See the *Amazing How-To Handbook* and *Authentic Assessment* for more on holistic, performance, and portfolio assessment.

RELATED RESOURCES

The Cat Came Back CD-ROM, Read Along Mode: Cyclones (pages 17-19).

AMAZING FACTS

Friend to Friend

LEVEL C, PAGE 22

KEY EXPERIENCES

- Recalling details
- Playing a game
- Finding other facts
- Making up new questions in groups

KEY LANGUAGE

- Review

1 INTRODUCE

MULTI-LEVEL TEACHING STRATEGIES

Activating prior knowledge. Ask students if they remember any of the Amazing Facts they read about in this unit. Prompt if necessary by mentioning topics covered, for example, *the name Smith, soccer in England, birthdays*, etc. Have students reread the Amazing Facts on pages 4 and 10. Include all the students by asking questions appropriate to each student's language stage. Here are some sample questions:

Speech Emergence: *Were soccer games in England big long ago? Do many people have the name Smith?*

Developing Fluency: *How many muscles does it take to speak to a friend?* (72) *What is about 78 percent water?* (a banana)

Reviewing days/weeks. Use a calendar. Point to each day of the week. Model, *Monday*, etc. Work **T-C**. Ask questions: *What day is before (Monday)? What day is after (Thursday)?* Work **T-C; T-S**. Follow the same procedure, substituting the months of the year: *January*, etc. Ask questions: *What month is before (April)? What month is after (October)?*

Reviewing time. Ask students about their daily schedules: *What time do you get up? What time do you leave for school?* etc. Use a large analog clock. Set the clock to various times. Ask: *What time is it?* Encourage students to respond: *It is 1: 30. It is 2:45*, etc.

2 EXPLORE

Describing the game. Ask students to open to page 22 of the Student Book and cover the questions. Begin by telling the students that they will play the Amazing Facts game in teams. Teams earn points by correctly answering questions on the quiz gameboard. The time limit is 5–10 minutes, depending on class level. Direct students' attention to the key at the top of the page. Point out how points and bonus points are earned. Explain that they will first work in teams to mark the answers to the questions. Then the teams will compete to answer the questions orally.

Playing the game. Divide the class into teams. Set the time limit and have the teams work together to answer the questions. Circulate and help as needed. At the end of the pre-set time period, have the teams compete for the correct answers orally. Read the questions in random order. The first team to raise their hands and answer the question correctly wins a point. The team with the most points at the end of play wins the game.

Extra challenge. For extra fluency practice, ask the students to answer the questions in complete sentences: *There are eleven people on a soccer team. There are twelve inches in a foot.*

SKILLS JOURNAL PAGE 20 **Creating a game.** Students create their own games to play with classmates. Teaching suggestions are provided in the Skills Journal annotation.

3 EXTEND

SOCIAL STUDIES Finding other facts. Choose a country for the students to learn about, or allow them to select one. Have students work in small groups. Brainstorm and then assign group topics such as food, geography, climate, products, or language. Have each group list two facts on a piece of paper. Emphasize that they do not need to write full sentences. Circulate and help as needed. Then have students add their facts to a bulletin board or make a poster. (CALLA: Resourcing)

Playing a facts game Divide the class into teams. Ask the class questions based on the facts the students have reported, for example, *What do people eat there?* The first student to raise his or her hand and answer the question correctly wins a point for his or her team. The team with the most points at the end of play wins the game.

ONGOING ASSESSMENT

PERFORMANCE Listening comprehension; oral language. Ask the questions from "Amazing Facts" in random order. Have the students answer orally. Can students understand the question easily? Do they answer using single words? Can they make complete sentences? Use the **Oral Language Checklist** in the *Amazing Assessment Package.*

STAFF DEVELOPMENT

See the *Amazing How-To Handbook* for more on using games in the ESL classroom.

MULTICULTURAL AWARENESS

You may want to have volunteers bring in examples of board games they have at home in their own languages. As an alternative, have students describe games played in their home cultures.

ASSESSMENT

You will find background information on the latest thinking in assessment as well as the assessment instruments for this theme in the *Amazing Assessment Package*.

You have been collecting assessment data through the ongoing and holistic assessment options (Oral Language Checklist, Reading Checklist, Writing Checklist, Anecdotal Record Form) in this theme. The following are specific end-of-theme assessment strategies that will help you evaluate your students' progress as well as adapt your instruction to meet their needs.

Student Self-Assessment. Self-assessment surveys are a means for students to have input into their own learning process. Students can use them to **reflect** on the work they have done and the learning strategies they have used during this theme.

Interpreting and Applying Assessment Data. As teachers, you collect assessment data in order to inform your instruction. Assessment information is a tool that helps you tailor your program to better meet the needs and interests of your students.

Evaluate the checklists, anecdotal records, portfolio collections, and test results from this theme as a means of informing your instruction.

- In which areas are students showing confidence and enthusiasm?
- In which areas are they hesitant or confused?
- Should you provide more classroom opportunities for oral language or writing?
- Would certain students (or the whole class) benefit from a focused mini-lesson on a certain area or skill?
- Remember to recycle skills as you teach the next theme and provide students with many opportunities to improve their competence.

Review the results of the **Student Self-Assessment** survey and incorporate students' interests as you plan your instruction for the next theme. What do they want to learn next? Which activities did they enjoy most? If your students particularly enjoyed choral reading, roleplaying, or working in partners, try to emphasize those kinds of activities in the next theme.

THEME CELEBRATION

The end of a theme study is a good time for students to share some of their accomplishments with others. Suggest to students that you hold a celebration to spotlight their work. This celebration can be an excellent opportunity to build stronger connections with other students and teachers in the school. Your students can share the secret codes they have written and demonstrate their knowledge of soccer. They may also want to share the Amazing Facts games they have researched and played. If possible, invite family members to the theme celebration.

END-OF-THEME READ-ALOUD BOOK

A Weekend with Wendell

by Kevin Henkes

New York: Greenwillow Books, 1986

In this story about two mouse friends, Wendell spends the weekend at Sophie's house while his parents are out of town. As he takes charge, Wendell's energetic and assertive manner annoys Sophie. She secretly wishes he would leave—until the end of his visit when Sophie finally makes the rules and finds that it can be fun playing with Wendell after all.

READING CORNER

It's important to get students excited about independent reading. Remember to distribute the Literature Links Bibliography for the next theme to your students and encourage them to use the *Amazing BookBytes* CD-ROM to respond to their reading.

Families Around the World

Theme 2 celebrates diversity in families of many cultures. Through literature, articles, poetry, and language activity pages in the Student Book, the students will learn about each other's families and about some animal families. They will read about the Chinese calendar, ant colonies, and a boy who likes to sleep at his grandma's house. The Skills Journal offers opportunities for further language practice, reading, writing, and research on a variety of theme-related topics.

Multi-Level Teaching Strategies integrated into each lesson plan insure that all students can participate in these class activities, each at his or her own level of language proficiency. **Home-School Connection** activities provide enjoyable extension activities for students and family members to do together.

The **Ongoing Assessment** suggestions in the lesson plans will help you keep track of your students' progress. On **Student Book** pages 42-43, the "Listen, Speak, Read, Write, Think" selection offers an opportunity for **holistic assessment**. The end-of-theme **Wrap-Up** page includes guidelines for implementing the full range of assessment tools and interpreting the results.

PLANNING TIPS

The **At-a-Glance Lesson Planner** on the next two pages provides an overview of the Key Experiences and Key Language presented in each lesson of the theme. Quickly scan the lesson plan Materials lists to see if there are materials to gather or prepare. Check the **Wrap-Up** page in case you want to plan ahead for the Theme Celebration.

The following **Read-Aloud Books** are recommended with this theme. Gather these titles and your own theme-related favorites. We encourage you to read aloud to your students every day. If possible, record the stories on tape and let students reread the books as they listen to the tapes.

- *My Song Is Beautiful* (poetry) selected by Mary Ann Hoberman

- *Everybody Cooks Rice* by Norah Dooley

- *Not So Fast, Songololo* by Niki Daly

- *Raven: A Trickster Tale from the Northwest* by Gerald McDermott

- *Mexicali Soup* by Kathryn Hitte and William Hayes

- *Dumpling Soup* by Jama Kim Rattigan (Wrap-Up page)

READING CORNER

Encourage independent reading for information and pleasure. If possible, set up a reading corner—a quiet, comfortable place that is just for reading (and perhaps listening to any books on tape you've collected). Make a bulletin board on which you can post book covers, students' BookBytes reviews and the Literature Links Bibliographies that support each theme. See the Appendix for the complete Literature Links Bibliography for this theme. It offers a variety of fiction and non-fiction choices **in English and in other languages.**

LESSON PLAN

1 **Student Book p. 23**
Theme Opener

2 **Student Book p. 24**
Communication 1A

3 **Student Book p. 25**
Communication 1B

4 **Student Book p. 26**
Read and Do

5 **Student Book p. 27**
My Family

6 **Student Book p. 28**
Communication 2A

7 **Student Book p. 29**
Communication 2B

8 **Student Book pp. 30-31**
Check This Out!

9 **Student Book p. 32**
Language Power A

10 **Student Book p. 33**
Language Power B

11 **Student Book pp. 34-35**
Hands-On Science

12 **Student Book pp. 36-41**
The Squeaky Door

13 **Student Book pp. 42-43**
Holistic Assessment

14 **Student Book p. 44**
Amazing Facts Game

KEY EXPERIENCES

Discussing families • Sharing personal experiences • Predicting what theme titles mean

Following conversational sequence • Writing a language experience story • Making fingerprint animal families

Identifying places in a house • Following conversational sequence • Discussing different kinds of homes • Making a drawing of a house

Reading a recipe • Scanning for information • Following directions • Measuring in recipes

Using art to make predictions • Learning about the Chinese calendar • Guided reading of a poem • Creating new verses

Describing location • Describing ongoing actions • Understanding subject/object pronouns • Playing TPR games

Identifying foods and containers • Adding and subtracting • Talking about food shopping • Roleplaying food shopping

Reading short selections • Using art to predict content • Discussing "Amazing Facts" • Reading about ants • Researching animal families

Identifying foods • Asking for and giving information • Discussing the food pyramid • Making a menu

Asking for and giving information • Describing quantity • Talking about family relationships

Identifying body parts • Reading about parts of the body • Following directions • Drawing a friend • Comparing skeletons

Making predictions • Guided reading of a play • Performing the play • Sharing folktales

Listening to a new story • Describing story events • Retelling the story • Thinking critically • Guided reading • Writing

Recalling facts/details • Reading for information • Playing "Amazing Facts" • Making charts about the body

LESSON PLANNER

KEY LANGUAGE

Family members: mother, father, sister, brother, aunt, uncle, grandparents • Parts of the body • ants, squeaky	Social Studies • Language Arts
Is your family big or small? • How many brothers/sisters do you have? • What are their names? • Do you have a pet? • birthday, hamster, pet	Art • Music • Social Studies • Language Arts
Where's (your brother)? • He's in the (kitchen). • What's he doing? • He's (eating cheese). • Rooms in a house • locations	Art • Social Studies • Language Arts
Peel the (bananas). • Cut the (bananas) . . . • peel, dip, heat up, fry, drain off, cool	Math • Social Studies • Language Arts
(I) was born . . ., so . . . • in the year of the (sheep) • dragon, monkey, rooster, sheep	Art • Social Studies • Language Arts
(He is) hiding. But I can see (him). • Can you see (me)? • behind, in front of, next to, under, on, in	Music • Social Studies • Language Arts
May I help you? • Yes, I need . . . • Yes, I'll have . . . • a pound of, a jar of, a gallon of • carrots, ice cream, jelly, juice, tomatoes, spaghetti sauce	Math • Language Arts
ants, attack, colonies, insects, queen, survive	Art • Math • Science • Social Studies • Language Arts
What are they eating? • They're eating (cereal). • apples, bananas, cheese, eggs, fish, oranges, rice, soup, sandwiches	Music • Science • Language Arts
How many (brothers) does she have? • She has (two brothers). • Do they have a pet? • Yes, they have a (bird). • hamster, pet, cousin	Social Studies • Language Arts
Body parts: arm, bone, elbow, fingers, hand, head, heart, knee, leg, muscles, neck, shoulder, skeleton, toes	Art • Music • Science • Social Studies • Language Arts
No, not me! • Animal sounds • scary/scariest • squeak/squeaky • tucked in, turned off	Art • Social Studies • Language Arts
butterfly • flower • fly • meadow • still • spread	Assessment
Review	Assessment

37

THEME OPENER

Families Around the World

LEVEL C, PAGE 23

KEY EXPERIENCES

- Discussing families
- Sharing personal experiences
- Predicting what theme titles mean

KEY LANGUAGE

- Family members: mother, father, sister, brother, aunt, uncle, grandparents
- parts of the body
- ants, squeaky

••• 1 INTRODUCE •••

MULTI-LEVEL TEACHING STRATEGIES

Building Background. Introduce the unit by discussing families. If possible, show the students a variety of photographs of families. Include various ethnicities and family sizes, from small nuclear to large extended. Also include photographs of single-parent households. Say, *These are all families.* Indicate family members, *mother, father,* etc. Ask students about their families. Expand the definition of family to mean those people with whom we live and share our lives.

Include all the students by asking questions appropriate to each student's language stage and family situation. Here are some sample questions:

Speech Emergence: *Do you have sisters? Do you have brothers? How old is your (sister)?*

Developing Fluency: *Whom do you live with? How many people are in your family? Tell me about an aunt or uncle of yours.*

ART Drawing families. Ask students to illustrate their families. Circulate and help students label the family members. Ask volunteers to present their families to the class: *This is my family. This is my mother.* etc.

••• 2 EXPLORE •••

Activating prior knowledge: Talking about families. Open to page 23 of the Student Book. Encourage students to comment on the photograph. Direct their attention to the unit theme, "Families Around the World." Read the title aloud. Ask students to tell you the names of countries around the world. As they say each country, write it on the board. Then have students locate it on a globe or world map. Say each name. Work **Teacher-Class.** Continue, *These are all countries in the world. What do you think we're going to learn about families around the world?*

Talking about ants. Direct students' attention to the second title, "All About Ants." Write *ants* on the board. Ask, *What do you know about ants?* To prompt, continue, *Where do they live? What do they eat? How do they move?*, etc. In small groups, have students discuss what they know about ants. Ask each group to make a **word web** about ants, then show it to the class. Then ask, *What else would you like to learn about ants?* List their ideas on the board. Gather up the word webs so that students will be able to reuse them later.

Talking about parts of the body. Play "Simon Says" **TPR** to review parts of the body. Tell students to touch various parts of their body. They should perform the action only if you say *Simon Says*, for example, *Simon Says touch your (head)*. The class starts out standing up. When you say, for example, *Touch your head* without also saying *Simon Says*, any students who perform the action sit down. The last child standing wins.

Talking about the literature. On the board, write the title "The Squeaky Door." Read it aloud and ask students to tell you what they think a story with this title will be about. Encourage students to use their imaginations. Ask **multi-level questions** to prompt them, *Where is the door? Is it a big door? What color is the door? What does a squeak sound like? Why does the door squeak?* (CALLA: Predicting)

Home-School Connection. Students do free writing on the unit theme of families. Teaching suggestions are provided in the Skills Journal annotation.

SOCIAL STUDIES Playing a geography game. Ask students to look at a globe or world map. Have each child write down the name of a country on a slip of paper. Gather the slips and put them in a pile. Write the names of the continents on the board. Then draw one slip from the pile. Read the name of the country to the class. Students say on which continent the country is located: *Kenya is in Africa. France is in Europe.*

MATH Counting ants. Make a simple worksheet of addition and subtraction problems about ants at a picnic. For example, *There were six ants at the picnic. Six more came. How many were there? There were 10 ants. Three left. How many were left?*

ONGOING ASSESSMENT

PERFORMANCE Oral language. Ask the students to tell you about their families. Observe different students' levels of participation. Use the **Oral Language Checklist** in the *Amazing Assessment Package*.

PORTFOLIO Independent writing. Have student save a copy of **Skills Journal** page 21 as an example of independent writing.

MULTICULTURAL AWARENESS
Discussing families may be difficult for students who have lost family members through war or political upheaval. Encourage those who want to participate, while being sensitive to those who appear uncomfortable.

COMMUNICATION 1A

Families Around the World

LEVEL C, PAGE 24

KEY EXPERIENCES

- Following conversational sequence
- Writing a language experience story
- Roleplaying fixed and free dialogues
- Making fingerprint animal families

KEY LANGUAGE

- *Is your family big or small?*
- *My family is big.*
- *How many brothers/sisters do you have?*
- *What are their names?*
- *Do you have a pet?*
- *big/small, birthday, hamster, pet*

MATERIALS

ink pads

40

••• 1 INTRODUCE •••

MULTI-LEVEL TEACHING STRATEGIES

Building Background. Cut out pictures of different cartoon families from newspapers. Mount the pictures on heavy construction paper. Cut the pictures apart to make puzzles. Have students work in pairs or small groups to assemble each puzzle. Circulate and encourage students to describe the family groupings.

Include all the students by asking questions appropriate to each student's language stage. Here are some sample questions:

Speech Emergence: *Is that the father? Is that the mother? Is it a big family or a small family?*

Developing Fluency: *How is this cartoon family different from a real family? Who is that?* Elicit full sentence responses, *That's the father. He's tall.*

ART Making fingerprint animal families. Students can make fingerprint animal families. Have students place their thumbs or fingers on an ink pad, and then on a piece of clean white paper. Then students draw faces, ears, legs, and tails on their fingerprints. Ask students to describe their fingerprint animal families. Model first: *A: Is your family big or small? B: My family is small. A: How many brothers do you have? B: I have one brother. A: What is his name? B: Daniel Duck.*

Writing a language experience story. Have students write stories about their fingerprint animal families. Encourage students to describe the family members. Ask students to share their writing in pairs or small groups.

••• 2 EXPLORE •••

Activating prior knowledge. Open to page 24 of the Student Book. Ask students to comment about the picture. Have students look and listen as you describe the page: *They are friends. They are having a conversation. They are talking about his family. She is asking him to describe his family.*

 **Look, listen, and talk.** Play the tape or read the text. Have students point to the lines as they listen. Check comprehension by asking **multi-level questions,** such as *Is his family big? How many brothers does he have? How many sisters?*, etc. Work **Teacher-Class; Teacher-Student.**

Practicing the conversation. Read the text or play the tape again, pausing for students to repeat. Divide the class into two groups. One group asks the questions, the other answers. Have students switch roles and repeat. (CALLA: Cooperation)

Reading for specific information: Amazing Facts. Direct students' attention to the bottom of the page. Give students time to read over the information. Ask **multi-level questions** appropriate to students' capabilities, for example, *How many of Johann Sebastian Bach's relatives were musicians? When do baby ducks learn to swim? Why do they learn so quickly? Do you move when you sleep? How often do you change positions?*

Data collection. Students conduct interviews, record the information in charts, and use it for paired conversation practice. Teaching suggestions are provided in the Skills Journal annotation.

Creating a conversation. In pairs, have students use the puzzle cartoon families from **Introduce** to create their own conversations. Have each child choose one of the puzzle families to be his or her family and then create a conversation modeled after the one in the book.

MUSIC Johann Sebastian Bach. Present the following background information on Bach and play a sample of his music, if possible. J.S. Bach came from a family that was musically active for seven generations. He was born in Germany in 1685 and died in 1750 at age 65. Bach wasn't recognized as a great composer until about 100 years after his death. He composed church music, mostly organ music. The *Brandenburg Concertos* are among his best known works.

SOCIAL STUDIES Adopting a grandparent. Contact your local Senior Center or agency to arrange to adopt a senior citizen as a class grandparent who can visit the class and share with the students on a regular basis. Alternatively, ask the Senior Center for a list of senior citizens who would like to receive visits from or be pen pals with your students. Help students write and exchange letters. Arrange a visit to the Senior Center if possible.

ONGOING ASSESSMENT

PERFORMANCE Oral language. Go around the class asking questions from the conversation on page 24 of the Student Book. Then ask about the students' families. Use the **Oral Language Checklist** in the *Amazing Assessment Package.*

PORTFOLIO Note-taking. Save **Skills Journal** page 22 as an example of oral/aural ability and note-taking.

MULTICULTURAL AWARENESS

Invite volunteers to tell the class about family living arrangements in their home cultures. For example, ask students to explain if they live in extended families. If they do, what is the housing like? How is the work divided?

TEACHER TO TEACHER

Encourage other teachers and students in the school to engage ESL students in conversations whenever possible. Conversation provides the natural context for practicing the rhythm and stress patterns of English. Through practice, students learn the words and expressions they need to engage in conversation with people outside of the classroom.

COMMUNICATION 1B

Families Around the World

LEVEL C, PAGE 25

KEY EXPERIENCES

- Identifying places in a house
- Following conversational sequence
- Discussing different kinds of homes
- Making a drawing of a house

KEY LANGUAGE

- *Where's (your brother)?*
- *He's in the (kitchen).*
- *What's he doing?.*
- *He's (eating cheese).*
- rooms in a house
- across from, between, next to

1 INTRODUCE

MULTI-LEVEL TEACHING STRATEGIES

Building background: Discussing locations in a house. On the board, make a simple drawing of a house or apartment. Say, *This is a house. Here is the kitchen. Here is the living room*, etc. As you say each room, write the word on the board. Have students repeat. Work **Teacher-Class.** Then hold up pictures of houses from various parts of the world. Identify each *(This is a house in Mexico)*, or ask students to guess where the house is. Ask them to tell you the reasons for their guesses *(I think it is in Guatemala. The trees and the flowers.).* Ask the students to describe the houses. (CALLA: Guessing)

Include all students in the activity by asking questions appropriate to each student's language stage. Here are some sample questions:

Speech Emergence: *Is this a big house? Is this house in a country where it is very cold?*

Developing Fluency: Encourage students to describe the houses without teacher prompts: *What does this house look like? Would you like to live in this house? Why or why not?*

ART Identifying places in a house. Use a large piece of butcher paper. Draw a floor plan of a house, or invite students to work cooperatively to draw one. Ask students to stand in a circle around the floor plan. Point out the *kitchen, the living room, bedrooms, bathroom, dining room, family room, garage*, etc. Encourage students to repeat each sentence: *This is the (living room).* Point to various rooms and ask, *What's this?* Model the answer: *This is the (kitchen).* Work chorally **(Teacher-Class)** and individually **(Teacher-Student).**

Playing a "Find It" game. Use the floor plan of the house and a small classroom object, such as an eraser or crayon. Have the students stand where they can all see the floor plan. Walk around the floor plan and drop the object. Ask, *Where's the (eraser)?* Encourage students to respond, *It's in the kitchen.* Continue with other rooms. Then divide the class into two teams. Have a member from one team drop the eraser and the other team describe its location.

2 EXPLORE

Activating prior knowledge. Open to page 25 of the Student Book. Ask students to comment on the picture. Ask, *Where's the (kitchen)?* and have students point to the correct room. Hold up your book and point to each room. Say the word *kitchen*. Emphasize the stress pattern (KIT-chen). Students repeat **chorally.**

Exploring the picture. Point to one room. Say, *This is the kitchen. What is it next to?* Continue asking about the other rooms, using *next to*, *across from*, *between*, etc. Work **T-C.**

 **Look, listen, and talk.** Play the tape or read the text. Have students point to the lines as they listen. Then read the text or play the tape again, pausing for students to repeat **chorally.**

Following conversational sequence. Check comprehension with **multi-level questions,** such as *Where's the baby brother? What's he doing?* Divide the class into two groups. One group asks the questions, the other answers. Have students continue, substituting other rooms and other family members. In pairs, have students practice the conversation, switching roles.

SKILLS JOURNAL PAGE 23 **Home–School Connection.** Students label the rooms of a house, draw family members, and say what each person is doing. Teaching suggestions are provided in the Skills Journal annotation.

3 EXTEND

Playing a TPR game. Make word cards for the rooms of a house. Give each card to a student volunteer. Ask the volunteers to come to the front of the class. Describe locations in an imaginary house. For example, *The kitchen is next to the bedroom. The living room is behind the kitchen.* The volunteers holding those cards position themselves accordingly. The rest of the class watches and corrects students if necessary (*No, between*). Next, tell all the volunteers to move around until you clap your hands and say *Freeze!* Then ask the class to describe the locations: *The living room is next to the bathroom*, etc. Continue.

SOCIAL STUDIES Discussing different kinds of homes. Lead a discussion of different kinds of homes (apartment above store, single-family, large apartment building) around the world. Show as many pictures of each as possible. Then ask students to draw a picture of where they live or of their dream house. (CALLA: Imagery)

- - - - - - ONGOING ASSESSMENT - - - - - -

PORTFOLIO Independent writing. Save **Skills Journal** page 23 as an example of oral proficiency and understanding of home vocabulary.

READ AND DO

Families Around the World

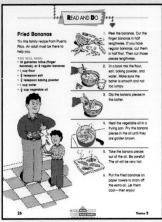

LEVEL C, PAGE 26

KEY EXPERIENCES

- Reading a recipe
- Scanning for information
- Following directions
- Measuring in recipes

KEY LANGUAGE

- *Peel the (bananas).*
- *Cut the (bananas) …*
- *In a bowl mix …*
- bananas, peel, dip, heat up, fry, drain off, cool, smooth/lumpy, golden, brown, paper towels

MATERIALS

- 8 bananas, 1 cup flour, $\frac{1}{2}$ teasp. salt, $\frac{1}{2}$ teasp. baking powder, 1 cup water, $\frac{1}{2}$ cup vegetable oil

●●● 1 INTRODUCE ●●●

MULTI-LEVEL TEACHING STRATEGIES

Building background. Bring to class a banana or a picture of a banana. If possible, also bring in a plantain. Ask, *Do you like bananas?* Invite students to make a **word web** about bananas. Encourage students to talk about the different ways they eat bananas in their home cultures.

Include all of the students in the discussion by asking questions appropriate to their language stage. Here are some sample questions:

Speech Emergence: *Are bananas sweet? Are bananas good? Do you like them?*

Developing Fluency: *What does a banana look like? Why do you like bananas? How do you eat bananas at home?*

SOCIAL STUDIES Talking about Puerto Rico. Explain to the students that you are going to learn a recipe from Puerto Rico. Ask, *Do you know where Puerto Rico is ?* Have a volunteer point it out on a globe or world map. Continue, *What do you know about Puerto Rico?* Encourage the students to share what they know. Keep a list of information on the board. Prompt if necessary. Give students the background information in the margin notes. (CALLA: Elaboration)

Talking about recipes. Write *recipe* on the board. Say, *A recipe tells us how to make something with food.* Continue, *Do you like chocolate milk? Do any of you know how to make it?* Together on the board list what you need: *milk, chocolate syrup or powder, a glass.* Then write down how to make it: *Pour milk in a glass. Measure two teaspoons of chocolate. Add the chocolate to the milk. Stir.* Use **TPR** to show the steps. Have students repeat. Note: You may substitute any simple recipe.

●●● 2 EXPLORE ●●●

Activating prior knowledge. Open to page 26 of the Student Book. Read the title "Read and Do" aloud. What do students think this means? Next, point to the recipe name and have students look for a word they know. What is the word? Invite students to comment on the rest of the page.

Scanning for specific information. Direct students' attention to "YOU WILL NEED." Ask *How many different things do you need?* (six) *What is the first thing you need? What is the (second) thing? How much water? How much (vegetable oil)?* Ask several questions, allowing time for students to answer **chorally.**

Following directions. Direct students' attention to the recipe on the right side of the page. Ask, *How many steps are there?* Next, ask the students quickly to scan each step and point to or copy the verbs. Model first. For Step 1, point to *peel* and *cut.* Check the rest of the answers: Step 2. *mix, make sure;* 3. *dip;* 4. *Heat up, fry;* 5. *take out;* 6. *put, let.* Maintain a rapid pace. (CALLA: Sequencing)

GUIDED READING Read the steps of the recipe as the students follow along in their books. Use **TPR** to demonstrate the steps as you read the recipe again, or have volunteers mime the actions: peel, cut, mix, dip, fry, take pieces out, put on paper towel.

Reading for a purpose; writing. Students read a paragraph and write answers to questions. Teaching suggestions are provided in the Skills Journal annotation.

MATH Measuring in recipes. Talk about the measurements used in the recipe. Bring measuring spoons and cups to class. Show students how to use them. Ask students to figure out how much they would need of each of the ingredients if they doubled or tripled the recipe. Bring other simple recipes to class for students to double and triple as well.

Home-School Connection: Making a cookbook. Invite students to take their books home and make fried bananas with an adult family member. Also have students find out the recipe for a family favorite. Ask them to write down their recipes and bring them to class. Students can illustrate their recipes and compile them in a class cookbook, *Our Favorite Things to Eat!*

ONGOING ASSESSMENT

PERFORMANCE Oral language. Ask students to explain how to make fried bananas. Prompt if necessary. Observe different students' levels of participation. Use the **Oral Language Checklist** in the *Amazing Assessment Package.*

PORTFOLIO Save **Skills Journal** page 24 as an example of reading comprehension.

MULTICULTURAL AWARENESS

People in many parts of the world distinguish between the smaller, sweeter bananas that are eaten as fruit and the larger plantains that are treated like a vegetable. Fruit bananas include not only the yellow variety familiar to people in the U.S., but also small, finger-sized bananas, some of which have dark, red skins. Plantains, which are very bitter if eaten raw, are used either ripe or green. Spanish-speaking students may refer to these as *maduros* or *plátanos verdes,* respectively. Plantains are eaten fried or baked, or they are added to soups and stews.

BACKGROUND INFORMATION

Puerto Rico is in the Caribbean, next to the Dominican Republic. It is a commonwealth of the United States. About three million people live there. The primary language is Spanish. The capital is San Juan. Puerto Rico exports many manufactured goods, plus sugar cane and coffee.

MY FAMILY

Families Around the World

LEVEL C, PAGE 27

KEY EXPERIENCES

- Using art to make predictions
- Learning about the Chinese calendar
- Guided reading of a poem
- Making logical connections
- Creating new verses

KEY LANGUAGE

- (I) was born …, so …
- in the year of the (sheep)
- dragon, monkey, rooster, sheep

1 INTRODUCE

MULTI-LEVEL TEACHING STRATEGIES

Activating prior knowledge. Use a calendar to review the months of the year. Point to a month. Ask, *What month is this? What month comes before/after (this month)?* Then review ordinal numbers by pointing to various dates and asking, *What date is it?* Work **T-C**. Follow with a discussion about birthdays.

Include all students in the discussion by asking questions appropriate to each student's language stage. Here are some sample questions:

Speech Emergence: *Is your birthday in (June)? When is your birthday? Do you like birthdays?*

Developing Fluency: *When were you born? Why do you like birthdays? What do you like to do on your birthday?*

Activating prior knowledge: Using art to make predictions. Ask students to open to page 27 in the Student Book. Ask them to cover the poem and look at the pictures carefully. Ask, *What do you see? You're going to read a poem. What do you think it will be about?* Make a list on the board of all of the animals on the page. In pairs, have students discuss what they think the poem is about. Ask volunteers for their ideas. *Do you think it is about animals? What animals?* (CALLA: Predicting)

Building background: Learning about the Chinese calendar. First, point out that the poem, "My Family," was written by a 9-year-old Japanese student named Ueda Akie. The Japanese use a calendar based on the Chinese system. Briefly explain the Chinese calendar. Each year is named for one of twelve animals: tiger, horse, snake, rat, pig, sheep, dragon, rooster, rabbit, monkey, ox, dog. Traditionally, people believe there is a connection between the year someone is born and the person's personality; for example, someone born in the year of the tiger is like a tiger. Make a list of the twelve animals. Ask students to think about themselves. Which animal are they most like? Why? Have them write one or two sentences. Ask students to share their writing in small groups.

2 EXPLORE

Guided reading of a poem. Ask the students to uncover the poem on page 27. Read or play the tape of the poem as the students follow along in their books. Do a **choral reading.** Read the poem with the class again, emphasizing the rhythm and intonation.

Talking about the poem. On the board, write: *I was born ..., so ...* Cue the students to make logical connections by pointing to each of the animal names in the poem, for example, *rooster*. Students answer, *I was born in the year of the rooster, so I wake up early.* Work **T-C.**

Creating new verses. Have students create new verses to the poem. This can be done as a whole group activity or by partners. The art on page 27 and the list of animal names on the board can serve as cues for additional verses. You may want to write on chart paper the words to the new verses the class creates. Later, students can illustrate the verses.

Home-School Connection. Students complete cloze poetry with free choice of words. Teaching suggestions are provided in the Skills Journal annotation.

Writing a poem. Ask students to write poems about their families, modeled after the poem in the book. Ask several volunteers to write their poems on the board. Then do **choral reading** of the poems.

SOCIAL STUDIES Learning more about the Chinese calendar. Have students use resource materials to learn more about the Chinese calendar. In which countries is it used? Who uses it? What is it used for? Discuss the information as a class. Students can draw or find pictures of the twelve animals. Display their work in the classroom. (CALLA: Resourcing)

ART Illustrating a poem. Ask students to illustrate one of the family members described in the poem on page 27, for example, the brother who likes to climb trees. In small groups have students share their work, then display it in the classroom.

ONGOING ASSESSMENT

PERFORMANCE Oral language. Ask the students to read the poem "My Family" again. Observe individual students' levels of participation. Use the **Oral Language Checklist** in the *Amazing Assessment Package.*

STAFF DEVELOPMENT
Refer to the *Amazing How-To Handbook* for more on literature-based instruction.

MULTICULTURAL AWARENESS
If any students are from Asian cultures that use a similar calendar, invite them to share something about it with the class. When were they born? What animal is associated with that year?

TEACHER TO TEACHER
If your students work with other teachers, you may want to suggest that they use choral and independent reading of poetry whenever possible. Poems provide an effective context for practicing the rhythm and intonation patterns of natural language.

BACKGROUND INFORMATION
The poem "My Family" appears in *Festival in My Heart,* a collection of poems written by Japanese school children. The poems were originally published as a daily feature in the leading Japanese newspaper, *Yomiuri Shimbun.*

COMMUNICATION 2A

THEME 2 • • • • • • •

Families Around the World

LEVEL C, PAGE 28

KEY EXPERIENCES

- Describing location
- Describing ongoing actions
- Understanding subject/object pronouns
- Playing TPR games

KEY LANGUAGE

- *He is/You are/I am hiding.*
- *But I can see (him/her/ you/them/me/us).*
- *Can you see (me)?*
- hiding, see
- behind, in front of, next to, under, on, in,
- playground equipment

---

1 INTRODUCE

MULTI-LEVEL TEACHING STRATEGIES

Building background. Play a version of Simon Says, using *please* as a cue word. Students follow the command only if you say *please* in the command, for example, *Please put your hands on your head.* Use commands with *in, on,* and *under.* Next, tell students to move their bodies around freely. When you say, *Freeze!* students stop and stay in position. Circulate and ask students about their positions.

Include all students in the activity by asking questions appropriate to their language stage. Here are some sample questions:

Speech Emergence: *Is your hand on your head? Is your hand on your knee?*

Developing Fluency: *Where is your (hand)?* Encourage students to respond in full sentences: *It's on my (elbow).*

Describing location. Print these prepositions on the board: *behind, in front of, next to, under, on, in.* Model and have students repeat as you show the positions. Then help students spell each word **chorally,** *u-n-d-e-r.* Ask students to copy the words on paper. Read **chorally, T-C.** Then use **TPR** commands with the prepositions, for example, *Stand in front of your desk, Put your pencil next to your eraser.*

Reading sight words. Make a set of cards with the following pronouns: *he, him, she, her, you, you, they, them, I, me, we, us.* Hold up the cards and have the students read them **chorally.** Place the cards along the chalkboard rail. On the board, write: *... wants the book. Please give it to ...* Point to the card with *he* and then to *him.* Hold up a book. Say, *He wants the book. Please give it to him.* Students repeat. Point to different pronouns. Have students make substitutions *(They want the book. Please give it to them)* etc. Prompt as needed. Work **T-C; T-S.**

2 EXPLORE

Activating prior knowledge. Open to page 28 of the Student Book. Engage students in a discussion of the playground scene. Ask, *What do you see?* Which of the pieces of playground equipment can they name?

Exploring key vocabulary. Point to the pictures of the balls and the boxes. Say, *The ball is behind the box, The ball is in front of the box,* etc. Point to each picture. Ask, *Where is the ball?* Encourage students to respond, *The ball is (behind) the box.* Bring a box and a ball to class. Place the ball in various positions and ask, *Where is the ball now?* Work **T-C.**

 **Look, listen, and talk.** As you play the tape or read the sentences at the top of the page, have students read along **chorally.** Then have partners talk about the scene. Have one student point to someone in the picture and ask an appropriate question, *Is she under the table?* Or *Where is she?* The other student answers. Then students switch roles.

SKILLS JOURNAL PAGE 26 **Describing locations.** Students practice describing locations using prepositions of place. Teaching suggestions are provided in the Skills Journal annotation.

Playing a Concentration game. Have groups of four students make a set of pronoun word cards like those used in **Introduce.** Students place the cards face down randomly on a table. The first player draws two cards and reads the words. If the words refer to the same person *(he/him),* the player keeps the cards. If the cards refer to different people *(he/she),* the cards go face down. The student with the most pairs at the end of play is the winner. For extra challenge, have students spell the pronouns. (CALLA: Imagery)

SOCIAL STUDIES Playing TPR Hide and Seek. Vary the traditional game of Hide and Seek, playing either outside or inside. One child is "IT" and searches for the other students. When a hidden child is found, "IT" says, *(She) was under the tree/behind the desk* Both "IT" and the child found run back to the home base.

 MUSIC "There's a Hole in the Bottom of the Sea." Play the tape or sing the song. (See the Tapescript in the Appendix.) Encourage students to sing along.

Home-School Connection. Ask the students to go home and observe one room in their house very carefully. What do they see? Ask them to make a drawing and bring it to class. In small groups, have students share what the rooms look like. Circulate and help with prepositions as needed.

- - - - ONGOING ASSESSMENT - - - -

PERFORMANCE Oral language. Have students ask and answer *where* questions referring to the baby in the Skills Journal or to objects placed around the classroom. Observe different students' levels, using the **Oral Language Checklist** In *The Amazing Assessment Package.*

TEACHER TO TEACHER

If your students work with other teachers, you may want to tell them that ESL students will master the prepositions more quickly if they are given opportunities to use them in real-life tasks. Asking students to help clean up the room is a good way to practice in context: *Please put the game on the bottom shelf,* etc.

RELATED RESOURCES

The Cat Came Back CD-ROM, Read Along Mode. Prepositions (page 19).

COMMUNICATION 2B

Families Around the World

LEVEL C, PAGE 29

KEY EXPERIENCES

- Identifying foods and containers
- Adding and subtracting
- Creating new conversations using the Data Bank
- Roleplaying food shopping

KEY LANGUAGE

- *May I help you?*
- *Yes, I need ....*
- *Yes, I'll have ...*
- *May I have ....?*
- a pound of, a jar of, a gallon of
- carrots, ice cream, jelly, juice, onions, pickles, tomatoes, spaghetti sauce, soft drink

MATERIALS

- puppets

1 INTRODUCE

MULTI-LEVEL TEACHING STRATEGIES

Building background. Bring to class several food items the students are familiar with. If possible, include a one-pound bag or box of some things (carrots, macaroni), as well as a gallon container of milk or juice. Hold up the items and ask, *What's this?* Students answer **chorally**. Prompt as needed. Place the food items on a table. Use two puppets; hold up one puppet and say, *(He) is going to the store to buy some food.* Hold up the other puppet and say, *(She) works at the store.* Model a conversation: P1: *May I help you?* P2: *Yes, I need a gallon of milk.* P1: *Here you are.* (Use one puppet to give the milk to the other puppet).

Continue, substituting several more food items you brought.

Pause and include all the students by asking each student questions appropriate to his or her language stage Here are some sample questions:

Speech Emergence: *What does he need? Does he need (milk)? Do you like milk?*

Developing Fluency: *How much (milk) does he need?* Encourage students to give a long answer, *He needs (a gallon of milk).*

MATH Adding and subtracting. On the board, write *one pound, one gallon.* Show what each measurement means. Have students repeat the words **chorally.** Then give the students simple word problems to answer orally. For example, *I need one pound of apples and one pound of bananas. How much fruit do I need?* Or, *I bought two pounds of apples. I gave one pound to a friend. How many pounds do I have now?* Alternatively, ask the students to each write one problem, then take turns reading them to the class.

Making observations. Bring to class colored food advertisements from the newspaper or magazines. Show them to the students. Encourage them to talk about what they see, *(I see) a jar of pickles*, etc.

2 EXPLORE

Activating prior knowledge. Open to page 29 of the Student Book. Encourage students to comment about the page. Point out the speech bubbles and ask students to show you which one belongs with each person.

 **Look, listen, and talk.** Play the tape or read the conversations as you use the puppets from **Introduce** to model each of the three conversational exchanges. (*May I help you?/Yes, I need*, etc.) Pause after each exchange for the students to repeat **chorally.** Divide the class into groups. Invite students to use the puppets, and have the groups do the exchanges again. Then have students switch roles.

Exploring key vocabulary. Include all students in the discussion by asking **multi-level questions,** such as *Whom do you see? Where are they? Does she need potatoes or carrots? What does the boy want to buy?* Introduce the vocabulary in the Data Bank at the bottom of the page. Ask students to repeat these words **chorally.** Hold up teacher-made vocabulary cards of the words in random order. Work **T-C**; then **T-S.**

Practicing the conversation. Model the conversations at the top of the page, substituting words from the Data Bank. Then encourage students to personalize by asking for other foods.

SKILLS JOURNAL PAGE 27 **Crossword puzzle.** Students work independently to complete a crossword puzzle, using food vocabulary. Teaching suggestions are provided in the Skills Journal annotation.

LIFE SKILLS Roleplaying food shopping. Set up a grocery store in the classroom. Bring empty food boxes or other realia if possible. Have students take turns being food shoppers and clerks.

Home-School Connection. Ask students to go home and write down the names of five foods that they find. Have students bring their lists to class and talk about what they saw, *I saw bread.* Together, **classify** the foods first by kinds of food and then by food containers or quantity, for example, *jars of, pounds of.* (CALLA: Classifying)

- - - - - ONGOING ASSESSMENT - - - - -

PORTFOLIO Save **Skills Journal** page 27 as an example of vocabulary mastery.

MULTICULTURAL AWARENESS

Invite volunteers to tell the class how food shopping is usually done in their parents' home cultures. For example, ask students if their parents shopped in stores or in open markets. Were certain days of the week market days? Did anything special happen on those days? Did parents buy a lot of food at once, or did someone go to the market every day? If students don't know or can't recall, encourage them to ask parents.

WRITING PROJECT

Writing Project 2A, *How to Make Butter,* is directly linked to this lesson. See the Process Writing Portfolio Program Teachers' Handbook, pages 12-13, for the Lesson Plan.

Students will find instructions and a Prewriting Sheet in the Writing Projects booklet inside the Portfolio.

CHECK THIS OUT!

Families Around the World

LEVEL C, PAGES 30-31

KEY EXPERIENCES

- Reading short selections
- Using art to predict content
- Discussing "Amazing Facts"
- Reading about ants
- Researching animal families

KEY LANGUAGE

- ants, attack, colonies, insects, queen, survive

1 INTRODUCE

MULTI-LEVEL TEACHING STRATEGIES

Building background: Discussing animal families. Engage students in a discussion of animals and animal families. Show students pictures of various animals. Ask, *What is this?* Prompt if necessary. Write the names of the animals on the board. Model, **T-C.** Talk about where the animals live, what the animals eat, and what their families are like.

Include all the students in the discussion by asking questions appropriate to each student's language stage. Here are some sample questions:

Speech Emergence: *Is this a lion? Is this a lion or a tiger? Where do lions live?*

Developing Fluency: *What do lions eat? Do lions live in groups? Are the groups big? Do you like lions? Why?*

Activating prior knowledge. Ask students to **brainstorm** about ants. Refer students to the **word web** for ants done in Lesson 1 for the Theme Opener. Together, come up with several questions about ants. Write the questions on the chart paper.

2 EXPLORE

Activating prior knowledge. Open to pages 30–31 of the Student Book. Read the lesson title, "Check This Out!" aloud. Ask if anyone knows what this expression means. As needed, explain that it means "Look at this." Help them to predict what the pages are about. (CALLA: Predicting)

GUIDED READING Using art to predict content. Direct students' attention to *Just Joking.* Read the text or play the tape. Then do a **choral reading.** Have students read it again independently. Check understanding. Ask, *What did the mother cat begin to do? Did the dog go away? What did the mother cat say to her kittens? Why?*

Repeat this procedure for the other articles.

SOCIAL STUDIES Amazing Facts. Have students look at the bottom of the page. Give them time to read briefly over the information on their own. Then ask **multi-level questions,** such as *What is the first "fact" about? How many sandwiches will the average kid eat? Do you eat* *peanut butter sandwiches? What holiday is the second "fact" about?,* etc. Have students compare what they have read to their own experiences. (CALLA: Comparing)

 GUIDED READING Finding factual information. Direct students' attention to the photograph of ants on page 31. Read the title aloud, "Unfriendly Families." Ask students to predict why ant families are called unfriendly. Tell students to listen for the information as you read or play the tape. Then do a **choral reading.** Have students read again independently.

SKILLS JOURNAL PAGE 28 **Reading for a purpose; appreciating cultural differences.** Students read and answer questions about differences between British and American English. **Cloze exercise.** Students listen and complete a cloze exercise. Teaching suggestions are provided in the Skills Journal annotations.

ART Summarizing a selection. Begin by having students make their own illustrations for *Unfriendly Families.* Then ask students to summarize the selection orally or in writing. (CALLA: Summarizing)

SCIENCE Learning about animal families. Help students find out about other animal families, such as lions, bees, or zebras. Have students work in small groups. Each group can select a different animal. Ask students to make posters illustrating what they learned; display in the classroom. (CALLA: Resourcing)

MATH Comparing prices. Ask students to tell you what a movie costs today. Then have students ask parents or older friends what a movie cost ten, twenty, or even fifty years ago.

ONGOING ASSESSMENT

PORTFOLIO Oral language. Ask students to present their summaries of *Unfriendly Families.* Observe different students' levels of participation. Use the **Oral Language Checklist** in the *Amazing Assessment Package.*

PORTFOLIO Listening. Save Skills Journal page 29 as an example of listening and writing abilities.

MULTICULTURAL AWARENESS
Ask volunteers to talk about holidays in their home cultures. Do they have Mother's Day? If so, is it celebrated the same day? What holidays do they have that are not celebrated in the U.S.?

TEACHER TO TEACHER
If your students work with other teachers, you may want to tell them that your students have been discussing, reading about, and researching ants in your class. Encourage your colleagues to allow students to share their information with other students, if possible.

STAFF DEVELOPMENT
See *The CALLA Handbook,* Chapter 9, for more on science in the ESL classroom.

RELATED RESOURCES
The Cat Came Back CD-ROM, Read Along Mode: Cats (pages 16-20); CD-ROM TG: Lesson 24, Cat Facts.

LANGUAGE POWER A

Families Around the World

LEVEL C, PAGE 32

KEY EXPERIENCES

- Identifying foods
- Asking for and giving information
- Roleplaying fixed and free dialogues
- Discussing the food pyramid
- Making a menu

KEY LANGUAGE

- *What are they eating?*
- *They're eating (cereal).*
- apples, bananas, beans, cereal, cheese, eggs, fish, ice cream, meat, oranges, peaches, rice, soup, sandwiches

••• 1 INTRODUCE •••

MULTI-LEVEL TEACHING STRATEGIES

Building background: Identifying foods. Make picture cue cards for the food vocabulary listed, *cereal, bananas,* etc. Show students each card, and say, *It's (cereal).* Students repeat.

Matching names. Make word cards for *cereal, bananas, rice, fish, meat, soup, eggs, beans, apples, sandwiches, oranges, peaches, ice cream, cheese.* Help students read all of the word cards. Work **T-C; T-S.** Then hide the picture cards throughout the room. Give each student a word card. Have students find the matching picture card as quickly as possible and place both on the chalk rail.

MUSIC Learning a food chant. Point to a picture card/word card pair *(cereal).* Say, *I like cereal,* as you clap to show the rhythm. Students repeat **chorally** as they clap. Do all the cards. Then circulate in the classroom; include all the students by asking questions appropriate to each child's language stage. Here are some sample questions:

Speech Emergence: *Do you like cereal?* Encourage the full response, *Yes, I like cereal.*

Developing Fluency: *Which do you like better, bananas or apples? When do you eat bananas?*

••• 2 EXPLORE •••

Activating prior knowledge. Open to page 32 of the Student Book. Encourage students to comment about the page. Find out how many of the foods students can identify.

Look, listen, and talk. Have students listen and point as you model the conversation or play the tape: *What are they eating? They're eating fish.* Read or play the tape again, pausing for students to repeat **chorally.** Then divide the students into two groups: one group asks the questions, the other answers. Point to *rice.* Group 1: *What are they eating?* Group 2: *They're eating rice.* Continue with the other pictures. Next, have partners take turns talking about the pictures.

SKILLS JOURNAL PAGE 30

Reading for a purpose; writing. Students read about food and write answers to questions. Teaching suggestions are provided in the Skills Journal annotation.

•••• 3 EXTEND ••••

Playing Word Scramble. Use the food vocabulary. Change the order of the letters in each word. Have students unscramble the letters and write the words correctly. For extra challenge, write *a few* and *a little* on the board. Help students decide which to use with each food *(a few eggs; a little cheese)*. (CALLA: Sequencing)

SCIENCE Discussing the food pyramid. Draw a food pyramid or use a copy of one from a cereal box or nutrition magazine. Ask students what this shape is called. Then explain that the food pyramid gives us information that can help us eat healthful food. We need to eat a lot of food from the bottom and only a little from the top. Grains are at the bottom, then fruits and vegetables, then proteins. Fats and sugar are at the top. Help the students decide where on the pyramid each food on page 32 belongs. Ask them to draw the food pyramid. (CALLA: Classifying)

HEALTH Making menus. Help students make their own menus. Encourage students to include their favorite food items, especially foods that are served in their homes. Have students illustrate their menus. Afterward, have students compare the items on their menus with the food pyramid. (CALLA: Comparing)

Building vocabulary. Use *Amazing English!* Word Attack 3 Interactive Vocabulary Games for practice with vocabulary.

ONGOING ASSESSMENT

PERFORMANCE Oral Language. Going in a chain around the class, have the students ask and answer the question, *What are they eating?*, pointing to pictures on the page. Have students draw pictures of people eating. Ask them to describe the pictures: *He is eating (rice and fish).* Observe different students' levels of participation. Use the **Oral Language Checklist** in the *Amazing Assessment Package*.

PERFORMANCE Writing. Save **Skills Journal** page 30 as a record of vocabulary mastery and comprehension.

MULTICULTURAL AWARENESS

Make a multicultural cookbook. Have students bring favorite recipes from home. Put the recipes into a class cookbook. Have students illustrate the recipes. Reproduce the cookbook for every student.

LANGUAGE POWER B

Families Around the World

LEVEL C, PAGE 33

KEY EXPERIENCES

- Asking for and giving information
- Describing quantity
- Talking about family relationships

KEY LANGUAGE

- *How many (brothers) does she have?*
- *She has (two brothers).*
- *Do they have a pet?*
- *Yes, they have a (bird).*
- bird, hamster, pet
- cousin

1 INTRODUCE

MULTI-LEVEL TEACHING STRATEGIES

Activating prior knowledge. Use one female and one male puppet. Divide the students into two teams. Give each team one puppet. The team describes one activity that their puppet likes to do and demonstrates the puppet doing the activity, *She likes to run.* Each team gets a point for an original sentence.

Cooperative learning. Make word cards: (1) 10 "he" pronoun cards; 10 "she" cards; (2) 4 sets of number cards from 1–8; (3) 8 relative cards each for *uncle, aunt, brother, sister, cousin.* Make 3 piles of cards: 1-pronoun cards; 2-number cards; 3-relatives cards. Work with the class in a chain game. Have student A draw one card from each of the three piles and ask student B a question based on the card selection, *Does he have one aunt?* Student B answers and then draws three cards and asks Student C a question. (CALLA: Selective Attention)

Include all the students by asking questions appropriate to each student's language stage. Here are some sample questions:

Speech Emergence: *Does she have a brother? Do they have a pet?*

Developing Fluency: Encourage students to add more information and also to use, *How many aunts does he have?*

Practicing writing. Put the pronoun cards, the number word cards, and the family member cards in three piles. Ask three volunteers to come to the front of the room. Ask each to pick a card from a pile and hold it up. Write a sentence on the board, using the cards as a guide, *He has one aunt.* Model the sentence. Have students read it **chorally,** then copy it onto a piece of paper. Have volunteers continue drawing cards and repeat.

2 EXPLORE

Activating prior knowledge. Open to page 33 of the Student Book. Encourage students to comment about the page. Involve each child in the discussion by asking **multi-level questions,** such as *At the top of the page, how many students do you see? What are they doing? Count the students at the bottom of the page. How many girls do you see?*

Look, listen, and talk. Point to the top picture. Say, *This is Rosa's family.* Introduce the family members, *two brothers, one sister, a pet* *bird.* Point to the bottom picture, and say, *This is George's family.* Then read or play the tape for the conversations. Have students repeat **chorally.** Continue with *one aunt, two aunts, three aunts, one cousin, two cousins, three cousins, four cousins, a hamster.*

Talking about family relationships. Have students point to each picture as you read the text. Then, divide the class into two groups. One group asks the questions, the other answers. Group 1: *How many brothers does she have?* Group 2: *She has two brothers,* etc.

Paired reading. Have students practice reading. One partner reads the questions and the other partner reads the answers. Have students switch roles and repeat. (CALLA: Cooperation)

Home-School Connection. Students practice writing questions and answers about family. Teaching suggestions are provided in the Skills Journal annotation.

SOCIAL STUDIES **Pet "Show and Tell."** Ask students to bring to class drawings or photographs of their pets. Have students take turns telling the class about their pets. Together make a **word web** about pets. Write "my pet" in the center. Have students include why they like their pets.

Interviewing and writing about classmates. Help students compile a list of questions to ask each other to find out about their families. Divide students into small groups. Have them interview each other. Help students write sentences and paragraphs describing the families of the students they interviewed. Then put the students into new groups and ask them to share the information, *Pedro has two brothers. He has two sisters, They have a dog.*

ONGOING ASSESSMENT

PERFORMANCE **Oral language.** Have students use the questions and answers from Exercise B in the Skills Journal to interview each other. Observe different students' levels of participation. Use the **Oral Language Checklist** in the *Amazing Assessment Package.*

STAFF DEVELOPMENT
See the *Amazing How-To Handbook* for other ways to implement cooperative learning.

HANDS-ON SCIENCE

Families Around the World

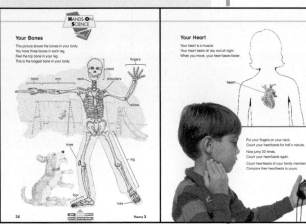

LEVEL C, PAGES 34-35

KEY EXPERIENCES

- Identifying body parts
- Reading about parts of the body
- Drawing a friend
- Comparing skeletons

KEY LANGUAGE

- Body parts: arm, bone, elbow, fingers, hand, head, heart, knee, leg, muscles, neck, shoulder, skeleton, toes

- longest, feel, count, jump, beat, move, faster

MATERIALS

- ink or poster paints

●●● 1 INTRODUCE ●●●

MULTI-LEVEL TEACHING STRATEGIES

Using TPR. Introduce these body parts: *neck, head, shoulder, elbow, arm, fingers, hand, leg, knee, toes, bone, muscles, heart.* Point to yourself and say, *This is my (head).* Then ask, *What's this?* Students respond by touching their own head and saying, *This is my head.* Continue. Include all students in the activity by asking questions appropriate to each student's language stage.

Speech Emergence: (Point to your heart.) *Is this my head? Is this your knee? Is this your leg or your arm?*

Developing Fluency: *What's longer, your arm or your leg? How many fingers and toes do you have?*

Building background: Thinking about the heart. Ask students to put their hands over their hearts. Ask, *what do you feel?* Next ask them to jump in place ten times, then feel their hearts again. *What do you feel now?* On the board, make a **word web.** In the center, write *heart.* Ask, *What do you know about the heart?* Add students' ideas to the word web.

●●● 2 EXPLORE ●●●

Activating prior knowledge. Direct students' attention to the illustrations on pages 34 and 35. Ask students to point to different parts of the body. Say, *Find the neck,* etc. Work **T-C.**

GUIDED READING Have students look and listen as you read the text on page 34. Ask, *What is the longest bone in your body?* Expand with **multi-level questions.**

Paired reading. Have pairs reread the text and review the parts of the body. One partner points to a body part and the other student reads the word. Students take turns.

GUIDED READING Direct the students' attention to page 35. Have students look and listen as you describe the heart. *This is a picture of the heart. Show me where your heart is. Let's read what it says about the heart.* Read the text at the top of the page. Then have students reread on their own. Check understanding with **multi-level questions.** (CALLA: Monitoring Comprehension)

 **Reading for a purpose; writing.** Students read about bones and write answers to questions. Teaching suggestions are provided in the Skills Journal annotation.

STAFF DEVELOPMENT

For more on science in the classroom, see *The CALLA Handbook.*

ART Drawing a friend. Partners draw full body outlines of each other on large pieces of paper. Encourage students to paint their body outlines and label different body parts.

MUSIC "Hands on Myself." Play the tape or sing the song. (See the Tapescript in the Appendix.).Encourage students to sing along.

SCIENCE Comparing skeletons. Show pictures or actual samples of various skeletons (cats, dogs, fish, dinosaurs, horses, cows, and birds). Cover the name of the animal. Allow students to examine the bone structure and decide what the animal is.

Doing an experiment. This experiment shows capillary action. Place a white carnation or piece of celery in a glass of water. Add twenty drops of blue food coloring. Take photographs or have students draw pictures of color changes at regular intervals.

SOCIAL STUDIES Hawaiian Menehune footprints. In Hawaiian mythology, Menehune were good little people who did nice things for others. Children can make Menehune footprints by dipping the base of the hand in ink or poster paints and placing it on white paper. Toes are made by inking a finger and pressing it on the paper five times.

ONGOING ASSESSMENT

PORTFOLIO Language experience writing. Students draw pictures of different body parts and write complete sentences about them, *My arm helps me throw balls.* To record students' progress, use the **Writing Checklist** in the *Amazing Assessment Package.* Save **Skills Journal** page 32 as a record of vocabulary mastery and comprehension.

THE SQUEAKY DOOR

Families Around the World

LEVEL C, PAGES 36-41

KEY EXPERIENCES

- Making predictions
- Guided reading of a play
- Performing the play
- Sharing folktales

KEY LANGUAGE

- *That scared the (cat) and (they both) jumped right out of bed.*
- *Grandma came running.*
- *So Grandma tucked the (cat) in with Sonny.*
- *No, not me!*
- animal sounds
- scary/scariest
- squeak/squeaky
- tucked in, turned off

1 INTRODUCE

MULTI-LEVEL TEACHING STRATEGIES

Building background. Engage students in a discussion about staying with relatives. Start, by saying, *When I was young, I liked to visit my (aunt and uncle) because (they had horses.)* Ask the students about their own experiences. Include all students in the discussion by asking questions appropriate to each student's language stage. Here are some sample questions:

Speech Emergence: *Who do you like to visit? Do you have a (cousin) you like you visit?*

Developing Fluency: *Why do you like to visit your grandparents? Do you do anything special there?*

2 EXPLORE

Activating prior knowledge. Ask students to look at the pictures on pages 36–41 in the Student Book. Read the title aloud, "The Squeaky Door." Ask the students to imitate the sound a squeaky door makes. Help the students to predict what happens in the play as you introduce the key vocabulary words *(scary/scariest, squeak/squeaky, tucked in, turned off)*. Ask **multi-level questions** that will help all students to join in.

Making predictions. Read the narrator's first three lines. Ask, *Why do you think Sonny didn't like to spend the night?* Encourage comments without making corrections. Finish reading the narrator's introduction. Repeat the question, *Why didn't he like to spend the night?* Next ask, *Does the grandmother solve the problem? How?* Have students look at the art again and predict what she does. (CALLA: Predicting)

GUIDED READING Read or play the tape of the whole play as the students follow along in their books. Then have students do silent **independent** reading without the tape. Ask students to demonstrate the sound each animal makes, for example, *What does the (cat) say?*

Guided discussion. Discuss the play with students. Ask literal and inferential questions that will enable students at all language stages to demonstrate how much they have understood. *What did Sonny hear? What did his grandma tell him to do the (first) time? Why? What did she tell him to do next? Why? What happened after the horse got in the bed? What did she notice in her tool kit? What did she do? Tell me why it was a good idea.*

Choral reading. Divide the students into eight groups. Assign parts: the narrator, Sonny, his grandmother, the cat, the dog, the rooster, the horse, and the door. Encourage the students to read with expression. Switch parts and repeat.

Cloze exercise; retelling a story. Students work independently to complete a cloze exercise, then work with a partner to check answers. **Recalling details; reading for a purpose.** Students work independently to answer questions on the reading. **Guided/creative writing; cloze story.** Students work independently to complete a cloze exercise on the reading, then write a new ending. Teaching suggestions are provided in the Skills Journal annotations.

ART Performing the play. Give students large sheets of paper so they can make their own scenery for the play. Have the students perform the play. If necessary, assign more than one child to be the narrator and the animals in order to include everyone. Perform for another class or for parents.

SOCIAL STUDIES Relating fiction to own experience. Ask students to do language experience writing about something they have been afraid of. *One time I was scared because ...* (CALLA: Comparing)

ONGOING ASSESSMENT

PERFORMANCE Oral language. Observe the students as they participate in the play. Use the **Oral Language Checklist** available in the *Amazing Assessment Package.*

PORTFOLIO Save **Skills Journal** pages 33 and 34 as a record of vocabulary mastery and comprehension ability.

MULTICULTURAL AWARENESS
Encourage students to share folk-tales from their home cultures. Ask them to bring a copy of their favorite folktale to class, or to briefly tell the class something about the tale.

STAFF DEVELOPMENT
See the *Amazing How-To Handbook* for more on reading strategies and cultural awareness.

WRITING PROJECT
Writing Project 2B, *Good Night!,* is directly linked to this lesson. See the Process Writing Portfolio Program Teachers' Handbook, pages 14-15, for the Lesson Plan

Students will find instructions and a Prewriting Sheet in the Writing Projects booklet inside the Portfolio.

HOLISTIC ASSESSMENT

Families Around the World

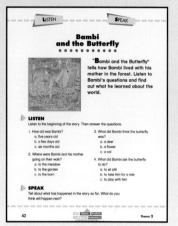

LEVEL C, PAGES 42-43

KEY EXPERIENCES

- Listening to a new story
- Describing story events
- Retelling the story
- Thinking critically
- Guided reading
- Writing

KEY LANGUAGE

- butterfly, flower, meadow, still, spread

MATERIALS

- construction paper
- glue

1 INTRODUCE

MULTI-LEVEL TEACHING STRATEGIES

These two pages offer a variety of assessment opportunities. The left-hand page consists of listening and speaking activities that follow a taped presentation. In the speaking activity, students are asked to summarize the story and make predictions based on what they have heard. The right-hand page consists of writing and critical thinking activities. These follow a reading passage that completes the listening component. You can use the activities to assess listening, speaking, reading, writing, and critical thinking skills. Have children work as a class or in small groups. Record your observations as appropriate on the **Anecdotal Record Form,** the **Reading Checklist,** and the **Writing Checklist** in the *Amazing Assessment Package.*

Building background. Begin by asking students if anyone has heard the story of Bambi the deer. If possible, bring in the original story by Felix Salten to share with students or show the movie *Bambi.* As an alternative, bring in photos of baby deer and invite students to discuss. Create a word web relating to deer. Assist with vocabulary as needed.

Ask **multi-level questions** to enable students at different proficiency levels to participate. Here are some sample questions:

Speech Emergence: *What is a baby deer called? Where do deer live?*

Developing Fluency: *How are fawns different from their mothers? Do real deer talk?*

SCIENCE Learning about butterflies. Bring in several books about butterflies for students to look through in their free time. You might also set up a bulletin board display about butterflies. Discuss the life of a butterfly from caterpillar, to chrysalis, to beautiful butterfly.

2 EXPLORE

Previewing the story. Open to Student Book pages 42–43 and let students comment on the pictures of the deer. Read the title aloud, "Bambi and the Butterfly." Ask students what they think this story will be about. Tell them they will listen to the story to find out what happened. (CALLA: Activating prior knowledge)

Preparing to listen. Tell the students they are going to hear the beginning of the story. Direct their attention to the listening questions. Do **choral**

reading of the listening questions before playing the tape. Give students time to do **independent reading** of the questions.

Listening to the story. Read or play the tape for the first part of "Bambi." You will find the tapescript in the Appendix.

Have students work independently to answer the listening questions. Read or play the tape again in segments; pause for students to check their work and make corrections.

Speaking. Ask **multi-level questions** about the story, for example, *What is the baby deer's name? What does Bambi ask his mother about the path? Does Bambi know that he is a deer?* If some students are struggling, play the tape again and retell the story once yourself.

Thinking. Invite students to predict what will happen. Ask, *What do you think Bambi will do? Will he talk to the butterfly? Why does Bambi think the butterfly is a flower?* (CALLA: Predicting)

GUIDED READING Read the rest of the story on page 43. Then ask students if their predictions were correct. Ask **multi-level questions,** such as *Did Bambi talk to the butterfly? What did he say? Did the butterfly play with Bambi? What did the butterfly do?* Use the **Reading Checklist** in the *Amazing Assessment Package.*

SKILLS JOURNAL PAGE 36 **Reading comprehension; cloze exercise.** Students work independently to finish cloze paragraphs using words from a Data Bank. Teaching suggestions are provided in the annotation. Save this page in the student's **Assessment Portfolio.**

♪♪

MUSIC "Over in the Meadow." Play the tape or sing the song. (See the Tapescript in the Appendix.)

ART Making butterflies. Show students how to make their own butterflies by folding a piece of construction paper in half and cutting out a butterfly shape. Legs and antennae can be made out of three strips of paper. Children can cut out pairs of different colored shapes to paste to both wings.

Writing. Invite students to write about other things Bambi saw in the meadow. To assess students' work, use the **Writing Checklist** in the *Amazing Assessment Package.*

AMAZING FACTS

Families Around the World

LEVEL C, PAGE 44

KEY EXPERIENCES

- Recalling facts/details
- Reading for information
- Playing "Amazing Facts"
- Making charts about the body

KEY LANGUAGE

- Review

1 INTRODUCE

MULTI-LEVEL TEACHING STRATEGIES

Building background. Ask students to open one of their textbooks to a unit they have already completed, or students can choose a science book from the Reading Corner. Ask them to scan the page and find a fact to share with the class. Give them time to write down the fact on a separate piece of paper. Discuss the facts they found.

Include all students in the discussion by asking questions appropriate to each student's language stage. Here are some sample questions:

Speech Emergence: *Did you find an interesting fact? Please read us your fact.*

Developing Fluency: *What is your fact? Why is that "amazing"?*

Recalling facts. Draw a food pyramid on the board. Ask, *What do you remember about the food pyramid?* Elicit ideas and list them on the board. Ask students to tell you their favorite foods and where they fit on the pyramid. (CALLA: Elaboration)

Using TPR. Play "Simon Says" to review the parts of the body, *Simon Says touch your knee,* etc.

Replaying a game. Use the pronoun cards, the number cards, and the family member cards from page 33 for a chain game. S1 draws one card from each pile and asks S2 a question: *Does she have two cousins?* S2 answers, *Yes, she has two cousins.* S2 then draws three cards and asks S3 a question, etc.

2 EXPLORE

Activating prior knowledge. Open to page 44 of the Student Book. Have students cover the questions. Ask, *Do you remember how to play the Amazing Facts game?* If necessary, review how to play. (They play in teams; teams earn points by correctly answering questions on the quiz game board. There will be a time limit of 5–10 minutes, depending on class level.)

Predicting the questions. Ask, *What have you learned about in this unit? What do you think the questions might be?* Elicit ideas from the class. Write student-generated questions on the board. (CALLA: Predicting)

Playing the game. Divide the students into teams. Set the time limit and have the teams work together to answer the questions. Circulate and help as needed. At the end of the pre-set time period, have the teams compete for the correct answers orally. Read the questions in random order. The first team to raise their hands and answer the question correctly wins a point. The team with the most points at the end of play wins the game.

Extra challenge. For extra fluency practice, ask the students to answer the questions in complete sentences: *Ants are social insects because they live and work together.*

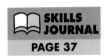 **Creating a game.** Students create their own Amazing Facts games to be played by classmates. Teaching suggestions are provided in the Skills Journal annotation.

SCIENCE Making charts about the body. Have students find out facts about another system in their body, such as the respiratory system or the digestive system. Students can write their facts on charts. Display in the classroom. (CALLA: Resourcing)

SOCIAL STUDIES Countries in the Caribbean. On a globe or world map, help students locate countries near Puerto Rico. Divide the students into groups and have each group choose one of the countries to research. Have the groups report five facts about their countries to the class. Students can use the facts to make a new facts game, "Countries in the Caribbean." (CALLA: Resourcing)

Home-School Connection. Have the students take home a copy of the "Amazing Facts" game they made in their Skills Journals. Encourage them to play it with their families and explain the facts if their family members need help.

ONGOING ASSESSMENT

PERFORMANCE Listening comprehension, oral language. Ask the questions from "Amazing Facts" in random order. Have the students answer orally. Can the student understand the questions easily? Does the student answer using single words? Can he/she make complete sentences? Use the **Oral Language Checklist** in the *Amazing Assessment Package.*

MULTICULTURAL AWARENESS
Invite volunteers to make up a game using facts from their home cultures. Ask them to present the game to the class, explaining the facts as needed.

Wrap Up

THEME 2

ASSESSMENT

You will find background information on the latest thinking in assessment as well as the assessment instruments for this theme in the *Amazing Assessment Package*.

You have been collecting assessment data through the ongoing and holistic assessment options (Oral Language Checklist, Reading Checklist, Writing Checklist, Anecdotal Record Form) in this theme. The following are specific end-of-theme assessment strategies that will help you evaluate your students' progress as well as adapt your instruction to meet their needs.

Student Self-Assessment. Self-assessment surveys are a means for students to have input into their own learning process. Students can use them to **reflect** on the work they have done and the learning strategies they have used during this theme.

Interpreting and Applying Assessment Data. As teachers, you collect assessment data in order to inform your instruction. Assessment information is a tool that helps you tailor your program to better meet the needs and interests of your students.

Evaluate the checklists, anecdotal records, portfolio collections, and test results from this theme as a means of informing your instruction.

- In which areas are students showing confidence and enthusiasm?
- In which areas are they hesitant or confused?
- Should you provide more classroom opportunities for oral language or writing?
- Would certain students (or the whole class) benefit from a focused mini-lesson on a certain area or skill?
- Remember to recycle skills as you teach the next theme and provide students with many opportunities to improve their competence.

Review the results of the **Student Self-Assessment** survey and incorporate students' interests as you plan your instruction for the next theme. What do they want to learn next? Which activities did they enjoy most? If your students particularly enjoyed choral reading, roleplaying, or working in partners, try to emphasize those kinds of activities in the next theme.

THEME CELEBRATION

The end of a theme study is a good time for students to share some of their accomplishments with others. Suggest to students that you hold a celebration to spotlight their work. This celebration can be an excellent opportunity to build stronger connections with other students and teachers in the school. Your students can make fried bananas for another class. They can share facts about unfriendly ant families and information about how to calculate heartbeats, as well as the Amazing Facts games they have researched and played. If possible, invite family members to the theme celebration.

END-OF-THEME READ-ALOUD BOOK

Dumpling Soup

by Jama Kim Rattigan

illustrated by Lillian Hsu-Flanders

Boston, Little, Brown and Company, 1993

In this story, seven-year-old Marisa tells about her family's celebration of the New Year. Marisa lives on Oahu, and her whole family gathers at Grandma's house every New Year's eve to celebrate and eat dumpling soup. This year it is Marisa's turn to learn to make dumplings.0Members of Marisa's family are Korean, Chinese, Japanese, Hawaiian, or *haole*, which is Hawaiian for white people. A glossary at the beginning of the book lists words from each language.

READING CORNER

It's important to get students excited about independent reading. Remember to distribute the Literature Links Bibliography for the next theme to your students and encourage them to use the *Amazing BookBytes* CD-ROM to respond to their reading.

Adventures in Space

Theme 3 takes students to the moon and the planets. Through literature, articles, poetry, and language activity pages in the **Student Book**, the students will learn some amazing facts about space and heighten their curiosity about space exploration. They will read about the adventures of two comic book heroes and about a woman astronaut. The **Skills Journal** offers opportunities for further language practice, reading, writing, and research on a variety of theme-related topics.

Multi-Level Teaching Strategies integrated into each lesson plan insure that all students can participate in these class activities, each at his or her own level of language proficiency. **Home-School Connection** activities provide enjoyable extension activities for students and family members to do together.

The **Ongoing Assessment** suggestions in the lesson plans will help you keep track of your students' progress. On **Student Book** pages 62-63, the "Listen, Speak, Read, Write, Think" selection offers an opportunity for **holistic assessment**. The end-of-theme **Wrap-Up** page includes guidelines for implementing the full range of assessment tools and interpreting the results.

PLANNING TIPS

The **At-a-Glance Lesson Planner** on the next two pages provides an overview of the Key Experiences and Key Language presented in each lesson of the theme. Quickly scan the lesson plan Materials lists to see if there are materials to gather or prepare. Check the **Wrap-Up** page in case you want to plan ahead for the Theme Celebration.

The following **Read-Aloud Books** are recommended with this theme. Gather these titles and your own theme-related favorites. We encourage you to read aloud to your students every day. If possible, record the stories on tape and let students reread the books as they listen to the tapes.

- *Kites Sail High* by Ruth Heller

- *This Same Sky: A Collection of Poems from Around the World* by Naomi S. Nye

- *Airmail to the Moon* by Tom Birdseye

- *Lost in the Solar System* by Joanna Cole

- *Christa McAuliffe, Teacher in Space* by Corinne J. Naden and Rose Blue

- *John Glenn, Space Pioneer* by Ann Angel

- *Alistair and the Alien Invasion* by Marilyn Sadler (Wrap-Up page)

READING CORNER

Encourage independent reading for information and pleasure. If possible, set up a reading corner—a quiet, comfortable place that is just for reading (and perhaps listening to any books on tape you've collected). Make a bulletin board on which you can post book covers, students' BookBytes reviews and the Literature Links Bibliographies that support each theme. See the Appendix for the complete Literature Links Bibliography for this theme. It offers a variety of fiction and non-fiction choices **in English and in other languages.**

LESSON PLAN

1 **Student Book p. 45**
Theme Opener

2 **Student Book p. 46**
Communication 1A

3 **Student Book p. 47**
Communication 1B

4 **Student Book p. 48**
Read and Do

5 **Student Book p. 49**
The Spaceship

6 **Student Book p. 50**
Communication 2A

7 **Student Book p. 51**
Communication 2B

8 **Student Book pp. 52-53**
Check This Out!

9 **Student Book p. 54**
Language Power A

10 **Student Book p. 55**
Language Power B

11 **Student Book pp. 56-57**
Hands-On Science

12 **Student Book pp. 58-61**
Tip Top Adventures

13 **Student Book pp. 62-63**
Holistic Assessment

14 **Student Book p. 64**
Amazing Facts Game

KEY EXPERIENCES

Talking about space travel • Sharing personal interests about space • Predicting what theme titles mean • Making a space facts chart

Talking about interests and preferences • Roleplaying fixed and free dialogues • Following conversational sequence • Reading for information

Discussing the solar system • Making a drawing/model of the solar system • Expressing preferences • Creating planet charts

Talking about air • Scanning for information • Reading/following directions • Making a rocket launcher • Experimenting with air

Making spaceships • Listening to a poem • Guided reading of a poem • Performing a poetry reading • Creating new verses

Identifying places in the community • Talking about the future • Describing errands • Roleplaying fixed and free conversations

Roleplaying fixed and free conversations • Identifying/counting coins • Creating new conversations • Asking for prices/making change

Predicting content • Reading short selections about space • Reading "Amazing Facts" • Researching meteors/stars

Talking about past ongoing actions • Problem solving • Previewing • Making observations

Describing ongoing actions • Expressing ownership • Identifying locations • Discussing what to do when lost • Going on a treasure hunt

Discussing ice/air • Performing experiments about ice/air • Following directions • Computing and comparing • Drawing conclusions

Guided reading of comic strips • Distinguishing between fantasy and reality • Enjoying humorous selections • Previewing past tense verbs

Listening to a new story • Describing story events • Retelling the story • Thinking critically • Guided reading • Writing

Recalling facts/details • Reading for information • Playing "Amazing Facts" • Creating a game

LESSON PLANNER

KEY LANGUAGE

adventures, space, spaceship

Do you like . . .? • Who's your favorite hero? • What's your favorite (TV show)? • I'd like to (travel). • I'd (go to the moon).

Do you want to . . .? • No, I don't. • I'd rather explore Mars. • Names of planets

fins, flexible, fold, jumbo, lift off, poke, stick, straw

Names of planets (R) • Milky Way, moonbeam, rings, spaceship, spacesuit

Where are you going? • I'm going to the library. • bank, check, groceries, library, mall, package, post office, supermarket

May I help you? • And how much is this game? • It's ($4.99). • Numbers 1-25 • cents, change, dime, dollar, penny, quarter, nickel

crater, gravity, meteor, orbit, sound waves, shrink, wish, brightest, nearest, hottest, coolest

What were you doing? • I was (driving a moon buggy). • rocks, space station

I am looking for my (hat). • Subject pronouns (R) • Possessive adjectives (R) • bat, bone, dog, hat, skate, socks, shoes, sweater

ice cube, speed, shaded, sunny, weight, react, temperature, seam

submarine, octopus, boxing gloves, sonic power, ladder, another close call, space skis, icicles, footprints, beast, the hatch

astronaut, at last, chosen, enjoyed, space shuttle

Review

CONTENT AREAS

Social Studies • Language Arts

Science • Language Arts

Art • Music • Science • Language Arts

Science • Language Arts

Science • Language Arts

Art • Music • Language Arts

Math • Language Arts

Science • Language Arts

Science • Language Arts

Social Studies • Language Arts

Science • Language Arts

Art • Science • Language Arts

Assessment

Assessment

THEME OPENER

Adventures in Space

LEVEL C, PAGE 45

KEY EXPERIENCES

- Talking about space travel
- Sharing personal interests about space
- Predicting what unit titles mean
- Making a space facts chart
- Exploring air and ice
- Illustrating predictions

KEY LANGUAGE

- adventures, space, spaceship

1 INTRODUCE

MULTI-LEVEL TEACHING STRATEGIES

Building background. Discuss the photograph of the astronaut on page 45 of the Student Book. Talk about what students already know about space and what they're curious about. Include all the students by asking questions appropriate to each student's language stage. Here are some sample questions:

Speech Emergence: *Would you like to travel in space? Where would you like to go? What do you think you would see?*

Developing Fluency: *Would you like to be an astronaut? Why? Do you think it would be hard?*

ART Drawing outer space. Ask students to draw a picture of themselves traveling in outer space. In small groups, have students take turns talking about their pictures.

SCIENCE Exploring weightlessness. Play "Simon Says." First say, *In space we don't weigh the same as we do on Earth. When we move, we feel like we're floating.* Demonstrate walking in space, using exaggerated movements. Then cue the students, *Simon Says walk*, etc. Encourage them to move freely.

2 EXPLORE

Activating prior knowledge. Read the title of the unit aloud, "Adventures in Space." Direct students' attention to the first topic of the unit, "The Spaceship." Then invite them to talk about what it would be like doing daily activities on a spaceship. Ask, *What do people do? Where do they sleep? What do they eat?* etc.

Cooperative learning. Divide students into groups. Have each of the groups choose a different daily activity such as sleeping, eating, doing scientific experiments, and exercising. Remind students about the weightlessness activity from **Introduce.** Have groups **brainstorm** how the activity is done on a spaceship, illustrate it, and write some captions or labels for the illustrations. Call on groups to report to the class.

Making a space facts chart. Have students make a chart in which they include the space facts they know. Ask, *What do we know about space?* Display in the classroom. Encourage students to add to the chart as they progress through the unit.

SCIENCE Exploring air and ice. Blow up a balloon. Ask, *What will happen if I put this balloon in a very warm place?* Elicit ideas. Talk about why the balloon might pop. (Hot air expands.) Next, show students a piece of ice or a drawing of a piece of ice. Ask, *What will happen if I put this ice in a very warm place?* Talk about how it will melt. (CALLA: Deduction)

Previewing. Explain that in "Tip Top Adventures," Tip and Top find a planet. Brainstorm with the class what the planet might be like. Encourage students to use their imaginations. *What do they see? Who do they see?* etc. (CALLA: Predicting)

SKILLS JOURNAL
PAGE 38

Prewriting. Students make word webs about space and use the words to write a paragraph. Teaching suggestions are provided in the Skills Journal annotation.

3 EXTEND

Using TPR. Have students take turns pantomiming for the class a weightless activity on a spaceship. The rest of the class identifies the activity, *You're brushing your teeth.*

SCIENCE Learning about space exploration. Share some of the highlights of the space race between the U.S. and Russia, such as July 20, 1969 when U.S. astronaut Neil Armstrong took the first steps on the moon. Display resource materials about the Kennedy Space Center and Cape Canaveral in the Reading Corner for students to look at in their free time. (CALLA: Resourcing)

ART Illustrating predictions. Ask students to illustrate what they think "The Tip Top Adventures" will be about. Encourage students to use their imaginations about what is on the planet. (CALLA: Imagery)

ONGOING ASSESSMENT

PERFORMANCE Oral language. Ask the students to describe for you their drawings about "Tip Top Adventures." Observe different students' levels of participation. Use the **Oral Language Checklist** in the *Amazing Assessment Package.*

PORTFOLIO Independent writing. Save **Skills Journal** page 38 as an example of independent writing.

TEACHER TO TEACHER

If your students work with other teachers, you may want to mention to them that students of limited language proficiency may have a good foundation in science from their home cultures. Ample hands-on science along with language support, provides valuable opportunities for those students to develop their self-esteem, while increasing their language skills.

COMMUNICATION 1A

Adventures in Space

LEVEL C, PAGE 46

KEY EXPERIENCES

- Talking about interests and preferences
- Roleplaying fixed and free dialogues
- Following conversational sequence
- Reading for information

KEY LANGUAGE

- *Do you like ...?*
- *Who's your favorite hero?*
- *What's your favorite (TV show)?*
- *I'd like to (travel).*
- *I'd (go to the moon).*

1 INTRODUCE

MULTI-LEVEL TEACHING STRATEGIES

Building background: Reading for information. Bring "how to" books to class about different types of hobbies, such as music, stamp collecting, and model trains. These books should be written at the K–2 reading levels. Set aside time for the students to look at the books. Show one of the books and talk about the hobby. Show students how to "read" the pictures as well as the words in the books. Discuss the students' hobbies and interests.

Include all students in the discussion, asking questions appropriate to each student's language stage. Here are some sample questions:

Speech Emergence: *Do you like sports? What is your favorite sport? Do you like music?*

Developing Fluency: *Do you play computer games? Tell the class about your favorite game. Why do you like it?*

Playing a game. Print on sentence strips, *What's your favorite color? What's your favorite toy? What's your favorite school subject? What's your favorite hobby? What's your favorite TV show? What's your favorite computer game?* Make enough copies so that each student has at least one strip. Help the students read the strips. Put the sentence strips in a hat. Read a strip to student 1, *What's your favorite color?* Student 1 answers. Student 1 then draws a strip and asks a question of Student 2. Continue with other students.

2 EXPLORE

Activating prior knowledge. Open to page 46 of the Student Book. Ask students to comment about the picture of the two students. Ask, *What do you see? What do you think they are talking about?*

Look, listen, and talk. Have students look and listen as you read or play the tape for the text at the top of the page. Check understanding by asking **multi-level questions:** *Who are their heroes? What are their favorite TV shows? Where do they want to go?*

Practicing the conversation. Read the text or play the tape again, pausing for students to repeat.

Reading for information: Amazing Facts. Direct students to the bottom of the page. Read or play the tape. Then give students time to reread the information on their own. Ask **multi-level questions,**

for example, *What is special about the Great Wall of China? How do male astronauts shave in space? What is special about the underwear of astronauts?* etc.

 **Data collection.** Students conduct interviews, record the information in charts, and use it for paired conversation practice. Teaching suggestions are provided in the Skills Journal annotation.

SKILLS JOURNAL PAGE 39

Show and Tell. Ask students to share examples of their favorite hobbies during Show and Tell. This might include stamps, stuffed animals, model cars, dolls, or baseball cards. Have students ask one another questions, *Do you like baseball cards?* Encourage students to show a partner or the class how to classify and organize baseball cards, how to mount a stamp, what their stuffed animals are, etc.

Language experience writing. Ask students to write about traveling to the moon. *What would they travel in? What would they take with them? Which favorite food/book/game would they take? How long would they stay there?* Have students draw pictures to accompany their writing.

SCIENCE Learning about space travel. Make a list of daily activities, such as eating, brushing your teeth, taking a shower, etc. Brainstorm how these activities might be done in space. Help students use resource materials to find the answers. Print the information on chart paper, *This is how you eat in space,* etc. Display in the classroom. (CALLA: Resourcing)

ONGOING ASSESSMENT

PERFORMANCE Oral language. Go around the class asking students about their preferences and favorites, *Do you like ...? What's your favorite ...?* Observe students' levels of participation. Use the **Oral Language Checklist** in the *Amazing Assessment Package.*

PORTFOLIO Note-taking. Save **Skills Journal** page 39 as an example of oral/aural abilities and note-taking.

MULTICULTURAL AWARENESS

Invite volunteers to tell the class about some of the TV shows they currently watch in English and in their primary languages (in those parts of the country where foreign language television is available). Ask students from other countries what they used to watch and which TV shows from the U.S. were popular in their home countries.

TEACHER TO TEACHER

If your students work with other teachers, you may want to mention to them that the students have been talking about heroes, hobbies, and space travel. Bringing up now-familiar topics in other classes lets ESL students use newly acquired language in a meaningful context.

STAFF DEVELOPMENT

Although television viewing should be limited, it does serve a useful purpose in language learning. See the *Amazing How-To Handbook* for more on this topic.

COMMUNICATION 1B

Adventures in Space

LEVEL C, PAGE 47

KEY EXPERIENCES

- Discussing the solar system
- Making a drawing/model of the solar system
- Expressing preferences
- Creating planet chants

KEY LANGUAGE

- *Do you want to ...?*
- *No, I don't.*
- *I'd rather explore Mars.*
- names of planets

MATERIALS

- styrofoam balls, straws, clay

1 INTRODUCE

MULTI-LEVEL TEACHING STRATEGIES

Building background: Discussing the solar system. Engage the students in a discussion of our solar system. Draw a circle on the board or on chart paper. Say, *This is the sun.* Write *sun* in the circle. Make a smaller circle away from the sun. Say, *This is Earth. This is where we live.* Write *Earth* under the circle. If available, you can attach labels to a mobile of the solar system instead. Elicit the names of the other planets in our solar system. Draw and label each in relative order and size. After you have drawn and labeled all the planets (Mercury, Venus, Earth, Mars, Jupiter, Saturn, Uranus, Neptune, Pluto), help students read the names **chorally** as you point to each planet.

Include all students in the activity by asking questions appropriate to each student's language stage. Here are some sample questions:

Speech Emergence: *Is Earth the closet planet to the sun? Do you know the name of the planet farthest from the sun? Do you think it is hot on Mercury?*

Developing Fluency: *What is the name of the planet closest to the sun? Which planet comes after Mercury? Can you spell Venus? Why is Mercury hotter than Venus? Do you think it would be more comfortable on Mars or Jupiter?*

ART Drawing the solar system. Ask students to make their own drawings of the solar system. Have them label the planets. In pairs, have students read the names of the planets and talk about their locations, *Venus is between Mercury and Earth; Mars is between Earth and Jupiter. Saturn comes after Jupiter,* etc. (CALLA: Imagery)

Playing letter scramble. Write the names of the planets on the board in random order. Scramble the letters of each name. Have students unscramble the letters. Then have the students number the planets from 1–9 according to their position from the sun. Read the names chorally. (CALLA: Sequencing)

2 EXPLORE

Activating prior knowledge. Open to page 47of the Student Book. Ask students to comment about the picture of the boys in the museum. What do they see? What do they think the students are talking about?

 **Look, listen, and talk.** Play the tape or read the conversation. Have students point to the lines as they listen. Read the conversation again, pausing for students to repeat **chorally.** Check comprehension, *Does (he) want to explore to the moon? Where would he rather go?* Work **Teacher-Class**.

Practicing the conversation. Divide the class into two groups. One group asks the question, the other answers. Switch roles and repeat. In pairs, have students practice the conversation. Then have them switch roles. Have partners continue practicing, substituting different planets, *Do you want to explore Venus?*

SKILLS JOURNAL PAGE 40 **Reading for a purpose; writing.** Students read about the planets and write answers to questions. Teaching suggestions are provided in the Skills Journal annotation.

Using TPR. Write the names of the planets and the sun on slips of paper. Make enough slips for everyone in the class. Cue the students, *Mercury touch your nose.* All students with the slip *Mercury* do the action. Continue, *touch your knee, pull your ear,* etc., naming a different planet each time. Then call out, *Sun stand next to the board. Planets line up!* Students line up in the correct order from the sun. Ask the students to spread out again and repeat. If there is more than one student per planet, students can make more than one line.

MUSIC Creating planet chants. Together create chants about the planets. Print them on chart paper. Help the students make the chants rhyme, for example, *Mercury, Mercury, touch your toes; Venus, Venus, wiggle your nose; Mars, Mars, turn to the right, Jupiter, Jupiter point to the light!* or *Earth, Earth touch your chin; Saturn, Saturn turn left and spin; Neptune, Neptune reach for the sky; Pluto, Pluto say good-bye!* Encourage the students to "orbit" in a circle as they do the actions and say the chant. Include rhyming pairs students have already studied, if possible.

SCIENCE Making a model. Have students make a model of the solar system using straws, clay, styrofoam balls or other materials available. Ask students to label the planets. Display in the classroom.

ONGOING ASSESSMENT

PERFORMANCE Oral language. Listen as students practice the conversation, substituting different planets. Observe different students' levels of participation using the **Oral Language Checklist** in the *Amazing Assessment Package.*

MULTICULTURAL AWARENESS

Invite volunteers to tell the class the names of the planets in their native languages. If several languages are represented, make a chart of the names in English and in other languages.

STAFF DEVELOPMENT

See the *Amazing How-To Handbook* and *The CALLA Handbook* for other suggestions on implementing CALLA in the classroom.

WRITING PROJECT

Writing Project 3A, *The Planets,* is directly linked to this lesson. See the Process Writing Portfolio Program Teachers' Handbook, pages 16-17, for the lesson Plan.

Students will find instructions and a Prewriting Sheet in the Writing Projects booklet inside the Portfolio.

READ AND DO

Adventures in Space

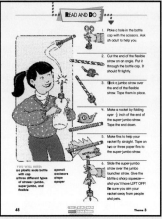

LEVEL C, PAGE 48

KEY EXPERIENCES

- Talking about air
- Scanning for information
- Reading/following directions
- Making a rocket launcher
- Experimenting with air

KEY LANGUAGE

- fins, flexible, fold, jumbo, lift off, poke, stick, straw

MATERIALS

- plastic soda bottles with caps; jumbo, super-jumbo, and flexible drinking straws

••• 1 INTRODUCE •••

MULTI-LEVEL TEACHING STRATEGIES

Building background. Hold up a ruler and a large sheet of paper. Lay the ruler on a table so that about one third of it lies over the edge. Spread the paper over the ruler. Ask, *What will happen if I hit the ruler?* Then hit the ruler and try to make the paper fly into the air. Discuss what happened to the paper. (The paper shouldn't fly up.)

Include all of the students by asking questions appropriate to each student's language stage:

Speech Emergence: *Did the paper move? Did it fly into the air?*

Developing Fluency: *What did the paper do? Why didn't the paper move? How could you make it move?*

Explain that the air presses down on the paper. Because the paper has a large area, there is a lot of air pressing down on the paper. This stops the paper from flying up.

Talking about air. Ask some general questions about air to help the students focus on the topic, such as *How does an airplane stay up in the air? How does air stay in a balloon? Why do balloons pop? How does a straw work?* Brainstorm ideas. Make a **word web** with *air* in the center. Help students think of other questions about air they would like to know the answers to, for example, *How much does air weigh? What happens when air gets warm?*

••• 2 EXPLORE •••

Activating prior knowledge. Open to page 48 of the Student Book. Invite students to comment on the page. What do they think the girl is doing? Direct students' attention to YOU WILL NEED. Say, *count how many things we need.* Make sure students include *three* types of straws. Ask students to read the list **chorally.** As the students say each item, hold it up. Demonstrate a flexible straw. (CALLA: Predicting)

GUIDED READING Following directions. Direct students' attention to the directions on the right side of the page. Say, *How many steps are there?* Next ask the students to scan each step *quickly* and identify the first word in each (all verbs). Check answers **chorally:** 1. *Poke;* 2. *Cut;* 3. *Stick;* 4. *Make;* 5. *Make;* 6. *Slide.* Have students mime the actions for 1, 2, 3, and 6. (CALLA: Sequencing)

Choral reading. Read the steps as the students follow along in their books. Read the steps again **chorally,** pausing to demonstrate each step. Ask **multi-level questions** such as, *Do you tape or glue the straws? What happens when you give the bottle a sharp squeeze? What should you be sure to do?* Demonstrate *aiming away* from people.

Cooperative learning: Making a rocket launcher. Divide the students into small groups. Distribute supplies for one rocket launcher per group. (Poke the holes in the bottle caps ahead of time). Have each group work together to make the rocket launcher. Circulate and encourage students to take turns reading the directions and doing the steps. Take the students outside or to a large space to launch the rockets. *Which rocket goes the highest?* (CALLA: Cooperation)

SKILLS JOURNAL PAGE 41

Reading for a purpose; writing. Students read paragraphs on space and write answers to questions. Teaching suggestions are provided in the Skills Journal annotation.

3 EXTEND

SCIENCE Lifting books with air. Lay a large plastic bag on a table and put a pile of books on top of the bag. Leave the open end of the bag sticking out. Ask students to predict what will happen if someone blows into the bag. Ask a student volunteer to do it, keeping the opening as small as possible. Discuss the results. (The books rise because the air in the bag is compressed.) Experiment further, varying the bag size and the amount of books. (CALLA: Predicting)

Home-School Connection: Another experiment. At home, have students take a glass, some water, and a square of cardboard slightly bigger than the glass. Tell them to fill the glass and wet the rim slightly, then lay the cardboard on top of the glass and turn the glass over. Ask them to report their results to the class. Encourage students to let family members watch the experiment as they explain what they are doing.

ONGOING ASSESSMENT

PERFORMANCE Oral language. Ask students to explain how to make the rocket launcher. Prompt as needed. Observe different students' levels of participation. Use the **Oral Language Checklist** in the *Amazing Assessment Package.*

PORTFOLIO Independent writing. Save **Skills Journal** page 41 as an example of reading comprehension.

STAFF DEVELOPMENT

See *The Amazing How-To Handbook* and *The CALLA Handbook* for additional ways to integrate science into the curriculum.

TEACHER TO TEACHER

If your students work with other teachers, you may want to mention to them that simple science experiments are good vehicles for involving less proficient ESL students in mainstream classroom activities. By pairing students of varying language abilities, more proficient ESL students or native English speakers can help less proficient students express their observations and experiment results.

RELATED RELATED RESOURCES

See *Eureka: Science Demonstrations for ESL Students* for more hands-on science activities you can do in your classroom.

THE SPACESHIP

Adventures in Space

LEVEL C, PAGE 49

KEY EXPERIENCES

- Making spaceships
- Listening to a poem
- Guided reading of a poem
- Performing a poetry reading
- Creating new verses
- Learning about space

KEY LANGUAGE

- names of planets (R)
- Milky Way, moonbeam, rings, spaceship, spacesuit

MATERIALS

- pipe cleaners, felt, colored paper, styrofoam

••• 1 INTRODUCE •••

MULTI-LEVEL TEACHING STRATEGIES

Building background. Tape a large piece of black paper to the chalkboard. Explain to the students that the piece of paper represents outer space. With white chalk or a white crayon, draw and introduce the following words and phrases from the poem: *spaceship, planets, Venus, Saturn, rings, moonbeam, Milky Way.* Ask what else students want you to draw in outer space. Include all students in the discussion by asking questions appropriate to each student's language stage. Here are some sample questions:

Speech Emergence: *Do we need the sun? The moon? Do you know the names of any stars?*, etc.

Developing Fluency: *What else is in space? Where should I draw the sun? How big should I make Venus?*

ART Making spaceships. Have students make spaceships out of empty milk cartons. Students can cover the milk cartons with aluminum foil and decorate in any way they choose. Encourage students to add doors and wings. They can also make astronauts out of pipe cleaners, felt, colored oak tag or construction paper, and styrofoam.

Listening to the poem. Play the tape or read the poem through once as students listen. Then ask them to listen again, this time paying close attention to rhyming words. Encourage students to try to write down any they hear. Then print all the rhyming words on the board: *me, see, rings, things, sun, fun, snack, back.* Help students read them. Ask, *Which words rhyme?* Model the pairs of rhyming words and have students repeat.

••• 2 EXPLORE •••

Activating prior knowledge. Have students open to page 49 of the Student Book. Read the title of the poem, "The Spaceship," aloud. Encourage students to comment about the page. Ask students what they think the girl is doing in each drawing. (CALLA: Predicting)

GUIDED READING Read or play the tape again as students read along in their books **chorally.** Emphasize the rhythm as you read. Ask **multi-level questions** such as *What did she dream? Did she go to the moon? Did she stay on Jupiter? Which planets are in the poem? What is the Milky Way? What does it have to do with a snack? Has anyone ever eaten a candy bar with that name?*

Exploring key vocabulary. Point to each verb on the page, *dreamed, built, flew, see, set, zoomed, landed, flashed, floated, rested, waved.* Model sentences using the verbs; work **T-C.** Ask students to pantomime the actions, using their spaceships where appropriate.

Performing a poetry reading. Divide the class into four groups. Try to put at least one strong reader in each group. Have each group practice reading one stanza. Encourage students to read with expression as they use gestures and move their spaceships to show what is happening. Bring the class back together. Have each group read and perform their verses in order.

Cloze poetry. Students write and illustrate a poem using words in the Data Bank or their own words. Teaching suggestions are provided in the Skills Journal annotation.

SCIENCE Learning about space. Help students use resource materials to learn more about our solar system and about the Milky Way. Before they begin, have them brainstorm a list of questions to think about, for example, *How close is the nearest star? Is our sun a star? How big is the Milky Way?* Ask groups or individuals to share what they learn with the class. Students can make posters of the solar system or the Milky Way with answers to one or more of their questions. Display in the classroom. (CALLA: Resourcing)

Creating new verses. Invite the class to create new verses to the poem. The art on page 49 can serve as cues for additional verses. You may want to do this as a whole group activity; write the verses on chart paper as students create them. Invite students to reread the verses with you. Later, students can add illustrations. Invite students to perform their verses for the class using gestures and their spaceships.

ONGOING ASSESSMENT

PERFORMANCE Oral language. Print the lines to "The Spaceship" on a piece of paper. Cut the lines into strips and put them in a pile in random order. Ask the students to put the lines into the correct order, then read the poem again. Observe different students' levels of participation. Use the **Oral Language Checklist** in the *Amazing Assessment Package.*

MULTICULTURAL AWARENESS

Ask students to share poems from their home cultures. After they present the poems in their native languages, have them explain the poems briefly, *It is about ...*

RELATED RESOURCES

The Cat Came Back CD-ROM, Read Along Mode: Space (pages 7-10)

COMMUNICATION 2A

Adventures in Space

LEVEL C, PAGE 50

KEY EXPERIENCES

- Identifying places in the community
- Talking about the future
- Describing errands
- Roleplaying fixed and free conversations
- Describing on-going actions

KEY LANGUAGE

- *Where are you going?*
- *I'm going to the (library).*
- *What are you going to do there?*
- *I'm going to (return a book).*
- bank, check, groceries, library, mall, package, post office, supermarket
- buy, cash, mail, shop

●●● 1 INTRODUCE ●●●

MULTI-LEVEL TEACHING STRATEGIES

Building background. Draw a map of an imaginary city with the following clearly labeled as signs on the buildings: *library, police station, fire station, supermarket, post office, gas station, toy store, bank.* Help students read the signs. Then explain that you need their help to locate the following: *a library card, a postage stamp, a toy animal, cheese, gasoline, a firefighter, money, books, letters.* Include all students in the activity by asking questions appropriate to each student's language stage. Here are some sample questions:

Speech Emergence: *Where can I find a toy animal? Is cheese at the bank or at the supermarket?*

Developing Fluency: *What other toys can I find at the toy store? What else can I find at the fire station?*

Roleplaying. Use puppets to roleplay conversations about going to and doing things at different community locations. Puppet 1: *Where are you going?* Puppet 2: *I'm going to the library.* Puppet 1: *What are you going to do there?* Puppet 2: *I'm going to return a book.* Have puppets make conversations about what they are going to do at the supermarket, the bank, the post office, and a shopping mall. For items to buy at the mall, review the Data Bank on page 9; for items at the at the supermarket, use the Data Bank page 29.

Language experience writing. Print TO DO at the top of the piece of chart paper. Ask students to share what they are going to do today. Print their responses on the chart: *I'm going to babysit my sister, I'm going to play soccer.* Have students read the list **chorally.** Ask students to copy the sentence about their own activity. Encourage students to draw a picture to accompany the sentence.

●●● 2 EXPLORE ●●●

Activating prior knowledge. Open to page 50 of the Student Book. Encourage students to comment on the page. Ask, *What do you see?* Read the introductory sentence aloud. Ask, *What year is it? How many years is that from now?*

 **Look, listen, and talk.** Play the tape or read the conversation on page 50. Point to each picture as you refer to it. Have students look at number 1 on page 50. Ask, *What's this?* Encourage students to respond, *It's a supermarket.* Continue, *What is she going to do there?*

Encourage students to respond, *She's going to buy groceries.* Repeat with numbers 2 to 4. Expand the conversation to meet the capabilities of your students.

Divide the students into two groups. One group asks the questions; the other answers. Group 1: *Where are you going?* Group 2: *I'm going to the library.* Group 1: *What are you going to do there?* Group 2: *I'm going to return a book.* Then, in pairs, have students roleplay conversations. Encourage students to practice the full conversation for each number and to personalize in any way they want.

 MUSIC **"The Street Beat."** Play the tape or sing (See the tapescript in the Appendix.) Then have students sing along with you.

SKILLS JOURNAL PAGE 43 **Home-School Connection.** Students match written language to pictures of places about town. Teaching suggestions are provided in the Skills Journal annotation.

ART Drawing space neighborhoods. In pairs or small groups, have students draw a neighborhood in space. First, brainstorm what stores or places might be there. Have students use their drawings to make new conversations, *Where are you going? / I'm going to the spacesuit store. / What are you going to do there? / I'm going to buy a new spacesuit for my sister.*

Home-School Connection. Ask the students to interview one or more people at home about the errands they plan to do the next weekend, for example, *Where are you going on Saturday?* Ask students to report to the class; work **T-S.** *Where is your sister going on Saturday, Tony? / She's going to the mall to buy a jacket.*

- - - - - - **ONGOING ASSESSMENT** - - - - - -

PERFORMANCE Oral language. Play a Chain Drill Game. Make the following word cards: *library, supermarket, mall, post office, bank, fire station.* Place the cards in a basket or hat. Have students sit in a circle. Ask Student 1, *Where are you going?* Student 1 draws a card and answers, *I'm going to the supermarket.* You ask Student 1, *Can I come, too?* Student 1 responds, *Yes, you can.* Students 1 and 2 conduct the same conversation, using a different card. Observe different students' levels of participation using the **Oral Language Checklist** in the *Amazing Assessment Package.*

TEACHER TO TEACHER

If your students work with other teachers, you may want to suggest that they ask students about their plans for the day or the week. Students can write out their schedules for the week and talk about them in pairs or small groups first, *On Monday I'm going to the post office. I'm going to send a birthday card to my grandmother.*

COMMUNICATION 2B

Adventures in Space

LEVEL C, PAGE 51

KEY EXPERIENCES

- Roleplaying fixed and free conversations
- Identifying/counting coins
- Creating new conversations using the Data Bank
- Asking for prices/making change
- Listening to/solving word problems

KEY LANGUAGE

- *May I help you?*
- *And how much is this game?*
- *It's ($4.99).*
- *Here's (a twenty dollar bill).*
- *And here's your change.*
- *Numbers 1–25*
- *cents, change, dime, dollar, penny, quarter, nickel*

●●● 1 INTRODUCE ●●●

MULTI-LEVEL TEACHING STRATEGIES

Building background. Bring a piggy bank to class with five pennies, five nickels, two dimes, four quarters, and dollar inside. Show students the bank and have them guess what is inside. Encourage students to lift it, shake it, and look inside. Then show students the money. Show each coin; show that five pennies equals a nickel, etc. Include all the students by asking questions appropriate to each student's language stage Here are some sample questions:

Speech Emergence: *What is this? Is this a penny? Is this a nickel or dime?*

Developing Fluency: *How many pennies equal a nickel? Which is more, a nickel or a dime?* Encourage students to answer with a long utterance, *A dime is more than a nickel.*

MATH Counting coins. Prepare these numeral cards: *1 one, 5 five, 10 ten, 25 twenty-five, 50 fifty, 75 seventy-five, 100 one hundred.* Help the students read the cards. Hold up a penny, *A penny is one cent.* Continue with the other coins and the dollar bill. Put the coins in various combinations. *(Two dimes and a nickel is 25 cents.)* On the board, write some problems. For example, *What is one nickel + five pennies?, one quarter = _____ cents, two quarters =_____ cents, How many quarters equal one dollar? How many nickels equal one quarter?*

●●● 2 EXPLORE ●●●

Activating prior knowledge. Open to page 51of the Student Book. Encourage students to comment on the page. Ask where the people are.

Exploring key vocabulary. Point to each vocabulary item in the Data Bank as you introduce it: *a penny, a dime,* etc. Ask students to repeat these words and phrases **chorally** and then **individually.**

▨ Look, listen, and talk. Students first listen and point to the pictures as you describe the situation. *He is shopping. He wants to buy two things. What does it look like he wants to buy? Do you think he will buy them?* Expand the questions to meet the capabilities of your students, for example, *Is he going to buy an action figure? Would you rather buy an action figure or a game?* (CALLA: Predicting)

Have the students follow along as you read the text or play the tape.

Then ask **multi-level questions,** such as *Who do you see? Are they at the bank? Where are they?* Next, have the students practice with partners. One partner is the shopper, the other is the store clerk. Then have the partners switch roles. Model the conversation again, substituting words from the Data Bank, *It's a quarter / It's only one dollar / Here's a ten dollar bill,* etc. Have students practice the conversation, substituting words from the Data Bank. Encourage partners to expand in any way they want.

 **Identifying coin values.** Students color in the correct coins for each person. Teaching suggestions are provided in the Skills Journal annotation.

LIFE SKILLS Asking for prices/Making change. Set up a store or supermarket in the classroom. Provide play money for the students to use. Have students take turns being the customers and the store clerk. Check that students ask for prices and make change correctly. Students can expand the roleplay so that shoppers "meet" on the way to the store and discuss their errands, *Where are you going? / I'm going to the supermarket. / What are you going to do there? / I'm going to buy a jar of peanut butter.*

MATH Listening to and solving word problems. Ask students to pretend they are in a store. Tell them how much money they have, for example, three quarters and a dime. Give them problems to solve, *You want to buy a pencil. It cost 25 cents. You also want an eraser. It costs 50 cents. Do you have enough money? How much do you have left?* For extra challenge, have students write problems to ask the class. (CALLA: Problem solving)

Home-School Connection. Ask students to look in a newspaper at home for food advertisements and to cut out pictures of items that cost $1.00 or less. Suggest that students work with family members and cut out items the family regularly buys. For extra challenge, expand into a classifying activity in which students cut out advertisements of various prices and group by price ($1.00 or less, $1.00–$2.00, over $2.00, etc.). Compile the advertisements in class and make a group chart.

CHECK THIS OUT!

Adventures in Space

LEVEL C, PAGES 52–53

KEY EXPERIENCES

- Predicting content
- Reading short selections about space
- Reading "Amazing Facts"
- Researching meteors/stars

KEY LANGUAGE

- crater, gravity, meteor, orbit, sound waves, shrink, wish
- brightest, nearest, hottest, coolest

1 INTRODUCE

MULTI-LEVEL TEACHING STRATEGIES

Building background: Using visual information. Ask students to open to pages 52–53 of the Student Book and look carefully at the pictures. Tell them you are going to find out how much they can remember. After one minute, have students close their books. Find out what students can recall about the pages. Include all the students in the discussion by asking questions appropriate to each student's language stage. Here are some sample questions:

Speech Emergence: *What did you see? Did you see a planet? Do you know the name of the planet?*

Developing Fluency: *Did you see someone looking out a window? Why was the child doing that? Did you see a big hole in the ground? What do you think made that hole?*

SCIENCE Discussing Saturn. Show the students drawings or photographs of Saturn. Find out what the students already know about Saturn. For example, point out the rings and ask students what they are called. Ask **multi-level questions,** *Is there air on Saturn? Are there trees and people? What are the rings made of? How long do you think it would take to go to Saturn? Would you like to visit it? Why or why not?*

2 EXPLORE

Activating prior knowledge. Open to pages 52–53 again. Have students comment on the two pages. Direct students' attention to the titles. Read the titles aloud, or call on volunteers to do so. For "Can You Hear Me?", ask the prereading question, *Why can't they hear him?* Encourage students to make predictions.

 **GUIDED READING** Read the text or play the tape for "Can You Hear Me?" Those students who are able should read **independently.** Check understanding. Ask **multi-level questions,** such as *What doesn't the moon have? What carries sound?*

Then have students look at "Have you ever wished on a star at night?" Repeat the above procedure, substituting the prereading question, *Which star can you wish on during the day?* and the comprehension question, *Why is the sun the brightest star you see?*

Direct students' attention to "UFO" Alert! Ask students to look at the picture and predict what the selection is about. Prompt with questions, *Who do you see? Where is he? Why is he looking behind him?* Play the tape or read the text as the students follow along in their books. Then do a **choral reading** of the text.

Reading for information: Amazing Facts. Read the facts or play the tape as students follow along in their books. Have students who are able read **independently.** Ask **multi-level questions:** *Do astronauts grow when they travel in space? How much do they grow? What happens when they come back to Earth? Why? What color are the hottest stars?*

Reading for information. Have students do a **paired reading** of "Ring Around Saturn" and "A Big Hit."

Reading for a purpose; writing. Students complete a cloze paragraph on meteors, then read about the moon and write answers to questions. **Following instructions.** Students make a group model of the solar system and write about making it. Teaching suggestions are provided in the Skills Journal annotations.

Language experience writing. Explain that we wish on a star for something we really want. What would students wish for? Have students write a paragraph of 2–3 sentences in which they describe what they want. Encourage students to make drawings of their wishes as well. To assess students' work, use the **Writing Checklist** in the *Amazing Assessment Package.*

SCIENCE Making a chart. Have students use resource materials to learn more about the colors of stars. Ask students to make a chart showing an example of each color of star, its temperature, and its distance from Earth. Discuss why stars are different colors. (CALLA: Resourcing)

ONGOING ASSESSMENT

PORTFOLIO Oral language. Ask students to tell you what happened in "A Big Hit!" Observe different students' levels of participation. Use the **Oral Language Checklist** in the *Amazing Assessment Package.*

PORTFOLIO Listening. Save **Skills Journal** page 45 as an example of reading comprehension.

LANGUAGE POWER A

Adventures in Space

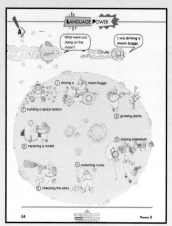

LEVEL C, PAGE 54

KEY EXPERIENCES

- Talking about past ongoing actions
- Problem solving
- Previewing
- Making observations

KEY LANGUAGE

- *What were you doing?*
- *I was (driving a moon buggy).*
- *rocks, space station*

MULTI-LEVEL TEACHING STRATEGIES

Building background. Use **TPR**. Prepare these word cards: *dancing, eating, jumping, running, hopping, drinking, playing, talking, singing, sewing, reading, writing, working, sleeping, washing.* Read the words with students. Place the word cards in a basket or a hat. Select a student to draw a card and pantomime the verb. The rest of the class guesses which verb is being pantomimed. Encourage students to respond, *He was dancing.* Include all the students by asking follow-up questions appropriate to each student's language stage. Here are some sample questions:

Speech Emergence: *Was he dancing? Do you like to dance?*

Developing Fluency: *Which do you like better, dancing or playing? Why?*

Problem solving. Before class, set a play clock to read 12:00. Display puppets with props associated with a variety of different activities (for example, a needle, paper and pencil, book, soap and towel, glass and plate). Explain to the students that the puppets were very busy and that all of a sudden, time stopped for them at noon. Have students use the props as clues to determine what the puppets might have been doing at 12:00. *She was reading. He was sewing.* Point to various puppets, *What was he doing?* Encourage students to respond with *He was eating a cookie,* etc.

2 EXPLORE

Activating prior knowledge. Open to page 54 of the Student Book. Encourage students to comment on the page. Ask students how many different activities there are on the page. Then call on different volunteers to read phrases 1–7. Encourage them to sound out the words by syllable and to look at the drawings for context clues.

Look, listen, and talk. Have students listen and point as you play the tape or model the conversation: *What were you doing on the moon? / I was driving a moon buggy.* Read it again, pausing for students to repeat **chorally.** Divide the students into two groups: one group asks the questions, the other answers. Group 1: *What were you doing on the moon?* Group 2: *I was growing plants.* Continue with the other pictures.

Personalizing. Next, have partners practice the conversation. Encourage them to add to the conversation by thinking of other activities that people might do on the moon.

Describing ongoing activities. Students answer questions about life on the moon and on Earth using the progressive. Teaching suggestions are provided in the Skills Journal annotation.

Reapply. Have partners use the poem, "The Spaceship," on page 49 to continue describing past ongoing actions. First have partners reread the poem together. Then have them ask each other questions stanza by stanza. For example, *What was she doing? She was flying around the planets.*

Making observations. Mount pictures of people involved in different activities on pieces of construction paper. Label each picture, *Last night.* On separate cards write one sentence to accompany each picture, *She was reading a book.* Have students match each picture with a sentence. (CALLA: Deduction)

Home-School Connection. Ask students to write about what they observe on their way home from school today. Suggest that they record their observations in a journal. In class have them list three things they saw, *a black dog, a city bus, three cats,* etc. Then have students write a paragraph, *When I was going home, I saw …* Encourage more proficient students to add to the descriptions, *I saw a big black dog. It was chasing a cat.* Encourage students to make illustrations for their stories. To assess students' work, use the **Writing Checklist** in the *Amazing Assessment Package.*

SCIENCE Learning about rocks. Help students find out information about the rocks on the moon. *What do they look like? What are they made of? Do they look like rocks on Earth?*

Building vocabulary. Use *Amazing English!* Word Attack 3 Interactive Vocabulary Games for practice with vocabulary.

- - - ONGOING ASSESSMENT - - -

PERFORMANCE Oral language. Going in a chain around the class, have students ask and answer the question, *What were you doing on the moon?* as they point to the pictures on the page. Then start a new chain; have the students ask and answer the question, *What were you doing at eight o'clock last night?* Observe different levels of participation. Use the **Oral Language Checklist** available in the *Amazing Assessment Package.*

PORTFOLIO Writing. Save **Skills Journal** page 47 as an example of past progressive and vocabulary mastery.

STAFF DEVELOPMENT
See the *Amazing How-To Handbook* for additional ways to develop problem-solving strategies.

STAFF DEVELOPMENT
Writing in a journal about daily observations and activities will enable students to develop both writing and observation skills.

LANGUAGE POWER B

Adventures in Space

LEVEL C, PAGE 55

KEY EXPERIENCES

- Describing ongoing actions
- Expressing ownership
- Identifying locations
- Discussing what to do when lost
- Going on a treasure hunt

KEY LANGUAGE

- *I am looking for my (hat).*
- subject pronouns (R)
- possessive adjectives (R)
- bat, bone, dog, hat, skate, socks, shoes, sweater

● ● ● **1 INTRODUCE** ● ● ●

MULTI-LEVEL TEACHING STRATEGIES

Building background. Print the following words on the board: *I, you, he, she, it, they.* Have the students read the pronouns. Ask groups to make pronoun stick puppets and label each puppet with the correct pronoun, front and back. Students may want to put names on the puppets as well. Display the puppets. Hide a variety of objects or picture cards throughout the classroom. Point to each pronoun puppet as you model the language with sentences, such as *I'm looking for my hat. They are looking for their sweaters.* Have students find the missing items for each puppet. Include all the students by asking questions appropriate to each student's language stage. Here are some sample questions:

Speech Emergence: *Am I looking for my hat? Is he looking for his scarf or his mittens?*

Developing Fluency: *What are they looking for? What is he looking for?*

Playing a spelling game. Use **TPR.** Play the "Find IT" spelling game. Explain to the students that the puppets lost their spelling words. Show students cards with spelling words on them. Be sure to include words students are currently studying. Select a student to be "IT." That child goes out of the room while the rest of the class hides the spelling word. "IT" comes back in and tries to find the spelling word. The class helps by continuously spelling the word, *(p-l-a-n-t).* They speak softly when "IT" is far away from the spelling card and louder and louder as "IT" gets nearer to the hidden word.

● ● ● **2 EXPLORE** ● ● ●

Activating prior knowledge. Open to page 55 of the Student Book. Read the line at the top of the page aloud and ask students what they think *belongings* are. Encourage students to comment on the page. Ask **multi-level questions,** such as *Where are they? Count the students. How many girls do you see? What are they doing?*

 **Look, listen, and talk.** Have students find each picture as you play the tape or read the text. Then read the text a second time chorally. Read the text a third time in unison, clapping out the rhythm. Encourage students to clap as well. Talk about the location of different

people, reviewing the prepositions, *next to, on, behind,* etc. *How many students are next to the tree? How many are on the blanket? Behind the picnic basket?*, etc. Encourage students to respond, *There are two students next to the tree.*

Then have students continue discussing the page with a partner. Have one student point to the objects while the other student reads the text. Have students switch roles and repeat. Encourage students to talk about the location of objects as well, *There are shoes under the picnic table.*

 **Review.** Students independently do exercises reviewing subject pronouns, possessives, and progressives. **PAGE 48** Teaching suggestions are provided in the Skills Journal annotation.

Acquiring new vocabulary. Use the illustration to explore more vocabulary if students are eager or ready to do so. Words might include *blanket, picnic basket, picnic table, thermos, tulips.*

SOCIAL STUDIES Going on a treasure hunt. Set up a treasure hunt for students. The treasure hunt may be done in your classroom or on the playground. The treasures could be a cache of stickers or special snack, for example. Make written clues on index cards. The cards should include directions on how to find other clues and the treasure. Try to use as many different prepositions as possible. Pair students of varying abilities to promote cooperative learning. (CALLA: Cooperation)

LIFE SKILLS Discussing what to do when lost. Discuss what students might do if they or their brothers or sisters get lost. Talk about the different strategies to use if they are lost in a shopping mall, the park, or on the street. Include people who are safe to turn to for help. Encourage students to roleplay being lost in different types of places.

ONGOING ASSESSMENT

PERFORMANCE Oral language Ask students to describe the students in the picture in on page 55. Point to different students and ask, *What are (they) looking for?* Observe different students' responses. Use the **Oral Language Checklist** in the *Amazing Assessment Package.*

STAFF DEVELOPMENT

See the *Amazing How-To Handbook* for other suggestions on ways to implement cooperative learning in the ESL classroom.

MULTICULTURAL AWARENESS

Ask students to tell the class about any special days in their home cultures when people have picnics. What days are considered good for picnics? Where do they go? What do they do? Do they play any special games? Do they eat any special foods? What are those foods?

HANDS-ON SCIENCE

Adventures in Space

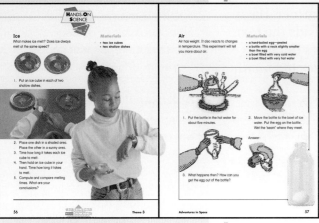

LEVEL C, PAGES 56–57

KEY EXPERIENCES

- Performing experiments about ice/air
- Following directions
- Computing and comparing
- Drawing conclusions
- Making predictions

KEY LANGUAGE

- ice cube, speed, shaded, sunny
- weight, react, temperature, seam

MATERIALS

- ice cubes, two shallow dishes
- a peeled hard-boiled egg, a bottle with a neck slightly smaller than the egg, two bowls
- a bottle, a balloon

1 INTRODUCE

MULTI-LEVEL TEACHING STRATEGIES

Building background: Discussing ice. Bring in several ice cubes. Have two or three volunteers wait outside the classroom. Bring each child in separately; have the child stand at the front of the room blindfolded. Give each an ice cube and have that child tell you what it is. Then pass the ice around and have the students think about how they would describe it to someone from a very hot planet who had never seen ice before. Write student ideas on the board or on chart paper as a **word web.** Include all students in the discussion by asking questions appropriate to each student's language stage.

Speech Emergence: *Is ice hard or soft? What makes ice melt? Will ice melt faster in the middle of the playground or in the shade?*

Developing Fluency: *Do you think ice melts faster in your hand or in the sun? Why? Do you think there is ice on Venus? Why or why not?*

Previewing. Direct students' attention to the illustrations on pages 56 and 57 of the Student Book. Ask students what other thing besides ice they are going to experiment with in "Hands-On Science." What can students tell you about air? With students, create another chart of words and phrases used to describe air, for example, *colorless, odorless, we need it to live, it has weight,* etc.

2 EXPLORE

Activating prior knowledge. Read the title and introduction for "Ice" aloud as students follow along in their books. Ask, *What are the two questions we are going to try to answer about ice?* Then direct students' attention to the title "Air" on page 57 and read the text underneath. Ask, *What does air have? What will this experiment tell us?*

GUIDED READING Following directions. Direct the students' attention to page 56. Have students look and listen as you read the directions. Then have students reread **independently.**

Cooperative learning. In small groups, have students do the experiment. Remind them to read the directions carefully. Have students compare their results with other groups and share their conclusions. Encourage students to help each other. (CALLA: Cooperation)

GUIDED READING Following directions. Direct students' attention to page 57. Ask them to look and listen as you read the list of materials and the directions. Have students read independently.

Cooperative learning. Do the experiment as a class. Encourage students to help each other set it up. Talk about the results. Discuss how they can get the egg out of the bottle.

Drawing conclusions. Explain to students that when air in the bottle cools, its pressure drops. The greater outside air pressure pushes the egg into the bottle. If you hold the bottle upside down, the egg will drop into the opening. Press the bottle opening to your mouth and blow hard. Quickly point the bottle away from you . . . or duck! The egg will rush out of the bottle because blowing into the bottle raises the pressure again. Check understanding, *Why does the egg go into the bottle? How can you get it out? Why does this work?* (CALLA: Deduction)

SKILLS JOURNAL PAGES 49–50 **Reading for a purpose; writing.** Students read about the Ice Age and write answers to questions. **Reading for a purpose; writing.** Students read about natural energy and write answers to questions. Teaching suggestions are provided in the Skills Journal annotations.

• • • 3 EXTEND • • •

SCIENCE Making predictions. Read the following experiment twice and tell students you want them to predict what will happen. *Put a balloon over the mouth of a bottle. Put the bottle in a bowl of very hot water. Wait several minutes. What happens? Now put the bottle into very cold water. What happens?* Ask students to write down their predictions in one or two sentences. If possible, do the experiment in class. Discuss the results. (Hot water: the air expands; the balloon inflates. Cold water: the air contracts; the balloon deflates.)

Home-School Connection. To reinforce the activities of this lesson, encourage the students to try the experiments again at home with adult supervision and report their results to the class.

ONGOING ASSESSMENT

PERFORMANCE Oral language. Ask the students to explain the steps and discuss the results of either experiment in the book. Observe different students' participation using the **Oral Language Checklist** available in the *Amazing Assessment Package.*.

STAFF DEVELOPMENT

See the *Amazing How-To Handbook* for more on developing critical thinking skills and CALLA strategies.

RELATED RESOURCES

See *Eureka: Science Demonstration for ESL Students* for more hands-on science activities you can do in your classroom.

TIP TOP ADVENTURES

Adventures in Space

LEVEL C, PAGES 58–61

KEY EXPERIENCES

- Guided reading of fantasy comic strips
- Distinguishing between fantasy and reality
- Enjoying humorous selections
- Previewing past tense verbs
- Creative/critical thinking

KEY LANGUAGE

- submarine, octopus, boxing gloves, sonic power, ladder, another close call
- space skis, icicles, footprints, beast, the hatch

••• 1 INTRODUCE •••

MULTI-LEVEL TEACHING STRATEGIES

Building background. Engage students in a discussion of travel in outer space. Begin, *Imagine you go to outer space. You find a planet. It is covered with water. What do you see there?* Encourage the students to use their imaginations. List student ideas on the board or on chart paper. Help with vocabulary as needed. Include all students in the discussion by asking questions appropriate to each student's language stage. Here are some sample questions:

Speech Emergence: *Is it cold there? Is it hot? Are there fish? Are there people? What else is there?*

Developing Fluency: *Do you think it would be colder than Earth or warmer? Why? Do you see anything special there?*

Previewing pictures. Ask students to look at the pictures on pages 58–61 in the Student Book. Read the titles, "Tip Top Adventures" and "More Tip Top Adventures." Explain that Tip and Top are the names of the two characters and that these are two different adventures. Ask students to predict what happens in the comic strips. Ask **multi-level questions** that will help all students to join in, *Where do they go first? What do they see? Does the second planet seem hot or cold? What is it covered with?*, etc.

Previewing past tense verbs. Make word cards for these past tense verbs: *put, dove, saw, lifted, pushed, chased, grabbed, dressed, slid, followed, moved, roared, slipped, jumped.* Help students read the word cards. Hold up the cards in random order. Students repeat **chorally.** Then place the word cards along the chalk rail where all of the students can see them. Say the present tense form *(dive);* together point to the past tense card and say the word *(dove)* **chorally.**

••• 2 EXPLORE •••

GUIDED READING Distinguishing between fantasy and reality. Read or play the tape for pages 58–59 of the comic strip as the students follow along in their books. Point out the sound words and dialogue in the speech bubbles. Ask if this is a real or imaginary planet. How do they know? Is this serious or funny? Then do a **choral reading.**

Roleplaying the story. Ask three volunteers to come to the front of the room. Assign parts: Tip, Top, and the octopus. As you read the part of the narrator, the volunteers pantomime the action in the comic strip. Encourage students to move freely but not to make physical contact.

 **GUIDED READING** Distinguishing between fantasy and reality. Read or play the tape for pages 60–61 of the comic strip as the students follow along in their books. Again ask students how they know this is a fantasy. Do a **choral reading.** Encourage students to read with expression.

SKILLS JOURNAL PAGES 51-54 **Reading for a purpose; cloze story.** Students work independently to complete cloze "Tip Top Adventures." **Retelling a story.** Students work independently to complete a "Tip Top Adventure" crossword puzzle. **Cloze story.** Students fill in blanks to complete the story. **Creative Writing.** Students work independently or with a partner to write and illustrate a 'Tip Top Adventure' of their own. Teaching suggestions are provided in the Skills Journal annotations.

3 EXTEND

SCIENCE Learning about the planets. Help students choose two planets in our solar system to research. As a class, concentrate on learning details about the surfaces of these planets. Together write the facts on chart paper. Then compare these planets with other real planets and with the imaginary planets Tip and Top visit. (CALLA: Cooperation)

ART Drawing the planets. Invite students to illustrate the surfaces of the two planets they learned about. Encourage them to add fantasy spaceships and the space travelers Tip and Top if they want. Display the drawings in the classroom.

ONGOING ASSESSMENT

PERFORMANCE Oral language. Ask the students to present their own Tip Top adventures orally, using the art they drew. Observe different levels of participation. Use the **Oral Language Checklist** in the *Amazing Assessment Package.*

PORTFOLIO Writing. Save **Skills Journal** pages 51 and 54 in students' folders.

MULTICULTURAL AWARENESS

Invite students to bring in examples of comic strips in their primary languages to share with the class. Invite others who do not speak the language to guess what is happening in the comic strips; then have the child who brought the strip in confirm their guesses or explain what the strip really says.

WRITING PROJECT

Writing Project 3B, *Comic Strip Adventure,* is directly linked to this lesson. See the Process Writing Portfolio Program Teachers' Handbook, pages 18–19, for the Lesson Plan.

Students will find instructions and a Prewriting Sheet in the Writing Projects booklet inside the Portfolio.

RELATED RESOURCES

The Cat Came Back, CD-ROM, Read Along Mode: Moon/Space (pages 7–10)

HOLISTIC ASSESSMENT

Adventures in Space

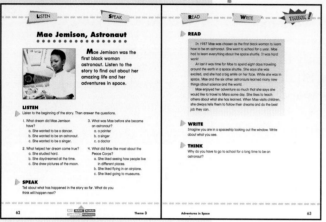

LEVEL C, PAGES 62–63

KEY EXPERIENCES

- Listening to a new story
- Describing story events
- Retelling the story
- Thinking critically
- Guided reading
- Writing

KEY LANGUAGE

- astronaut, at last, chosen, enjoyed, space shuttle

• • • 1 INTRODUCE • • •

MULTI-LEVEL TEACHING STRATEGIES

These two pages offer a variety of assessment opportunities. The left-hand page consists of listening and speaking activities that follow a taped presentation. In the speaking activity, students are asked to summarize the story and make predictions based on what they have heard. The right-hand page consists of writing and critical thinking activities. These follow a reading passage that completes the listening component. You can use the activities to assess listening, speaking, reading, writing, and critical thinking skills. Have children work as a class or in small groups. Record your observations as appropriate on the **Anecdotal Record Form,** the **Reading Checklist,** and the **Writing Checklist** in the *Amazing Assessment Package.*

Building background. Begin by asking students if anyone has ever thought of being an astronaut. Invite students to brainstorm some of the qualities, abilities, and skills that an astronaut would need. Ask **multi-level questions** to enable students at different proficiency levels to participate.

Speech Emergence: *Where did you see a photograph of a real astronaut in this theme? Would you like to be an astronaut? Why or why not?*

Developing Fluency: *Where do astronauts study? What things do you think they learn? Do you know anyone who would be a good astronaut?*

SCIENCE Discussing types of spacecraft. Bring in photos of several different types of manned and unmanned spacecraft, including a space shuttle, satellites, the *Voyager* probes, the *Apollo* lunar landing modules, and early U.S. and Soviet space capsules. Invite volunteers to identify the different types and say what they know about them.

• • • 2 EXPLORE • • •

Previewing the story. Open to Student Book pages 62–63 and let students comment on the picture. Read the title aloud, "Mae Jemison, Astronaut." Then have students read the first sentence of the introduction **independently.** Ask students what they think this story will be about. (CALLA: Activating prior knowledge)

Preparing to listen. Tell the students they are going to hear the beginning of the story. Direct their attention to the listening questions. Do **choral reading** of the listening questions before playing the tape.
Give students time to do **independent reading** of the questions.

 **Listening to the story.** Read or play the tape for the first part of "Mae Jemison, Astronaut." You will find the tapescript in the Appendix.

Have students answer the questions in the book. If some students are struggling, play the tape again and retell the story once yourself.

Retelling the story. Encourage the students to retell the story up to this point. Do not look for word-for-word retelling here, not even from your best students. (CALLA: Summarizing)

Thinking. Ask, *Do you think Mae Jemison was a good student? How do you know? Do you think she had to work hard? Do you think a lot of girls play football?* Have students predict what they are going to read about next. (CALLA: Predicting)

GUIDED READING Read the rest of the story on page 63 or have students read it with you. Then ask students if their predictions were correct. Ask **multi-level questions** such as *For how long did Mae Jemison go to astronaut school? What type of spacecraft did she fly in?* Use the **Reading Checklist** in the *Amazing Assessment Package*.

SKILLS JOURNAL PAGE 55 **Reading comprehension.** Students work independently to complete cloze paragraphs using words from the Data Bank. Teaching suggestions are provided in the Skills Journal annotation. Save this page in the student's **Assessment Portfolio**.

3 EXTEND

Writing. Students imagine they are in a spaceship looking out the window. They write about what they see. Invite students to also draw some of the images. To assess students' work, use the **Writing Checklist** in the *Amazing Assessment Package*.

LIFE SKILLS Learning about space careers. Help students learn about some of the types of jobs people interested in space might pursue. Encourage students to think about the people who design and build the spacecraft, those who train the astronauts, and the support people on the ground during a launch. Help students find appropriate resource materials.

MULTICULTURAL AWARENESS

As you discuss whether any of the students have ever thought of becoming an astronaut, try to make a special effort to draw the more reticent girls into the conversation. Keep in mind that girls from very traditional cultures may need of encouragement to discuss and explore non-traditional career options.

Keep in mind that much of the rest of the world calls soccer "football," so students may not understand that Mae Jemison actually played American football. While many girls now play soccer, it is still highly unusual for a girl to play American football.

AMAZING FACTS

Adventures in Space

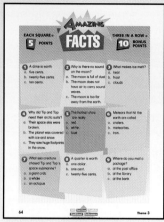

LEVEL C, PAGE 64

KEY EXPERIENCES

- Recalling facts/details
- Reading for information
- Playing "Amazing Facts"
- Creating a game

KEY LANGUAGE

- Review

MATERIALS

- *two jars, a towel*

1 INTRODUCE

MULTI-LEVEL TEACHING STRATEGIES

Describing activities. Use the word cards from Lesson 6 (bank, post office, library, etc.) Hold up a card. Practice conversations such as *Where are you going to go? / I'm going to the (bank). / What are you going to do there? / I'm going to cash a check.* Prompt as needed. Work **T-C**; then **T-S**.

Recalling facts. Engage the students in a discussion of the experiments on ice and air. On the board draw two ice cubes on saucers and an egg in a bottle to prompt the discussion. Make sure they include reasons for the results. Include all students in the discussion by asking questions appropriate to each student's language stage. Here are some sample questions:

Speech Emergence: *Where did we put one of the ice cubes? Did we put the other ice cube in the sun, too? Where did we put it? We put the bottle in water. One bowl had hot water. What was in the other bowl?*

Developing Fluency: *Which ice cube melted faster? Tell us why it did. What happened to the egg? Why? What did we do to get the egg out of the bottle?*

Talking about money. Hold up money (penny, nickel, quarter, one dollar bill). Ask, *What's this?* Encourage students to respond, *It's a penny.* Continue, *A nickel is worth 5 pennies. What is a (dime) worth?*, etc. Work **T-C**; **T-S**.

2 EXPLORE

Activating prior knowledge. Open to page 64 of the Student Book. Have students cover the questions. Ask, *How do you play the Amazing Facts game?* Prompt if necessary. (They play in teams; teams earn points by correctly answering questions on the quiz game board. There will be a time limit of 5–10 minutes, depending on class level.)

Making predictions. Ask, *What did you learn about in this unit? What are some questions you would ask?* Encourage students to share what they remember.

Playing the game. Divide the students into teams. Set the time limit and have the teams work together to answer the questions. Circulate and help as needed. At the end of the pre-set time period, have the teams compete for the correct answers orally. Read the questions in random order. The first team to raise their hands and answer the question correctly wins a point. The team with the most points at the end of play wins the game.

Extra challenge. For extra fluency practice, ask the students to answer the questions in complete sentences: *A quarter is worth twenty-five cents.*

Creating a game. Students create their own "Amazing Facts" games to be played by classmates. Teaching suggestions are provided in the Skills Journal annotation.

Making content area Learning Logs. Show students how to keep Learning Log notebooks for different subjects: science, social studies, math. Have students keep track of concepts they learn. Set aside a specific time each day for the students to write or draw in their Learning Logs. Also encourage students to include concepts or words they find confusing. Go over the Learning Logs with individuals on a regular basis to determine what they are learning and what is confusing. (CALLA: Self-assessment)

ART Making a comic strip. Have students create a few comic book frames of a story with a space theme. They might talk about a typical day in space or a special adventure. Students can work in pairs or small groups. Display in the classroom.

SCIENCE Doing another experiment. Place two jars of warm water where it is cold, either outside or in a refrigerator. Wrap one in a towel. Record the temperature of the water at regular intervals. Why does the jar without the towel get cooler faster? (CALLA: Comparing)

Home-School Connection. Have the students take home the "Amazing Facts" game they made in their Skills Journal. Encourage them to play it with their families and explain the facts.

ONGOING ASSESSMENT

PERFORMANCE Listening comprehension, oral language. Ask the questions from "Amazing Facts" in random order. Have the students answer orally. Can they understand the question easily? Do the students answer using single words? Can they respond with complete sentences? Use the **Oral Language Checklist** in the *Amazing Assessment Package.*

STAFF DEVELOPMENT

For more on Learning Logs, see *The Amazing How-To Handbook.* Encourage the students to add to their content area Learning Logs on a regular basis. Help them feel it is a place where they can remember interesting information as well as let you know where they need help.

ASSESSMENT

You will find background information on the latest thinking in assessment as well as the assessment instruments for this theme in the *Amazing Assessment Package*.

You have been collecting assessment data through the ongoing and holistic assessment options (Oral Language Checklist, Reading Checklist, Writing Checklist, Anecdotal Record Form) in this theme. The following are specific end-of-theme assessment strategies that will help you evaluate your students' progress as well as adapt your instruction to meet their needs.

Student Self-Assessment. Self-assessment surveys are a means for students to have input into their own learning process. Students can use them to **reflect** on the work they have done and the learning strategies they have used during this theme.

Interpreting and Applying Assessment Data. As teachers, you collect assessment data in order to inform your instruction. Assessment information is a tool that helps you tailor your program to better meet the needs and interests of your students.

Evaluate the checklists, anecdotal records, portfolio collections, and test results from this theme as a means of informing your instruction.

- In which areas are students showing confidence and enthusiasm?
- In which areas are they hesitant or confused?
- Should you provide more classroom opportunities for oral language or writing?
- Would certain students (or the whole class) benefit from a focused mini-lesson on a certain area or skill?
- Remember to recycle skills as you teach the next theme and provide students with many opportunities to improve their competence.

Review the results of the **Student Self-Assessment** survey and incorporate students' interests as you plan your instruction for the next theme. What do they want to learn next? Which activities did they enjoy most? If your students particularly enjoyed choral reading, roleplaying, or working in partners, try to emphasize those kinds of activities in the next theme.

THEME CELEBRATION

The end of a theme study is a good time for students to share some of their accomplishments with others. Suggest to students that you hold a celebration to spotlight their work. This celebration can be an excellent opportunity to build stronger connections with other students and teachers in the school. Your students can demonstrate their rocket launchers, make a Tip Top Adventures comic book of all their original stories, and share the Amazing Facts games they have researched and played. If possible, invite family members to the theme celebration.

END-OF-THEME READ-ALOUD BOOK

Alistair and the Alien Invasion by Marilyn Sadler

illustrated by Roger Bollen

New York: Simon & Schuster, 1994

Alistair is a most unusual boy genius—he irons his shoelaces and thanks his teacher for assigning homework. While working on a science project, he encounters aliens invading Earth. Luckily, his unique solution saves the planet.

READING CORNER

It's important to get students excited about independent reading. Remember to distribute the Literature Links Bibliography for the next theme to your students and encourage them to use the *Amazing BookBytes* CD-ROM to respond to their reading..

Across the USA

In Theme 4, students explore life, recreation, and history in America. Through literature, articles, music, and language activity pages in the **Student Book**, the students will learn about different kinds of houses, the immigrant experience, and Native American art. They will sing a Woody Guthrie song and read about special pen pals. The **Skills Journal** offers opportunities for further language practice, reading, writing, and research on a variety of theme-related topics.

Multi-Level Teaching Strategies integrated into each lesson plan insure that all students can participate in these class activities, each at his or her own level of language proficiency. **Home-School Connection** activities provide enjoyable extension activities for students and family members to do together.

The **Ongoing Assessment** suggestions in the lesson plans will help you keep track of your students' progress. On **Student Book** pages 82-83, the "Listen, Speak, Read, Write, Think" selection offers an opportunity for **holistic assessment**. The end-of-theme **Wrap-Up** page includes guidelines for implementing the full range of assessment tools and interpreting the results.

PLANNING TIPS

The **At-a-Glance Lesson Planner** on the next two pages provides an overview of the Key Experiences and Key Language presented in each lesson of the theme. Quickly scan the lesson plan Materials lists to see if there are materials to gather or prepare. Check the **Wrap-Up** page in case you want to plan ahead for the Theme Celebration.

The following **Read-Aloud Books** are recommended with this theme. Gather these titles and your own theme-related favorites. We encourage you to read aloud to your students every day. If possible, record the stories on tape and let students reread the books as they listen to the tapes.

- *As the Crow Flies: A First Book of Maps* by Gail Hartman

- *The House that Jack Built* by Jenny Stow

- *This Is the Way We Go to School* by Edith Baer

- *Over the River and Through the Woods* illustrated by Brinton Turkle

- *Could Be Worse* by James Stevenson

- *Houses and Homes* by Ann Morris (Wrap-Up page)

READING CORNER

Encourage independent reading for information and pleasure. If possible, set up a reading corner—a quiet, comfortable place that is just for reading (and perhaps listening to any books on tape you've collected). Make a bulletin board on which you can post book covers, students' BookBytes reviews and the Literature Links Bibliographies that support each theme. See the Appendix for the complete Literature Links Bibliography for this theme. It offers a variety of fiction and non-fiction choices **in English and in other languages.**

LESSON PLAN

KEY EXPERIENCES

1 **Student Book p. 65**
Theme Opener

Talking about U.S. geography and people • Sharing travel interests • Learning names of states • Predicting meaning of theme titles

2 **Student Book p. 66**
Communication 1A

Talking about self • Following conversational sequence • Reading "Amazing Facts" • Making personal address books

3 **Student Book p. 67**
Communication 1B

Learning names of states • Talking about U.S. geography • Comparing modes of transportation • Playing a geography game

4 **Student Book p. 68**
Read and Do

Discussing magnets • Reading and following directions • Writing an adventure story • Making a course

5 **Student Book p. 69**
This Land Is Your Land

Singing a traditional song • Creating new song verses • Looking at U.S. landscapes • Making musical instruments

6 **Student Book p. 70**
Communication 2A

Describing work • TPR describing occupations • Discussing occupations • Interviewing about occupations

7 **Student Book p. 71**
Communication 2B

Writing/talking about after-school activities • Playing occupations Tic-Tac-Toe • Making a graph • Talking about exercise

8 **Student Book pp. 72-73**
Check This Out!

Guided reading of a poem • Identifying rhyming words • Reading short selections • Using visual information

9 **Student Book p. 74**
Language Power A

Describing actions • Sequencing • Making observations • Retelling a story

10 **Student Book p. 75**
Language Power B

Discussing stamps • Learning about pen pals • Sequencing and summarizing • Classifying stamps

11 **Student Book pp. 76-77**
Hands-On Social Studies

Learning about the Chippewa • Following directions • Making a dream catcher • Critical thinking

12 **Student Book pp. 78-81**
My Home

Comparing places • Reading/discussing an essay • Critical thinking • Learning about farm workers • Illustrating the story

13 **Student Book pp. 82-83**
Holistic Assessment

Listening for information • Reading factual information • Predicting outcomes • Expressing opinions • Learning about the Anasazi

14 **Student Book p. 84**
Amazing Facts Game

Recalling details • Reading for information • Playing a game • Creating a game

KEY LANGUAGE

CONTENT AREAS

KEY LANGUAGE	CONTENT AREAS
Names of states • across, dream catcher, paddle, raft, river, trucker,	Social Studies • Language Arts
Where were you born? • I was born in (Chicago). • When did you move here? • address, area code, phone number	Math • Social Studies • Language Arts
Is it by bus? • No, it isn't. • Guess again! • by airplane/bus/ camper/car/van/train/truck/motorcycle/ship • north, south, east, west	Art • Social Studies • Language Arts
magnet, mast, pins, sails, sheet of foam or cork, vertically	Science • Social Studies • Language Arts
forest, island, land, made, waters	Art • Music • Social Studies • Language Arts
chef, farmer, mail carrier, truck driver, writer, doctor • cook(s), drive(s), grow(s), help(s), write(s), deliver(s)	Art • Social Studies • Language Arts
(He) works in a (restaurant) • After work, (he) likes to (play hockey) • after, before, baseball, glove, helmet, skates, hockey, jog, running shoes	Math • Music • Language Arts
north, south, east, west, pen pal	Art • Music • Social Studies • Language Arts
Present verbs with -es • and, but	Social Studies • Language Arts
countries, fun, kids, (pen) pals, special, stamps	Social Studies • Language Arts
dream catcher, bad dreams, good dreams, web, feathers, crisscross	Art • Science • Social Studies • Language Arts
border, bunk beds, fields, hills, trailer	Art • Social Studies • Language Arts
beans, celebrated, corn, descended, gathered, harvest, reservoir, squash	Assessment
Review	Assessment

THEME OPENER

Across the USA

LEVEL C, PAGE 65

KEY EXPERIENCES

- Talking about U.S. geography and people
- Sharing personal travel interests
- Learning names of states
- Predicting meaning of unit titles
- Brainstorming ideas

KEY LANGUAGE

- across, dream catcher, paddle, raft, river, trucker
- Names of states

1 INTRODUCE

MULTI-LEVEL TEACHING STRATEGIES

Activating prior knowledge. Discuss the photograph on page 65 of the Student Book. Ask students what this child is doing. Do they think this is a boy or a girl? Why? Where do they think this child might be? Assist with vocabulary relating to rafting if students seem ready to explore the topic further. Then ask students where they have lived or visited in the U.S. Help them locate these places on a large map of the U.S. Include all the students by asking questions appropriate to each student's language stage. Here are some sample questions:

Speech Emergence: (Point to the map.) *What is the name of this state? Have you been there? Where would you like to go?*

Developing Fluency: *What is your favorite place in the U.S.? Why?* (Point to a state.) *This is (Colorado). What is the name of a state next to (Colorado)?*

Learning the names of the states. Begin working with names of states. Make the following word cards: *Texas, California, Colorado, Florida, Missouri, New York, Iowa, Maine, Oregon,* and *Georgia*. If the class seems ready, use more. Read the names of the states aloud as you point them out on the map. Work **Teacher-Class (T-C).** Read the cards again. Ask, *Where's (California)?* Have students point out the states. Ask the students to make comparisons, *Which is bigger, California or Maine?*

Word Scramble. Print on the board the names of the states from the word cards. Scramble the letters of each state. In pairs, have students unscramble the letters and print the words on a piece of paper. Read the names of the states chorally.

2 EXPLORE

Brainstorming. Direct students' attention to the first topic of the unit, "Houses." Talk about what kinds of houses there are. Together make a **word web** of ideas about houses. Encourage students to think about feelings they associate with houses as well as housing types.

Predicting. Have a volunteer read aloud the title of the second topic, "Trucker Buddies." Elicit that a buddy is a friend and that a trucker is a person who drives a truck for a living. What do they think this selection will be about? (CALLA: Predicting)

Cooperative learning. Divide the class into small groups. Ask groups to discuss the kinds of houses they would like to live in. Then have students illustrate the houses in group posters of a community. Ask groups to present their community posters to the class. (CALLA: Cooperation)

SOCIAL STUDIES Discussing dream catchers. Direct students' attention to the third title, "Dream Catchers." Explain that dream catchers are used by the Chippewa people. A dream catcher is hung over a child's bed. Ask, *What do you think dream catchers are used for? What kind of dreams do they catch? Why would you want to catch dreams?* Brainstorm ideas. (CALLA: Brainstorming)

Talking about a home. Read the title "My Home." Ask, *What is a home?* Work together to make a list of ideas, *A home is where you sleep. A home is where your family lives,* etc.

Using background knowledge. Students list the states and capitals they know. Teaching suggestions are provided in the Skills Journal annotation.

SKILLS JOURNAL PAGE 57

3 EXTEND

Playing a states game. Place the word cards of the states in a pile in random order. Hold up a card, *Maine.* Students locate it on a map of the U.S. Then they read the name aloud. You may also want to have students spell the names out loud or have a states spelling bee.

ART Drawing my home. Ask students to draw pictures of their own homes. Encourage them to include details showing the type of building it is, for example, wood, brick, adobe. Display the drawings in the classroom.

ART Illustrating predictions. Ask students to illustrate what they think a dream catcher looks like. They may want to depict one hanging over a child's bed as it catches dreams. Then invite volunteers to share their illustrations with the class. Save the illustrations in students' **portfolios** to discuss again when the class makes dream catchers.

MULTICULTURAL AWARENESS

Encourage students to describe the houses in their native cultures and, if possible, to bring photographs or pictures to class. Ask students to make comparisons among the homes in various places and to think about how climate affects housing types.

TEACHER TO TEACHER

If your students work with other teachers, you may want to suggest that they display large maps of the U.S. in their classrooms. Also suggest that they look for opportunities to have ESL students locate places on a map as often as possible.

COMMUNICATION 1A

LEVEL C, PAGE 66

KEY EXPERIENCES

- Talking about self
- Roleplaying conversations
- Following conversational sequence
- Reading "Amazing Facts"
- Making personal address books

KEY LANGUAGE

- *Where were you born?*
- *I was born in (Chicago).*
- *When did you move here?*
- *What's your phone number/address?*
- address, area code, phone number

MATERIALS

- shoe boxes, envelopes

1 INTRODUCE

MULTI-LEVEL TEACHING STRATEGIES

Building background: Making a chart. Take a class survey. Find out where each student was born and compile the information in a chart. You may also want to help students locate each of the places on a world map or globe. Find out how old they were when they moved to your community. Include all the students by asking questions appropriate to each student's language stage. Here are some sample questions:

Speech Emergence: *Where were you born? How old were you when you moved here? How old are you now?*

Developing Fluency: *Where were you born? How many years ago did you move here? How old were you?*

MATH Classifying information. Students can also classify the information on the chart, *How many of us were born in (Mexico)?*, etc. Encourage students to illustrate the chart with pictures of their countries. (CALLA: Classifying)

Reading sentence strips. Make the following sentence strips: *Where were you born? When did you move here? What's your address now? What's your phone number?* Read the sentences aloud. Work **Teacher-Class; Teacher-Student.** Display the sentence strips. Read the sentences aloud **chorally,** clapping out the rhythm. For each sentence, clap loudest on the word receiving the most stress *(born/move/address/phone).* Ask students to tell you the words on which you clapped the loudest. If necessary, repeat.

2 EXPLORE

Activating prior knowledge. Open to page 66 of the Student Book. Ask students to comment about the picture. *Who is in the picture? What are they doing?*

Look, listen, and talk. Have students look and listen as you read the text or play the tape of the conversation. Check understanding with **multi-level questions,** such as *Where was she born? When did she move? What's her address?*, etc. Ask if anyone knows what an area code is. To help explain what an area code is for, show students the map of area codes in your local phone book.

Practicing the conversation. Read the text or play the tape again for the conversation, pausing for students to repeat. Then divide the class into two groups. One group asks the questions, the other answers. Have groups switch roles and repeat. Next, have partners practice the conversation, substituting information about themselves.

Reading for specific information: Amazing Facts. Direct students' attention to the bottom of the page. If possible, show students pictures of a California condor and of the Southwest. Write the following questions on the board: *Who uses a lot of pencils? How many pencils are used a year? How far can a California condor fly?, How much do the temperatures drop at night in the desert?* Have students read **independently** to locate the answers. Then reread the Amazing Facts **chorally.**

Data collection. Students conduct interviews, record the information in charts, and use it for paired conversation practice. Teaching suggestions are provided in the Skills Journal annotation.

SOCIAL STUDIES Class mailboxes. Student may enjoy making class "mailboxes" out of shoe boxes with home addresses printed on them. Students can write short notes to one another. Show students how to address envelopes. Include all the students by writing your own notes to them about special things they have done. Remind students that if they mail real letters, they have to use stamps.

Playing a chanting game. Each student makes a "letter." Students stand in a circle and chant: *I'm sending a letter to my friend. Who can it be? Who can it be?* The person who is "IT" skips around the outside of the circle and "drops" his or her letter behind a classmate. The classmate must pick up the letter, chase, and try to tag "IT" before "IT" gets to the empty space in the circle. If the classmate doesn't succeed, he or she becomes "IT" for the next round.

ONGOING ASSESSMENT

PERFORMANCE Oral language. Listen to the students practicing the conversation as they talk about themselves. Observe students' levels of participation. Use the **Oral Language Checklist** in the *Amazing Assessment Package.*

PORTFOLIO Note-taking. Save **Skills Journal** page 58 as an example of oral/aural abilities and note-taking.

MULTICULTURAL AWARENESS
Invite volunteers to tell the class about how addresses are written in their home cultures. Ask them to write examples on the board, or bring in envelopes with addresses written on them. Compare how it is done in different countries.

105

COMMUNICATION 1B

Across the USA

LEVEL C, PAGE 67

KEY EXPERIENCES

- Learning names of the states
- Talking about U.S. geography
- Comparing/drawing modes of transportation
- Playing a geography game

KEY LANGUAGE

- *Is it by bus?*
- *No, it isn't.*
- *Guess again!*
- by airplane/bus/camper/ car/van/train/truck/motor- cycle/ship
- north, south, east, west

●●● 1 INTRODUCE ●●●

MULTI-LEVEL TEACHING STRATEGIES

Building background: Problem solving. Make a puzzle by mounting a large map of the U.S. on tag board or construction paper. Cut apart the map by region or state to make a puzzle. Give each student one or more pieces of the puzzle. Hide the puzzle pieces of Alaska and Hawaii. Have the students put the puzzle together. Help the students read the names of the states **chorally** as you point to each state. Talk about the location of the states. Include all the students by asking questions appropriate to each student's language stage. Here are some sample questions:

Speech Emergence: *Where is Kentucky? Point to Ohio. What is the name of the state between California and Washington?*

Developing Fluency: (Point to a state.) *What is the name of this state? Which state is between Colorado and Missouri?*

SOCIAL STUDIES Comparing modes of transportation. Use two puppets. Display a map of the U.S. Explain that the puppets want to go from New York to Los Angeles. Show students pictures of different ways of going: *car, bus, truck, motorcycle, van, ship, camper, airplane, train.* Have the puppets talk about how they will travel. P 1: *I want to go by car.* P 2: *I want to go by plane. It will be faster.*

Have the puppets discuss the comfort, speed, and cost of the different kinds of travel. Encourage students to help them decide which mode is best. (CALLA: Comparing)

Matching words and pictures. Locate pictures of each of the following types of transportation and make separate word cards: *car, bus, truck, motorcycle, van, ship, camper, airplane, train.* Help students read the word cards and match the cards to the pictures.

●●● 2 EXPLORE ●●●

Activating prior knowledge. Open to page 67 of the Student Book. Ask students to comment about the page. *What is this a map of? What do you see on the map?*

 **Look, listen, and talk.** Have students point to each mode of transportation as you identify it, *by bus,* etc. Students look and listen as you read the conversation or play the tape. Check understanding: *Is it by bus?*, etc.

Practicing the conversation. Read the conversation. Have students point to the lines as they listen. Read the conversation again, pausing for students to repeat. Divide the class into two groups. One group asks the question, the other answers.

Group 1: *Guess which way I'm crossing the U.S.A?*
Group 2: *Is it by bus?*
Group 1: *No it isn't. Guess again.*

Switch roles and repeat. In pairs, have students practice the conversation, switching roles. Have them continue practicing, substituting different modes of transportation.

Student 1: *Guess which way I'm crossing the U.S. A.*
Student 2: *Is it by motorcycle?*
Student 1: *No it isn't. Guess again.*

Reading a map; learning state names. Students find states and write their names. Teaching suggestions are provided in the Skills Journal annotation.

ART Drawing modes of transportation. Ask students to imagine they are traveling to a place they would like to visit. Then ask them to think about all the different types of transportation they would need to use to get there. Invite students to illustrate the journey, showing all the modes of transportation. Later, have the class discuss whether the drawings are realistic for the destination; for example, do students realize they would need an airplane or ship for a trip across the ocean? (CALLA: Deduction/induction)

Home-School Connection. Encourage students to discuss with parents or other family members all the forms of transportation they used to travel to the U.S. when they first came here. Later, have students share stories about the trip with the class.

SOCIAL STUDIES Playing a geography game. Have students play Twenty Questions about the map of the U.S. Have Student 1 begin, *I'm thinking of a state.* Student 2: *Is it in the north?* Student 1: *No, it's not*, etc. Before students begin, present vocabulary for the concepts *north, south, east, west*. Write the words on the board. Help students read the words as you point to the appropriate section of the map.

MULTICULTURAL AWARENESS

Encourage volunteers to tell the class about any modes of transportation used in their home cultures that aren't used in the U.S. Also discuss which types of transportation are the most popular in a given country or region.

When discussing the specifics of journeys to the U.S., keep in mind that some students may have experienced extreme hardships or personal losses.

RELATED RESOURCES

The Cat Came Back, CD-ROM Read Along Mode: Trains (pages 11-14); Write Along Mode: Modes of Transportation

READ AND DO

Across the USA

LEVEL C, PAGE 68

KEY EXPERIENCES

- Discussing magnets
- Reading and following directions
- Writing an adventure story
- Making a course

KEY LANGUAGE

- magnet, mast, pins, sails, sheet of foam or cork, vertically

MATERIALS

- magnet, plastic tray, pins, tape, ruler, paper, thin sheet of foam or cork

1 INTRODUCE

MULTI-LEVEL TEACHING STRATEGIES

Building background: Discussing magnets. Hold up a magnet and a paper clip. Ask, *What is this? What happens if we put the magnet and paper clip together?* Walk around the room. Have students test for things magnets are attracted to in the classroom. Include all the students by asking questions appropriate to each student's language stage. Here are some sample questions:

Speech Emergence: *Will the magnet stick to this? What happens if I put the magnet on this?*

Developing Fluency: *Why didn't the ruler stick to the magnet? Why do these things stick, but those things don't?*

SCIENCE Exploring magnets. Help students explore how magnets work by introducing the words *repel* (push apart) and *attract* (pull together). If possible, hold two magnets together. Hold them so that the north poles are touching; and then so that north and south poles are touching. Each time, ask, *What happens?* Explain that any magnet has two poles, north and south. Demonstrate how opposite poles attract (north pulls on south) and similar poles repel (north pushes away north). Help students make a **concept map** about magnets. Encourage them to add to the map as they learn more about magnets.

Making a magnetism chart. Make a class chart with two columns: *Things that are magnetic* and *Things that aren't magnetic*. Have students work together to classify the classroom objects. Ask students to try to come up with characteristics of magnetic objects. (CALLA: Classifying)

2 EXPLORE

Activating prior knowledge. Open to page 68 of the Student Book. Have students skim the page. Ask, *What are we going to do? How many steps are there?*

Exploring new vocabulary. On the board, write the words for the materials needed for the magnetic sailboats. Hold up each thing and model the word; students repeat. Work **T-C; T-S.**

GUIDED READING Following directions. Read and demonstrate the directions. Remind students that directions often start with simple verbs. Ask the students to scan the directions and identify these verbs plus any accompanying prepositions, such as *Cut from, Push into, Move* *under*, etc. Read again as students follow along in their books. Then have students read the directions to assemble their boats. Encourage students to ask questions for clarification. (CALLA: Questioning for clarification)

Cooperative learning. In pairs, students compare their boats. Students reread the directions. Encourage students to help one another make corrections. (CALLA: Comparing)

Reading for a purpose; writing. Students read a paragraph about magnets and write answers to questions. Teaching suggestions are provided in the Skills Journal annotation.

Writing an adventure story. Have students write adventure stories about traveling in their magnetic sailboats. Brainstorm ideas first. Encourage students to use a world map or globe to find the names of bodies of water they might travel on or places they might go. You may also suggest that they use their magnetic boats to go on another Tip Top Adventure. Have students work in pairs to critique each other's writing and suggest improvements. Use the **Writing Checklist** in the *Amazing Assessment Package.*(CALLA: Cooperation)

SOCIAL STUDIES Making a water course. In pairs, students make courses for their boats to follow, with, for example, bridges, buoys, and landmarks. Encourage students to use a geography book or other resource material to create a course in a specific place, for example, *Tokyo*. Have students take turns giving each other directions on the course. (CALLA: Resourcing)

SCIENCE Electromagnetic fields. Help students begin to learn about electromagnetic fields. Discuss some of the many electronic devices around us that operate on the principles of electromagnetism, including computers, television, and radio. Place simple books with illustrations and diagrams in the Science Center and allow students to explore the topic in their free time. (CALLA: Resourcing)

ONGOING ASSESSMENT

PERFORMANCE Oral language. Ask students to demonstrate how to make magnetic sailboats. Prompt as needed. Observe different students' levels of participation. Use the **Oral Language Checklist** in the *Amazing Assessment Package.*

PORTFOLIO Reading comprehension. Save **Skills Journal** page 60 as an example of reading comprehension.

THIS LAND IS YOUR LAND

Across the USA

LEVEL C, PAGE 69

KEY EXPERIENCES

- Singing a traditional song
- Creating new song verses
- Looking at U.S. landscapes
- Making musical instruments

KEY LANGUAGE

- forest, island, land, made, waters

MATERIALS

- empty frozen juice cans, streamers

1 INTRODUCE

MULTI-LEVEL TEACHING STRATEGIES

Activating prior knowledge. Direct students' attention to a map of the U.S. Have them point to California and New York. Find out what the students know about these states. Include all the students by asking questions appropriate to each student's language stage. Here are some sample questions:

Speech Emergence: *Is California in the west? Where is New York?*

Developing Fluency: *Which is bigger, California or New York? Where would you rather live? Why?*

SOCIAL STUDIES Looking at U.S. landscapes. Bring in several books and magazines with photos showing places all around the U.S. Encourage students to look for names of states or cities in the captions. As students look through the books and magazines, move around the room, answering questions and providing assistance with vocabulary. Also ask students questions about what they see in the photos.

MUSIC Making musical instruments. Have students make different types of shakers to keep rhythm when singing or listening to "This Land Is Your Land." Students can fill empty frozen juice cans with dried beans, buttons, or coins and tape them closed. Encourage students to decorate the shakers with colored paper and streamers.

2 EXPLORE

Activating prior knowledge. Open to page 69 of the Student Book. Read the title, "This Land Is Your Land," aloud and ask students how they know this is a song (musical notes on song pages). Encourage students to comment about the page. Can anyone identify the figure in the upper right? (the Statue of Liberty) Where is this statue located?

MUSIC "This Land Is Your Land." Play the tape or sing the song. Try to bring pictures of a California redwood forest, New York City islands (for example, Manhattan and Ellis), and the Gulf Stream waters. Point to the different pictures as you sing the song. Present the song again and have students clap in time to the music. Then have students read the words in the book **chorally.** Next have students sing the song as a group.

Creating new song verses. Print the words of the song on the board. Work together to substitute words in the song with places in your community. For example,

> *This land is your land,*
> *This land is my land,*
> *From Central Street,*
> *To the great big playground,*
> *From the corner bus stop,*
> *To the basketball courts,*
> *This town was made for you and me.*

Copy the song on chart paper. Sing together.

Learning language through song. Students change key words in "This Land Is Your Land" and make more new verses about their town, classroom, or school. Teaching suggestions are provided in the Skills Journal annotation.

ART Illustrating the new song verses. Have students illustrate the class's new song verses. Have students describe their pictures to the rest of the group.

SOCIAL STUDIES Making a mural. Have students make a giant mural of the U.S. Encourage students to refer to pictures of different parts of the U.S. in books and magazines you have brought in and to locate others in the library. Students can use a variety of media: paint, chalk, crayons, and markers. (CALLA: Imagery)

ONGOING ASSESSMENT

PERFORMANCE Oral language. Print the words to "This Land Is Your Land" on a piece of paper. Cut the lines into strips. Ask students to put the lines into the correct order, then read or sing the song. Observe different levels of participation. Use the **Oral Language Checklist** in the *Amazing Assessment Package.*

MULTICULTURAL AWARENESS

Ask students to share songs from their home cultures. Encourage them to bring in shakers or other percussion instruments that are used there.

STAFF DEVELOPMENT

For more about using music in the ESL classroom see the *Amazing How-To Handbook.*

TEACHER TO TEACHER

Songs provide an effective context for practicing the rhythm and intonation patterns of natural language. Make songs available for students to listen to and encourage students to sing.

WRITING PROJECT

Writing Project 4A, *My Song,* is directly linked to this lesson. See the Process Writing Portfolio Program Teachers' Handbook, pages 20-21, for the Lesson Plan.

Students will find instructions and a Prewriting Sheet in the Writing Projects booklet inside the Portfolio.

COMMUNICATION 2A

Across the USA

LEVEL C, PAGE 70

KEY EXPERIENCES

- Describing work
- TPR describing occupations
- Discussing occupations
- Interviewing about occupations

KEY LANGUAGE

- chef, farmer, mail carrier, truck driver, writer, doctor
- cook(s), drive(s), grow(s), help(s), write(s), deliver(s)

1 INTRODUCE

MULTI-LEVEL TEACHING STRATEGIES

Building background: Describing work. Show students a picture of a scene where people are performing a variety of work-related activities. You might choose a scene on a farm, for example. Talk about and list all the things a farmer does: milk the cows, clean the barn, pick the corn, plant the vegetables. Ask students if anyone has ever been on a farm. Include all the students by asking questions appropriate to each student's language stage. Here are some sample questions:

Speech Emergence: *What time of day is it? How do you know? What is the farmer doing here?*

Developing Fluency: *Would you like to live on a farm? What could you do there? Which do you like better, living on a farm or living in a city? Why?*

TPR describing occupations. Make word cards for occupations: *chef, farmer, writer, truck driver, mail carrier, police officer, bus driver, doctor*, etc. Help students read the cards. Then put the cards in a pile in random order. Have students pick a card and pantomime tasks associated with the occupation, such as cooking or driving a truck. Ask the rest of the class to guess the occupation. *She is a truck driver.* (CALLA: Guessing)

2 EXPLORE

Activating prior knowledge. Open to page 70 of the Student Book. Encourage students to comment about the page. How many occupations can they identify?

 **Look, listen, and talk.** Have students listen and point to the appropriate pictures as you play the tape or read the text, *She's a doctor. She helps sick people.* etc. Point to each picture again. Ask, *What is her job?* Encourage students to respond, *She's a doctor.* Continue *What does she do?* Encourage students to respond, *She helps people.* Continue with the other occupations and tasks.

GUIDED READING Have students read along with you **chorally.** Next divide the students into two groups. One group reads the occupations; the other reads the tasks. Have groups switch roles and repeat. Help students practice the conversation by substituting all the different occupations and tasks in the pictures.

SOCIAL STUDIES Discussing occupations. Invite students to discuss women and men in traditional and non-traditional occupations. Remind students about Mae Jemison, the astronaut, by returning to pages 62–63. As needed, prompt discussion by asking specific questions, such as *Do you know any women who are construction workers or truck drivers? Do you know any men who are nurses or day care workers?*

 **Matching written language to pictures.** Students match written language to pictures of occupations and write answers to questions. Teaching suggestions are provided in the Skills Journal annotation.

ART Making a collage. Have students make an occupations collage. Encourage them to cut out pictures from magazines. Ask students to write one sentence on a strip of paper naming the occupation and describing a task that person does, for example, *She is a police officer. She helps people in trouble.* Place the labels underneath the photos.

Home-School Connection: Interviewing about occupations. Ask students to interview two people at home or in the community about their occupations. In preparation, have students brainstorm some interview questions: *What is your job? What do you do?* Students may interview people in the primary language if they prefer. Ask students to share their information in small groups, then report to the class. Encourage students to ask one another, *Who did you talk to, (Tina)? What is your aunt's job? What does she do?* On the board, compile a list of occupations.

- - - - **ONGOING ASSESSMENT** - - - -

PERFORMANCE Oral language. Use the word cards: *chef, police officer,* etc. Place the cards in a basket or hat. Ask S1, *What is her job?* S1 draws a card and answers, *She's a doctor.* Continue, *What does she do?* S1 responds, *She helps people.* Have S2 draw a new card. S1 and S2 conduct the same conversation, using the occupation on the new card. Observe different students' levels of participation. Use the **Oral Language Checklist** in the *Amazing Assessment Package.*

MULTICULTURAL AWARENESS

Ask students to share with the class information about occupations in their parents' home countries. Find out if their parents are from fishing areas, the mountains, mining or agricultural economies, etc. Encourage students to bring photographs to share with the class.

TEACHER TO TEACHER

If your students work with other teachers, you may want to plan a Jobs Fair with them. If possible, invite people from several different professions and of diverse cultural backgrounds to come as guest speakers.

COMMUNICATION 2B

Across the USA

LEVEL C, PAGE 71

KEY EXPERIENCES

- Writing/talking about after-school activities
- Playing Occupations Tic-Tac-Toe
- Making a graph
- Talking about exercise

KEY LANGUAGE

- *(He) works in a (restaurant).*
- *After work, (he) likes to (play hockey).*
- *(He) has (his) (skates and a helmet).*
- after, before
- baseball, glove, helmet, skates, hockey, jog, running shoes, restaurant, tape recorder, towel

• • • 1 INTRODUCE • • •

MULTI-LEVEL TEACHING STRATEGIES

Activating prior knowledge. Play Occupations Tic-Tac-Toe. Draw a tic-tac-toe grid on a piece of chart paper. In each square print a number, the pronoun *he* or *she*, and an occupation. Form two teams, X and O. A member of one team requests a square by number (5). The rest of the team responds in unison, *He's a farmer.* A member of the same team then says where the job may be performed, *He works on a farm.* If both answers are correct, that team puts an X or O in the square. At the end of play, review the squares with the class. Include all the students by asking questions appropriate to each student's language stage. Here are some sample questions:

Speech Emergence: (Point to a square.) *What is her job? Where does she work?*

Developing Fluency: *Who works in a restaurant? How many occupations are on the board?*

Writing about after-school activities. Ask students to bring in items they use for after-school activities. Ask volunteers to show the items and discuss what the items are used for and when: *I have a baseball. After school, I play baseball.* Print on the board, *I have a … After school, I like to ….* Students copy the sentences on paper and complete them. Then have them exchange their papers with a partner for corrections.

• • • 2 EXPLORE • • •

Activating prior knowledge. Open to page 71 of the Student Book. Encourage students to comment about the page. Ask, *Who do you see in the (first) picture? Where does (he) work,?, What is (he) carrying? What do you think (he) likes to do after work?* etc.

Exploring key vocabulary. Point to the pictures and introduce unfamiliar items, *hockey, skates, helmet, running shoes, towel, glove, baseball, tapes, tape recorder.* Help students read each word **chorally.**

Look, listen, and talk. Have students listen and point to the appropriate pictures as you read the text or play the tape. Ask **multi-level questions,** such as *Look at number one. What does he like to do after work? Who likes to jog?*

Practicing the conversation. Play the tape or read the conversation at the bottom of the page. Have students read each sentence **chorally.** Then divide the class into two groups. One group asks the questions; the other reads the answers.

Group 1: *Does he work in a grocery store?.*
Group 2: *No he doesn't.*
Group 1: *Where does he work?.*
Group 2: *He works in a restaurant.*

Have groups switch roles and repeat. Then help students practice the conversation in pairs, substituting the other locations on the page.

 **Matching written language to pictures.** Students match written language to pictures and write answers to questions. Teaching suggestions are provided in the Skills Journal annotation.

SKILLS JOURNAL
PAGE 63

 MUSIC "The Worker's Song." Play the tape or sing the song. (See the tapescript in the Appendix.) Invite students to sing along.

Home-School Connection. Ask students to interview people they know and write short paragraphs about their work and leisure activities. On the board, write a model: *My (neighbor's) name is ... She works in a/an ... After work, she likes to ....* Ask students to share their paragraphs in small groups and help one another make corrections. Use the **Writing Checklist** in the *Amazing Assessment Package.*

MATH Making a graph. Make a graph of the top five leisure activities of the people interviewed. Discuss the results, *What is the most popular activity? What is the most unusual activity? What activity would you like to try?* (CALLA: Grouping)

- - - - - **ONGOING ASSESSMENT** - - - - -

PERFORMANCE Oral language. Circulate as students practice the conversation in pairs, substituting different occupations and activities. Observe different students' levels of participation. Use the **Oral Language Checklist** in the *Amazing Assessment Package.*

MULTICULTURAL AWARENESS

Ask students to share with the class information about leisure activities in their home cultures. Find out if there are special seasonal activities or activities associated with holidays. Encourage students to make drawings or bring objects associated with the activities to share with the class.

TEACHER TO TEACHER

If your students work with other teachers, you may want to share with them some ways to help ESL students read for fun. Teachers can help the students apply for library cards at the local library and encourage students to participate in any special activities offered there. They can set up a Reading Corner or arrange a visit to a local bookstore.

CHECK THIS OUT!

Across the USA

LEVEL C, PAGES 72–73

KEY EXPERIENCES

- Guided reading of a poem
- Identifying rhyming words
- Reading short selections
- Using visual information
- Reading "Amazing Facts"

KEY LANGUAGE

- north, south, east, west
- pen pals

MATERIALS

- toothpicks, popsicle sticks, baker's clay, modeling clay

1 INTRODUCE

MULTI-LEVEL TEACHING STRATEGIES

Building background: Recalling details. Ask students to open to pages 72–73 of the Student Book and look carefully at the pictures. After one minute, have students close their books. Engage students in a discussion of the illustrations. Include all the students by asking questions appropriate to each student's language stage. Here are some sample questions:

Speech Emergence: *What did you see? Did you see a truck driver? Who was with him?*

Developing Fluency: *Do you think the truck driver and the kids are friends? What can you tell me about Mount Rushmore? Did you see faces? Do you know whose faces they were?*

Discussing trucks. Preview "Truckers and Students Are Pen Pals!" by showing students photographs of large trucks. Talk about the job of a trucker, *What do truckers do? Where do they go? Where do they sleep? Do they get to go home each night? Do you think it is a fun job?* etc. Tailor your questions to the language stages of your students. (CALLA: Previewing)

Talking about Mount Rushmore. On a map, point out South Dakota and the Black Hills. Find out if any students have been there. If so, have them describe the area. Use the book to point out the four presidents represented there. Brainstorm ideas about the construction process. Ask, *How do you think this monument was made?* (CALLA: Brainstorming)

2 EXPLORE

Activating prior knowledge. Open to pages 72–73 again. Read the names of the short selections aloud or call on volunteers to do so.

GUIDED READING Focusing on rhyming. Read the poem on page 72 or play the tape. Read or play it again as the students read along in their books. Ask **multi-level questions,** such as *What types of houses are there? Where are there houses? What are houses made of?* On the board, write: *sticks, low, west.* Ask, *Can you find a word in the poem that rhymes with each of these words?* Do a **choral reading** of the poem. Check the rhyming pairs, *What rhymes with sticks?* etc. Print the pairs on the board, *sticks/bricks, low/row, west/best.* Read the

116

pairs, **T-C.** Do a final reading of the poem **chorally,** clapping on the rhyming pairs.

Reading for the main idea. On page 73, direct students' attention to "Truckers and Students Are Pen Pals!" Have students do **independent reading,** then **partner reading.** Ask, *What is the Trucker Buddy program? How can someone join?*

Using visual information. Direct students' attention to "Mount Rushmore." Ask students to look at the picture as you read the text. Do a **choral reading** of the text. Check comprehension, *Where are the heads carved? Which presidents are they?* etc.

Reading for information: Amazing Facts. Play the tape or read the facts as students follow along in their books. Then have students read **independently.** Ask **multi-level questions** such as *How much do most Americans eat? How many pounds are in a ton?*

SKILLS JOURNAL PAGES 64-65 **Rewriting a poem.** Students write a new poem modeled on "Houses." **Reading for a purpose; writing a postcard.** Students complete a cloze exercise and write a postcard to a friend. Teaching suggestions are provided in the Skills Journal annotations.

•••• 3 EXTEND ••••

SOCIAL STUDIES Learning about Mount Rushmore. Help students use resource materials to find out more about Mount Rushmore. Have each student write a short paragraph and illustrate it. As an alternative, students can use clay to sculpt their own Mount Rushmore. (CALLA: Resourcing)

ART Making a house. Have students construct houses out of different materials, such as toothpicks, popsicle sticks, baker's clay, and modeling clay. Ask students which houses feel most durable and which would be most appropriate for various climates. Display in the classroom. (CALLA: Comparing)

MUSIC "America the Beautiful." Play the tape or sing the song (See the tapescript in the Appendix.) Then sing again and invite students to join in.

- - - - ONGOING ASSESSMENT - - - -

PORTFOLIO Save **Skills Journal** page 65.

MULTICULTURAL AWARENESS
Make a mural of houses from around the world. Have students label where the houses are from, what they are made of, and, if students are able, how that housing style fits local climate.

TEACHER TO TEACHER
If your students work with other teachers, you may want to mention to them that students have been discussing housing styles in different parts of the U.S. and around the world.

LANGUAGE POWER A

Across the USA

LEVEL C, PAGE 74

KEY EXPERIENCES

- Describing actions
- Sequencing
- Making observations
- Retelling a story

KEY LANGUAGE

- and, but
- Present verbs with -es

• • • **1 INTRODUCE** • • •

MULTI-LEVEL TEACHING STRATEGIES

Building background: Describing TPR actions. Prepare and number cards as follows: *1 - wake up, 2 - brush teeth, 3 - wash face, 4 - get dressed, 5 - eat breakfast, 6 - put on jacket, 7 - open the door, 8 - go to school.* Read the cards with students. Place the cards in a basket or a hat. Select a student to draw a card and pantomime the verb. The rest of the class guesses which activity it is. Include all the students by asking questions appropriate to each student's language stage. Here are some sample questions:

Speech Emergence: (Indicate a student who pantomimed an activity.) *Was she eating breakfast? What time do you eat breakfast?*

Developing Fluency: *What was she doing? What do you like to do first, eat breakfast or get dressed?*

Sequence scramble. Place the word cards on the chalk rail in random order. Ask the students to help you put the activities in order. Help the students read the cards. Then have partners read the cards to each other in correct order, using the pronoun I, for example, *I wake up, I brush my teeth.* (CALLA: Sequencing)

Previewing. Prepare these word cards: *brushes, washes, dresses, rushes, misses, chases, catches.* Help students read the word cards as volunteers mime the activities. Display the cards along the chalk rail. Explain, *We are going to read about Ben. Ben has a bad day. He wakes up late. What do you think happens? He usually rides the bus to work. Do you think he misses the bus today? What is the opposite of "misses" it?*

• • • **2 EXPLORE** • • •

Activating prior knowledge. Open to page 74 of the Student Book. Encourage students to comment about the sequence of pictures.

 **Look, listen, and talk.** Have students cover the text and look at the pictures as you read the text or play the tape. Ask the students to examine the pictures carefully. Ask questions: *Look at number one. What does Ben do?* Encourage students to respond, *He wakes up.* Continue with the other pictures.

GUIDED READING Read the text or play the tape again as students follow along in their books. Then ask students to reread **independently** and copy the verbs on another piece of paper. Check by reading the verbs **chorally,** *brushes, washes,* etc.

Practicing the conversation. Read or play the tape for the conversation at the bottom of the page. Help students read each sentence chorally. Then divide the students into two groups. One group asks the question; the other reads the answer. Have groups switch roles and repeat. Then help students substitute vocabulary for each picture, using all the present tense verbs.

Describing present actions using simple present tense. Students supply correct verb forms. Teaching suggestions are provided in the Skills Journal annotation.

Making observations. Prepare (or have students prepare) sets of four sequence cards. Some events you may want to include are an ice cream cone being eaten, a balloon being blown up, a plant growing from seed, an ice cube melting. Students practice putting the cards in correct order and describing the sequence to one another. (CALLA: Sequencing)

SOCIAL STUDIES Sequencing. Have students practice doing tasks that must be done in a specific order, such as tying shoelaces, making a peanut butter sandwich, brushing teeth. In pairs, students practice giving instructions to one another. Circulate and help as needed. The student getting the instructions can give feedback on the right order. Put on the board these sequence words: *first, next, then, last.* Help students use them. (CALLA: Sequencing)

Building vocabulary. Use *Amazing English!* Word Attack 3 Interactive Vocabulary Games for practice with vocabulary.

- - - - - - - ONGOING ASSESSMENT - - - - - - -

PERFORMANCE Retelling the story; oral language. Have students use the drawings to describe the sequence in Ben's day. Check for appropriate use of verb forms in the present. Use the **Oral Language Checklist** in the *Amazing Assessment Package.*

PORTFOLIO Save **Skills Journal** page 66 as an example of verb mastery.

STAFF DEVELOPMENT

See the *Amazing How-To Handbook* for additional ways to develop reading strategies.

TEACHER TO TEACHER

If your students work with other teachers, you may want to mention to them that having ESL students give sequenced instructions for classroom tasks will help reinforce the concepts and vocabulary presented in this lesson.

LANGUAGE POWER B

Across the USA

LEVEL C, PAGE 75

KEY EXPERIENCES

- Discussing stamps
- Learning about pen pals
- Sequencing and summarizing
- Classifying stamps

KEY LANGUAGE

- countries, fun, kids, (pen) pals, special, stamps

••• 1 INTRODUCE •••

MULTI-LEVEL TEACHING STRATEGIES

Building background: Discussing stamps. Bring to class as many kinds of U.S. postage stamps as possible. Show the stamps and ask what they are used for. Discuss how many stamps are needed to send a letter across town or across the country, to Canada and Mexico, or overseas. Encourage students to sort the stamps. Include all the students by asking questions appropriate to each student's language stage. Here are some sample questions:

Speech Emergence: *What is this? What do you use it for?*

Developing Fluency: *How much does this stamp cost? Which stamp costs more, this one or that one?*

Learning about pen pals. Before class, prepare a letter such as this one:

January 3

Dear Matilda,

    I like you very much. You're my best friend. You're special. Thank you for playing with me on the weekend. It was fun skating. Please come again.

Your pal,
Desdemona

Print the letter on a large piece of paper. Address an envelope. Explain that Matilda received a letter from her pen pal Desdemona. Say that Matilda and Desdemona are pen pals, friends who write letters to each other. Show the letter and envelope and talk about the format. Read the letter aloud. Ask students if they have ever received a letter and how they felt about it.

Cooperative learning. Students dictate sentences to you for the reply letter to Desdemona. Print the sentences in a letter format. Have students copy the letter, then exchange papers and read to each other. Display in the classroom.

••• 2 EXPLORE •••

Activating prior knowledge. Open to page 75 of the Student Book. Encourage students to comment about the page.

GUIDED READING Read or play the tape for the text at the top of the page. Next ask students to reread **independently.** Then have students scan the text to locate new vocabulary. Check comprehension with **multi-level questions,** such as *What does she belong to? What do they save? Do they put the stamps in a book or a box?*

Reading for specific information. Read or ask a volunteer to read from the text: *Here are some stamps from our book. Do you know where they are from?* Students read and observe the stamps to find out what countries they're from.

Practicing the conversation. Read or play the tape for the conversation at the bottom of the page. Divide the students into two groups. One group asks the question; the other reads the answer. Have groups switch roles and repeat. Extend the practice by substituting the pronouns *he* and *she.* Encourage students to personalize in any other way they choose.

Completing a crossword puzzle. Students complete sentences with verbs from a Data Bank and use the verbs to complete the crossword puzzle. Teaching suggestions are provided in the Skills Journal annotation.

Sequencing. Print each sentence of the text on page 75 on separate sentence strips. Mix up the strips. Have students work in pairs to put the sentences into correct order. Pair students of varying abilities to promote cooperative learning. Have students turn to page 75 to check their work and make corrections to the sequence. Students then can take turns rereading out loud. (CALLA: Cooperation)

SOCIAL STUDIES Classifying stamps from around the world. Ask students to bring to class stamps from letters they have received and bring as many of your own as possible. Talk about the different countries the stamps are from. Help students locate the countries on a world map or globe. Then ask students to sort the stamps by country. They can also be sorted by cost, color, size, or theme, for example, famous people, animals, landmarks. (CALLA: Classifying)

ONGOING ASSESSMENT

PERFORMANCE Oral language; summarizing. Ask students to summarize what the kids do in the Pen Pal Club. Observe different students' levels of detail in their descriptions.

HANDS-ON SOCIAL STUDIES

Across the USA

LEVEL C, PAGES 76–77

KEY EXPERIENCES
- Learning about the Chippewa
- Following directions
- Making a dream catcher
- Critical thinking

KEY LANGUAGE
- dream catcher, bad dreams, good dreams, web, feathers, crisscross

MATERIALS
- white paper plates, 12 inch sections of yarn, beads, feathers, masking tape, pencil, scissors

••• 1 INTRODUCE •••

MULTI-LEVEL TEACHING STRATEGIES

Building background: Discussing dreaming. Discuss dreaming with the students. Encourage the students to share their ideas and personal experiences. Have students create a **word web** of dreaming ideas.

Include all the students by asking questions appropriate to each student's language stage. Here are some sample questions:

Speech Emergence: *Do you think everyone dreams? Do you dream every night? Do you think dogs and cats dream?* (They do.)

Developing Fluency: *How often do you think you dream? Do you like to dream? Have you had a funny dream? Do you want to tell the class about your dream?*

SOCIAL STUDIES Learning about the Chippewa. Explain that students are going to make Chippewa dream catchers. On a map, point out where the Chippewa lived (from Minnesota to the area around the Great Lakes). Also ask students to think about how they could catch a dream. Then ask students to draw their own ideas about what a dream catcher looks like.

••• 2 EXPLORE •••

Activating prior knowledge. Open to pages 76 and 77 of the Student Book. Have students look at the illustrations. What do they think this is?

GUIDED READING Read the introduction on page 76 aloud. Then have students reread the introduction **independently.** Check understanding with **multi-level questions,** such as *What do you use to make dream catchers? What gets caught in the web? Where do good dreams go? Where do you think you hang a dream catcher?* Have students **skim** the page. Ask, *What are we going to do? How many steps are there?*

Exploring new vocabulary. On the board, write the words for the items needed for the dream catcher. Hold up each item, model the word, and have students repeat. Work **T-C; T-S.**

Following directions. Read aloud and demonstrate the directions. Remind students that directions often start with simple verbs. Ask the students to scan the directions and identify verbs such as *Draw, Cut* out, *Punch*, etc. Read aloud and demonstrate again. Make sure students understand what *crisscrossing* means. Have students do **independent reading.**

Cooperative learning. In pairs, students help each other make the dream catchers, rereading the directions as needed. Encourage them to make corrections and suggestions. (CALLA: Cooperation)

Research; writing. Students work with a partner to find out more about the Chippewa people and write answers to questions. **Creative writing.** Students record a bad dream and a good dream they had. Teaching suggestions are provided in the Skills Journal annotations.

SKILLS JOURNAL
PAGES 68-69

3 EXTEND

SCIENCE Dreaming. Help students use resource materials to look up REM (rapid eye movement) sleep and find out what happens to our bodies when we dream. Challenge more proficient students to find out what happens if we don't dream. Compile the information on a chart. Pair students of varying abilities and have them write a paragraph about what they learned. (CALLA: Resourcing)

Language experience writing. Encourage students to keep their own "dream logs." Tell them to keep a pencil and some paper next to their beds. As soon as they wake up, they write down what happened in their dreams. If they want, after a week, they can bring their "dream logs" to the class to share, or they can choose just one dream to share. Keep in mind that students who have experienced personal trauma may not want to share troubling dreams.

ART Displaying the dream catchers. Help the students make a display of their dream catchers in a hall of the school for all to admire. Ask volunteers to find out more information about the Chippewa to include in the display.

ONGOING ASSESSMENT

PERFORMANCE Oral language. Ask individual students to explain how to make a dream catcher. Observe different students' levels. Use the **Oral Language Checklist** in the *Amazing Assessment Package.*

TEACHER TO TEACHER
If your students work with other teachers, you may want to arrange for your ESL students to show other classes how to make dream catchers.

MY HOME

LEVEL C, PAGES 78–81

KEY EXPERIENCES

- Comparing places
- Reading/discussing an essay
- Critical thinking
- Learning about farm workers
- Illustrating the story

KEY LANGUAGE

- border, bunk beds, fields, hills, trailer

1 INTRODUCE

MULTI-LEVEL TEACHING STRATEGIES

Building background: Comparing places. Lead students in a discussion comparing their current homes with other places they have lived. Show students how to make a **Venn diagram** showing similarities and differences. Be sensitive to students who may have experienced or may be experiencing personal hardship.

Include all the students by asking questions appropriate to each student's language stage. Here are some sample questions:

Speech Emergence: *Where did you live before? Did you live in a house or an apartment?*

Developing Fluency: *How long have you lived here? What did your house look like in (Laos)?*

2 EXPLORE

Activating prior knowledge. Open to pages 78–81 of the Student Book. Read the title aloud, "My Home." Ask students to comment on the photograph on page 78. Ask the students to predict what this selection might be about. (CALLA: Predicting)

GUIDED READING Explain that this selection is from a book called *Voices from the Fields.* Ask students what they think the book might be about. Write the following questions on the board and ask students to listen for the answers: *Where did the boy live before? How old was he when his family came to the U.S.?* Read or play the tape of the essay all the way through. Then pause and ask students the answers to the two questions you wrote on the board.

Have students reread the essay **independently.** Then ask **multi-level questions** to check comprehension: *Do you think this is a real story? Why or why not? Which house was bigger, the one in Mexico or the one in the U.S.? What is a bunk bed? Can you draw a picture on the board? How many brothers does Manuel have? How many sisters? What fruit does the family pick? What does Manuel want to do when he grows up?*

Paired reading. Have partners read the story together, alternating pages. As they read, have students look for the answers to any of the questions they could not answer earlier. Then have partners practice summarizing the story for each other. (CALLA: Summarizing)

SKILLS JOURNAL PAGES 70-73

Retelling a story in sequence. Students complete a cloze activity of the story. **Recalling details; drawing conclusions.** Students answer comprehension questions. **Describing a drawing.** Students draw a house and then write about where family members sleep. **Home-School Connection.** Students draw their own dream houses. Teaching suggestions are provided in the Skills Journal annotations.

Critical thinking. Help students find specific words and phrases in the text that indicate how Manuel feels. Make a list on the board or invite a volunteer to do so. Then ask the students to write two or three sentences about how he feels and why. Suggest the following as a writing starter: *I think ... because ...* (CALLA: Deduction)

SOCIAL STUDIES Learning about farm workers. Help the students use resource materials to learn about farm workers. Before they begin, brainstorm a list of questions, such as *Which states have the most farm workers? Where do the farm workers live? Where do the students go to school?* Have students work in groups to locate information for one or two of the questions. Afterward, have the groups share what they discovered. (CALLA: Resourcing)

ART Illustrating the story. Ask students to select something from "My Home" to illustrate. Help students write captions for their illustrations. Display in the classroom.

ONGOING ASSESSMENT

PORTFOLIO Save **Skills Journal** page 71 as an example of comprehension ability, and page 73 as an example of creative writing.

MULTICULTURAL AWARENESS

Keep in mind that some students in your class may be from migrant worker families. If this is the case, ask students to share their own experiences only if they seem willing to do so.

RELATED RESOURCES

The Cat Came Back, CD-ROM
Read Along Mode:
Farm/Countryside (page 9)

EXCERPTED LITERATURE

"My Home" is excerpted from *Voices from the Fields: Children of Migrant Farm Workers Tell Their Stories* by S. Beth Atkin. Copyright © 1993 by S. Beth Atkin, by permission of Little, Brown and Company.

Rationale: This excerpt is meant to stimulate interest in reading the full-length book.

WRITING PROJECT

Writing Project 4B, *Home Sweet Home,* is directly linked to this lesson. See the Process Writing Portfolio Program Teachers' Handbook, pages 22-23, for the Lesson Plan.

Students will find instructions and a Prewriting Sheet in the Writing Projects booklet inside the Portfolio.

HOLISTIC ASSESSMENT

Across the USA

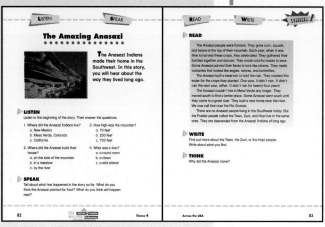

LEVEL C, PAGES 82–83

KEY EXPERIENCES

- Listening for information
- Reading factual information
- Predicting outcomes
- Expressing opinions
- Learning about the Anasazi

KEY LANGUAGE

- beans, celebrated, corn, descended, gathered, harvest, reservoir, squash

1 INTRODUCE

MULTI-LEVEL TEACHING STRATEGIES

These two pages offer a variety of assessment opportunities. The left-hand page consists of listening and speaking activities that follow a taped presentation. In the speaking activity, students are asked to summarize the story and make predictions based on what they have heard. The right-hand page consists of writing and critical thinking activities. These follow a reading passage that completes the listening component. You can use the activities to assess listening, speaking, reading, writing, and critical thinking skills. Have children work as a class or in small groups. Record your observations as appropriate on the **Anecdotal Record Form,** the **Reading Checklist,** and the **Writing Checklist** in the *Amazing Assessment Package.*

Building background: Introducing the Anasazi. Begin by asking students if anyone has heard of the Anasazi Indians. On a map of the U.S., point out New Mexico, Colorado, Arizona, and Utah. Tell students that the Anasazi lived in this area, the Southwest U.S., more than 500 years ago. Ask questions appropriate to each student's language stage. Here are some sample questions:

Speech Emergence: *Where did the Anasazi live? Point to the states on the map.*

Developing Fluency: *Who can name some states in the Southwest? Have you been to any of those states? Tell us about them.*

2 EXPLORE

Previewing the topic. Open the Student Book to page 82 and let the students comment on the photograph. Tell the students that they will hear about the Anasazi people. Give students time to read the listening questions.

 **Listening to the story.** Read or play the tape for the story. You will find the tapescript in the Appendix.

Have students work independently to answer the listening questions. Read or play the tape again for students to check their work.

Speaking. Ask **multi-level questions** as you encourage the students to talk about what happened in the story so far, *Did the Anasazi live in California? Where did they build their houses?* Have them predict what will happen next in the story. (CALLA: Predicting)

GUIDED READING. Read the second part of the story on page 83 as the students listen and follow along in their books. Then have the students do **partner reading,** alternating paragraphs. Use the **Reading Checklist** in the *Amazing Assessment Package.*

Retelling the story. Encourage the students to retell the story. Focus on the key ideas in each paragraph. Prompt the students by asking **multi-level questions**, for example, *What did the Anasazi grow? Why couldn't they live in Mesa Verde any longer?*

Observing the students. As you discuss the story, notice the level of participation and the particular abilities of each child. What new words have they learned? What language structures do they use? Which students can answer *why* questions? You may want to add progress notes to students' **portfolios** at this time. Use the **Anecdotal Record Form** in the *Amazing Assessment Package.*

Reading comprehension. Students work independently to complete cloze sentences, using words from a Data Bank. Teaching suggestions are provided in the Skills Journal annotation. Save this page in the student's **Assessment Portfolio.**

SOCIAL STUDIES **Learning about other Native Americans.** Help students use resource materials to find out about the Tewa, Zuni, or the Hopi people. Ask the students to write about what they learn. Encourage them to exchange papers and help each other make corrections. Use the **Writing Checklist** in the *Amazing Assessment Package.* (CALLA: Resourcing)

Critical thinking. Ask the students to consider why the Anasazi moved. Encourage them to reread the story to find the reason(s). Have students discuss their ideas in small groups then share their ideas with the class. (CALLA: Deduction)

ART **Drawing a cliff house.** Invite students to draw their own representations of what the cliff houses looked like when the Anasazi still lived in them.

MULTICULTURAL AWARENESS

Try to bring in some photos of the remarkable cliff dwellings of the Southwest for students to look at and comment on. Encourage students to describe unusual dwellings they have seen in other parts of the world.

STAFF DEVELOPMENT

See the *Amazing How-To Handbook* and *Authentic Assessment* for more on holistic assessment and other assessment topics.

AMAZING FACTS

Across the USA

LEVEL C, PAGE 84

KEY EXPERIENCES
■ Recalling details
■ Reading for information
■ Playing a game
■ Creating a game

KEY LANGUAGE
■ Review

MATERIALS
■ iron nails, small magnets

1 INTRODUCE

MULTI-LEVEL TEACHING STRATEGIES

Activating prior knowledge. Engage the students in a discussion of Chippewa dream catchers. Also encourage students to describe how they made their own dream catchers. Include all the students by asking questions appropriate to each student's language stage. Here are some sample questions:

Speech Emergence: *Who uses dream catchers? Do dream catchers catch bad dreams or good dreams?*

Developing Fluency: *What happens to bad dreams? What happens to good dreams? What do you use to make a dream catcher? Is it difficult?*

Using TPR. Use the word cards for occupations: *chef, farmer, writer, truck driver, mail carrier, police officer, bus driver, doctor,* etc. from Student Book page 70. Put the cards in a pile in random order. Have students draw a card and pantomime tasks associated with the occupation, such as cooking or driving a truck. Ask, *What is she doing?* Encourage students to respond, *She is cooking.* Then have students guess the occupation. *She is a chef.* Encourage students to add, *She cooks food.*

Playing a game: Freeze! Review the word cards: *brushes, washes, dresses, rushes, misses, chases, catches* from Student Book page 74. Display the cards along the chalk rail. Ask four volunteers to come to the front of the room. Assign each of them one of the verbs to pantomime. After twenty seconds, say, *Freeze.* The rest of the class guesses what each volunteer was doing. Change volunteers and continue.

2 EXPLORE

Activating prior knowledge. Open to page 84 of the Student Book. Have students cover the questions. Review how to play the Amazing Facts game. Prompt if necessary.

Predicting the questions. Ask, *What did you learn about in this theme?* Encourage students to share any facts they remember. Write student ideas for questions on the board.

Playing the game. Divide the students into teams. Set the time limit and have the teams work together to answer the questions. Circulate and help as needed. At the end of the pre-set time period, have the teams compete for the correct answers orally. Read the questions in random order. The first team to raise their hands and answer the question correctly wins a point. The team with the most points at the end of play wins the game.

Challenge. For extra fluency practice, ask the students to answer the questions in complete sentences: *The Anasazi built a reservoir to hold the rain.*

Creating a game. Students create their own Amazing Facts games, researching answers if necessary. Teaching suggestions are provided in the Skills Journal annotation.

Sharing Learning Logs. Ask students to share their Learning Logs with partners or small groups. Encourage students to talk about interesting facts they have learned, to note things they have found difficult, and to ask their peers for help with the things they find confusing. (CALLA: Self-Monitoring)

SOCIAL STUDIES Planning a trip. Have the students work in pairs or small groups to plan a cross-country trip. Brainstorm the names of cities and points of interest they might visit. Help students decide which modes of transportation they will use. Encourage them to make a drawing of the U.S. and show their route.

SCIENCE Magnetizing a nail. Provide the students with iron nails and magnets. Demonstrate how they can make a nail into a temporary magnet by tapping it hard against the magnet. Provide paper clips for students to pick up.

ONGOING ASSESSMENT

SELF-ASSESSMENT Listening comprehension. Suggest that students monitor their own listening comprehension by asking themselves the following questions: *How well do I understand? Do I ask for clarification when I do not understand? Do I listen for context clues? Do I look for clues in the speaker's face and body language?*

STAFF DEVELOPMENT

See the *Amazing How-To Handbook* for more suggestions on how to use "Amazing Facts."

ASSESSMENT

You will find background information on the latest thinking in assessment as well as the assessment instruments for this theme in the *Amazing Assessment Package*.

You have been collecting assessment data through the ongoing and holistic assessment options (Oral Language Checklist, Reading Checklist, Writing Checklist, Anecdotal Record Form) in this theme. The following are specific end-of-theme assessment strategies that will help you evaluate your students' progress as well as adapt your instruction to meet their needs.

Student Self-Assessment. Self-assessment surveys are a means for students to have input into their own learning process. Students can use them to **reflect** on the work they have done and the learning strategies they have used during this theme.

Interpreting and Applying Assessment Data. As teachers, you collect assessment data in order to inform your instruction. Assessment information is a tool that helps you tailor your program to better meet the needs and interests of your students.

Evaluate the checklists, anecdotal records, portfolio collections, and test results from this theme as a means of informing your instruction.

• In which areas are students showing confidence and enthusiasm?
• In which areas are they hesitant or confused?
• Should you provide more classroom opportunities for oral language or writing?
• Would certain students (or the whole class) benefit from a focused mini-lesson on a certain area or skill?
• Remember to recycle skills as you teach the next theme and provide students with many opportunities to improve their competence.

Review the results of the **Student Self-Assessment** survey and incorporate students' interests as you plan your instruction for the next theme. What do they want to learn next? Which activities did they enjoy most? If your students particularly enjoyed choral reading, roleplaying, or working in partners, try to emphasize those kinds of activities in the next theme.

THEME CELEBRATION

The end of a theme study is a good time for students to share some of their accomplishments with others. Suggest to students that you hold a celebration to spotlight their work. This celebration can be an excellent opportunity to build stronger connections with other students and teachers in the school. Your students can share pen pal letters, display their dream catchers, or give a report about the Anasazi Indians. Students can also share with other classes the Amazing Facts games they have researched and played. If possible, invite family members to the theme celebration.

END-OF-THEME READ-ALOUD BOOK

Houses and Homes

by Ann Morris

photographs by Ken Heyman

New York: Simon & Schuster, 1994

Simple text accompanies striking photographs showing houses around the world. Children will identify with houses that look like theirs or that share some characteristic. They will learn that, whatever a house looks like, it is a home. A map and index indicate where each photograph was taken and provide some context.

It's important to get students excited about independent reading. Remember to distribute the Literature Links Bibliography for the next theme to your students and encourage them to use the *Amazing Book Bytes* CD-ROM to respond to their reading.

Animals Wild and Tame~

With Theme 5, students enter the world of animals. Through literature, articles, music, and language activity pages in the **Student Book**, the students will learn the animals in the Chinese calendar, imagine they are circus animal trainers, and do research about lions. They will make a chart of animal habitats and learn how a famous gorilla uses American Sign Language. The **Skills Journal** offers opportunities for further language practice, reading, writing, and research on a variety of theme-related topics.

Multi-Level Teaching Strategies integrated into each lesson plan insure that all students can participate in these class activities, each at his or her own level of language proficiency. **Home-School Connection** activities provide enjoyable extension activities for students and family members to do together.

The **Ongoing Assessment** suggestions in the lesson plans will help you keep track of your students' progress. On **Student Book** pages 102-103, the "Listen, Speak, Read, Write, Think" selection offers an opportunity for **holistic assessment**. The end-of-theme **Wrap-Up** page includes guidelines for implementing the full range of assessment tools and interpreting the results.

PLANNING TIPS

The **At-a-Glance Lesson Planner** on the next two pages provides an overview of the Key Experiences and Key Language presented in each lesson of the theme. Quickly scan the lesson plan Materials lists to see if there are materials to gather or prepare. Check the **Wrap-Up** page in case you want to plan ahead for the Theme Celebration.

The following **Read-Aloud Books** are recommended with this theme. Gather these titles and your own theme-related favorites. We encourage you to read aloud to your students every day. If possible, record the stories on tape and let students reread the books as they listen to the tapes.

- *Q Is for Duck* by Elting and Folsom

- *Quick As a Cricket* (poetry) by Audrey Wood

- *Koko's Kitten* by Francine Patterson

- *The Day the Goose Got Loose* by Reeve Lindburg

- *Maii and Cousin Horned Toad* by Shonto Begay

- *I Am the Dog, I Am the Cat* by Donald Hall (Wrap-Up page)

READING CORNER

Encourage independent reading for information and pleasure. If possible, set up a reading corner—a quiet, comfortable place that is just for reading (and perhaps listening to any books on tape you've collected). Make a bulletin board on which you can post book covers, students' BookBytes reviews and the Literature Links Bibliographies that support each theme. See the Appendix for the complete Literature Links Bibliography for this theme. It offers a variety of fiction and non-fiction choices **in English and in other languages.**

LESSON PLAN

1 Student Book p. 85
Theme Opener

2 Student Book p. 86
Communication 1A

3 Student Book p. 87
Communication 1B

4 Student Book p. 88
Read and Do

5 Student Book p. 89
Do the Dog Walk

6 Student Book p. 90
Communication 2A

7 Student Book p. 91
Communication 2B

8 Student Book pp. 92-93
Check This Out!

9 Student Book p. 94
Language Power A

10 Student Book p. 95
Language Power B

11 Student Book p. 96-97
Hands-On Science

12 Student Book pp. 98-101
Koko's Computer

13 Student Book pp. 102-103
Holistic Assessment

14 Student Book p. 104
Amazing Facts Game

KEY EXPERIENCES

Talking about animals • Previewing/drawing habitats • Sharing personal interests about animals • Predicting meaning of theme titles

Talking about pet preferences • Roleplaying conversations • Personalizing a conversation • Reading "Amazing Facts"

Describing/following a sequence • Reading a narration • Describing actions in the past • Roleplaying the story

Discussing saving money • Scanning for information • Reading/following directions • Making a piggy bank • Planning ways to save

Learning/comparing animal sounds • Identifying baby and grown animals • Singing a TPR song • Creating new verses

Comparing past and present • Reading about a dream • Talking about circus life/circus animals

Touring the school library • Roleplaying checking out books • Creating new conversations using a Data Bank • Using the local library

Using titles to predict content • Reading short selections • Recalling details • Scanning • Reading "Amazing Facts" • Discussing animals

Guided reading • Identifying a sequence • Using map skills • Retelling a story • Learning about seeing-eye dogs

Expressing ownership • Talking about pets • Reviewing pet vocabulary

Identifying animals • Learning about animal habitats • Reading/following directions • Making a chart • Comparing habitats

Reading a nonfiction selection • Learning about gorillas • Relating Koko's language learning to students' own experiences

Learning about lions • Listening for information • Reading factual information • Predicting outcome • Expressing opinions

Predicting questions • Recalling details • Playing a game • Creating a game

LESSON PLANNER

KEY LANGUAGE

gorilla, habitat, tame, wild, zoo • north, south, east, west (R)
What's your favorite (wild animal)? • Is there a good book about animals? • female, male, pet
Did she . . .? • Yes, she did./No, she didn't. • Past tense verbs • first, second, third, next, last (R)
cork, paste, newspaper, tube, cover, cut, glue, press, repeat, tear
duckling, frog, kitten, puppy, tadpole
Past tense verbs: clapped, dreamed, lived, traveled, stayed, loved, cheered, whistled, stamped • animal trainer, fans
Can I help you? • I want to (borrow a book). • CD, cassette tape, library card, magazine, painting, stories, videotape, borrow, check out, take out
cicada, cricket, grasshopper, grip
Past tense verbs: traveled, waited, loaded, collected, patted, boarded, counted, started up, shouted • passengers • seeing-eye dog
This is my/his dog. • This is your/her cat/parrot. • These are our gerbils. • Those are their turtles. • Pets
Names of animals • Habitats
American Sign Language • mad, mittens, icon, symbol
captivity, cubs, hunting, leap, outrun, preserves, pride
Review

CONTENT AREAS

Social Studies • Language Arts
Art • Social Studies • Language Arts
Social Studies • Language Arts
Math • Language Arts
Art • Music • Language Arts
Social Studies • Language Arts
Math • Language Arts
Art • Science • Language Arts
Science • Language Arts
Music • Science • Language Arts
Science • Language Arts
Science • Social Studies • Language Arts
Assessment
Assessment

THEME OPENER

Animals Wild and Tame

LEVEL C, PAGE 85

KEY EXPERIENCES

- Talking about animals
- Previewing/drawing habitats
- Sharing personal interests about animals
- Predicting meaning of theme titles
- Brainstorming ideas

KEY LANGUAGE

- gorilla, habitat, tame, wild, zoo
- north, south, east, west (R)

1 INTRODUCE

MULTI-LEVEL TEACHING STRATEGIES

Building background. Discuss the photograph on Student Book page 85 of a gorilla named Koko. Find out if any of the students have heard of Koko. Ask students to predict where she is and what she is doing. Include all the students by asking questions appropriate to each student's language stage. Here are some sample questions:

Speech Emergence: (Point to the picture.) *This is Koko. Is Koko in a forest or a zoo? What do you see next to Koko?*

Developing Fluency: *Where is Koko? What is she doing? Why is there a computer next to her? Is she thinking? What is she thinking about?*

Previewing habitats. Direct students' attention to the title, "Animal Habitats." Write the word *habitat* on the board and model the word **Teacher-Class.** Say, *Wild gorillas live in central and western central Africa. That is their habitat. Koko doesn't live in Africa. She was born in a zoo. Now she lives in California. She lives at a place where people study gorillas. That place is Koko's habitat.* Continue, *Tell me the names of some animals you know. Where do they live?* Give examples: *A whale lives in the ocean. A cow lives on a farm. My cat lives at my house.* Brainstorm a list of animals and their habitats. Write them on the board. Help students arrive at the distinction between *wild* and *tame.* (CALLA: Deduction/induction)

ART Drawing habitats. Ask students to draw a picture of an animal in its habitat. Circulate. Encourage students to use their imaginations and add details. In small groups, have students take turns talking about their pictures.

2 EXPLORE

Activating prior knowledge. Use **TPR.** Make word cards for the animals the students named: *dog, cat, elephant,* etc. Help students read the word cards. Ask, *How does a dog walk? How does a cat walk?*, etc. Have the whole class move about and pantomime the animals walking.

Talking about the Chinese calendar. Reread the poem, "My Family" (Theme 2, page 27). Ask students which animals are named in the poem. Remind students that the Chinese calendar is based on twelve animals. Ask students to guess what the other animals are. Make a list on the board. (CALLA: Imagery)

Previewing. Explain that in "Koko's Computer" they will read about how Koko uses a computer. Brainstorm with the class what Koko uses the computer for. Encourage students to use their imaginations. Ask **multi-level questions** such as *How does she use it? What does she use it for? Can she read the computer keys?*, etc.

SKILLS JOURNAL PAGE 76
Writing about a photo; predicting. Students write a description of the theme opener photo and what they think the Koko story will be about. Teaching suggestions are provided in the Skills Journal annotation.

•••• **3 EXTEND** ••••

STAFF DEVELOPMENT

For more on resourcing, see *The CALLA Handbook*. Set up a Reading Corner with books and magazines about tame and wild animals. Encourage students to browse in their free time.

Using TPR. Put the animal word cards in a basket or hat. Have students take turns pantomiming for the class one of the animals. The rest of the class identifies the animal, for example, *Lion* or *You're a lion.*

Language experience writing. Ask students to write a paragraph of three or four sentences about a trip they have taken to a zoo, a farm, or an animal park. Brainstorm ideas first. Write a model on the board: *I went to ...I saw ... It was ...*, etc. Encourage students to add illustrations. In pairs, have students share their stories and help each other make corrections. (CALLA: Cooperation)

SOCIAL STUDIES Learning habitat names. Use a globe or world map. Review the names of the continents, *This is Africa*, etc. Talk about names of countries, *Is this Brazil? What country is this? What country is east of Guatemala?* Review *north, south, east, west.* Students copy the names on a piece of paper. Use a geography book or photographs to point out different habitats, such as *savanna, rain forest, desert.*

ONGOING ASSESSMENT

PERFORMANCE Oral language. Circulate and observe the students as they share their stories about their animal trips. Observe different students' levels of expression. Use the **Oral Language Checklist** in the *Amazing Assessment Package.*

PORTFOLIO Writing. Save **Skills Journal** page 76 as an example of independent writing.

COMMUNICATION 1A

Animals Wild and Tame

LEVEL C, PAGE 86

KEY EXPERIENCES

- Talking about pet preferences
- Roleplaying conversations
- Personalizing a conversation
- Reading "Amazing Facts"
- Making a pet collage

KEY LANGUAGE

- *What's your favorite (wild animal)?*
- *Is there a good book about animals?*
- *There are lots.*
- *female, male, pet*

••• 1 INTRODUCE •••

MULTI-LEVEL TEACHING STRATEGIES

Building background. Display pictures of animals that are pets. If possible, include pictures of pets with their owners. Engage the students in a discussion of the pictures and of pets in general. Include all students in the discussion, asking questions appropriate to each student's language stage. Here are some sample questions:

Speech Emergence: (Point to a picture.) *What is this? Do you think this is a good pet? Do you have a pet? What is your pet's name?*

Developing Fluency: (Point to a picture.) *Does this boy like his pet? How do you know? What are they doing? Do you have a pet? Do you like having a pet? Tell one thing good about your pet.*

Brainstorming. Discuss what it means to have a pet. Together make a **word web** on the board. Make a circle and write *a pet* in the center. Prompt the students to include good things about a pet as well as the responsibilities. Ask, *How does a pet make you feel? What do you need to do for your pet?*

ART Drawing a pet. Ask students to draw a picture of their pet or of an animal they would like to have as a pet. Encourage them to write the animal's name and a sentence about the pet. *This is ... I like her because ...* or, *I like this (dog). I want her for a pet because ....* Invite students to share their drawings with the class.

••• 2 EXPLORE •••

Activating prior knowledge. Open to page 86 of the Student Book. Ask students to comment about the picture. *What do you see?*

Look, listen, and talk. Have students look and listen as you read the text or play the tape of the text at the top of the page. Introduce the words *male* and *female* to help students talk about pets. Check understanding with **multi-level questions,** such as *What's her pet's name? Is her pet a male or a female? How do you know? Are there a lot of books about animals?*

Practicing the conversation. Read the text or play the tape again, pausing for students to repeat. Divide the class into two groups. One group asks the questions, the other answers. Have groups switch roles and repeat. (CALLA: Cooperation)

Reading for specific information: Amazing Facts. Show students a picture of a caterpillar and of an ostrich. Ask them to guess how many muscles a caterpillar has and how much an ostrich egg weighs. Write their guesses on the board. (CALLA: Guessing)

Direct students' attention to the bottom of the page. Do **choral reading.** Then give students time to reread **independently.** Ask, *How many muscles does a caterpillar have? How much can an ostrich's egg weigh? Whose guess was the closest? Would Koko like a banana? Why?*, etc. Tailor the questions to the capabilities of your students.

Data collection. Students conduct interviews, record the information in charts, and use it for paired conversation practice. Teaching suggestions are provided in the Skills Journal annotation.

Interviewing: Home-School Connection. Have students interview friends and relatives at home about their favorite wild animals and pets. Encourage students to ask for reasons, *Why are elephants your favorite animal?* Make a class chart showing the most common responses. Discuss the chart, *How many people like elephants?* (CALLA: Classifying)

ART Making a pet collage. Use a large piece of butcher paper and ask students to mount photographs of their pets or the drawings of the pets they would like to have. Display in the classroom.

SOCIAL STUDIES Playing a Chain Game. Ask Student 1, *What's your favorite wild animal?* Student 1 answers, then asks the question of Student 2. S2 turns to S3 and says: *(S1)'s favorite wild animal is (a tiger). My favorite wild animal is (a giraffe). What's your favorite wild animal?* Students continue asking and answering in a chain.

ONGOING ASSESSMENT

PERFORMANCE Oral language. Go around the class asking students about their favorites, *What's your favorite (wild animal)?* Observe students' levels of participation. Use the **Oral Language Checklist** in the *Amazing Assessment Package.*

PORTFOLIO Note-taking. Save **Skills Journal** page 77 as an example of oral/aural abilities and note-taking.

MULTICULTURAL AWARENESS
Invite volunteers to tell the class about pets in their home cultures. Ask students which animals are the most popular. Encourage students to draw or bring in photographs of animals they used to have as pets. Are there any animals that people here keep as pets that are never kept as pets in their home cultures?

COMMUNICATION 1B

Animals Wild and Tame

LEVEL C, PAGE 87

KEY EXPERIENCES

- Describing/following a sequence
- Reading a narration
- Describing actions in the past
- Roleplaying the story

KEY LANGUAGE

- *Did she ...?*
- *Yes, she did. No, she didn't.*
- Past tense verbs
- *first, second, third, next, last* (R)

• • • 1 INTRODUCE • • •

MULTI-LEVEL TEACHING STRATEGIES

Building background. Ask the students to open to page 87 of the Student Book and cover the text. Give them time to look carefully at the pictures. Discuss each picture. Ask students to predict what the story is about. Include all students in the discussion by asking questions appropriate to each student's language stage. Here are some sample questions:

Speech Emergence: (Point to each picture.) *Who you see? Does she open the refrigerator door?*

Developing Fluency: *What does she do here? What is in the back yard? What does she do after she washes her dog?*

After you have discussed each picture, write *first, second, third, next,* and *last* on the board. Review the sequence. Point to the first square, *First she rushed home from school.* Continue with the other pictures.

Describing a sequence. Have students work in pairs. Have one student tell the other student the steps involved in brushing teeth. Before students begin, put key words on the board: *toothpaste, toothbrush, put, squeeze, turn on water, rinse.* Demonstrate with **TPR** actions as you model the words. Remind the students to listen carefully and do only what their partner says. Encourage students to use gestures. Ask pairs to demonstrate for the class.

Writing past tense verbs. Print on the board: *rushed, kissed, opened, asked, answered, washed, dried, brushed, trimmed, tied, looked.* Point to the *-ed* at the end of each word. Underline the base form of each verb *(rush,* etc.). Help the students read the words. Listen for correct pronunciation of the ending. Point out how *y* changes to *i* in *dried* and *tied.* Have students copy each of the words, then exchange papers to make sure the spelling is correct. Encourage students to keep a daily log of their activities to give them further practice in using past tense verbs. *(Yesterday I ....)*

• • • 2 EXPLORE • • •

 **Look, listen, and talk.** Have students uncover the text at the top of page 87. Ask students to point to each picture as you read the text or play the tape. Ask, *What happened in the first picture?* Encourage students to respond, *She opened the refrigerator door.* Continue with other **multi-level questions** to elicit both short and long responses in the past tense.

Choral reading. Read the text or play the tape again and have students follow along **chorally.** Divide the class into groups. Have the first group read the first paragraph; ask which pictures go with it. Continue in the same way.

Practicing the conversation. Read or play the tape for the conversation at the bottom of the page. Have students point to the lines as they listen. Read the conversation again, pausing for students to repeat. Help students substitute other phrases for "*...rush home from the library*" so that all the past tense verbs are practiced in context. Example: *Did she open the closet door? No, she didn't. She opened the refrigerator door.*

Describing past actions. Students make the verbs in the Data Bank past tense and use them to complete a cloze story. Teaching suggestions are provided in the Skills Journal annotation.

Spelling practice. Print on the board the simple forms of the verbs used in the story: *rush, kiss,* etc. Ask students to write the past tense form of each verb. Circulate and check spelling. For extra challenge, ask the students to put the verbs in alphabetical order. (CALLA: Sequencing)

SOCIAL STUDIES Roleplaying the story. Students roleplay the story on page 87, using picture cards and other objects as props. Assign roles to students. Read the text, one sentence at a time, and have students roleplay what was just said. They can roleplay several parts.

Retelling the story. Have students work in pairs. One student covers the text and retells the story using the illustrations. The other student listens and prompts as needed, using the text. Students switch roles and repeat.

ONGOING ASSESSMENT

PERFORMANCE Listening comprehension; oral language. Have students open their books to page 87. Read the following sentences and ask students for the matching picture: *I opened the refrigerator door. I washed him from head to tail. I trimmed the hair around his eyes. I tied a beautiful ribbon around his neck.*

MULTICULTURAL AWARENESS

Keep in mind that people in many parts of the world feel that Americans go overboard in the way we pamper our pets, especially dogs. Some cultures do not keep dogs as pets; other cultures may tolerate dogs, but would never allow them in the house.

READ AND DO

Animals Wild and Tame

LEVEL C, PAGE 88

KEY EXPERIENCES

- Discussing saving money
- Scanning for information
- Reading/following directions
- Making a piggy bank
- Planning ways to save

KEY LANGUAGE

- cork, paste, newspaper, tube,
- cover, cut, glue, press, repeat, tear

MATERIALS

- corks, oranges, paste or glue, newspaper, paint, toothpaste tube tops

---

1 INTRODUCE

MULTI-LEVEL TEACHING STRATEGIES

Building background: Discussing saving money. Bring several small banks to class if, possible. Elicit the word *bank* or provide the word yourself; write it on the board. Ask what you do with a bank, and write the words *save money* on the board. Ask students if they have their own banks and have them describe them. Include all of the students by asking questions appropriate to each student's language stage. Here are some sample questions:

Speech Emergence: *What do you put in your bank?* (Hold up a bank.) *Does your bank look like this?*

Developing Fluency: *What do you plan to do with your money? How much do you save each week?*

Brainstorming about money. Have the students brainstorm why saving money is important. List the reasons on the board. Also make a list of ways to earn money, *cut lawns, wash cars, walk a neighbor's dog, feed a neighbor's pet while the neighbor is on vacation,* etc. (CALLA: Brainstorming)

MATH Problem solving. Choose one of the reasons for saving money (for example, to buy a new bike). Discuss how much money students might earn doing various jobs (for example, $5 to cut someone's lawn, $2 to walk a dog) and how long it will take to buy what they want. Then ask the students to decide one thing they each want to buy, how they could earn the money, and how long they would have to work. Pair students to work together. Circulate and help as needed. (CALLA: Problem solving)

2 EXPLORE

Activating prior knowledge. Open to page 88 of the Student Book. Have students look at the pictures and scan the page. Ask, *What are we going to do? How many steps are there?*

Exploring new vocabulary. On the board, write the vocabulary words for the things needed to make the piggy bank. Hold up each item, point to the word, model it, and have students repeat.

GUIDED READING Following directions. Read the directions aloud. Pantomime to demonstrate the verbs, or have volunteers do so. Note that some students may, for religious reasons, prefer making a bunny bank rather than a piggy bank; allow them to do so.

Paired reading. Have the students take turns reading the directions to each other. As one partner reads, the other pantomimes the steps. In pairs, students help each other make the piggy banks, rereading the directions as needed. Circulate and help them. (CALLA: Cooperation)

Reading for a purpose; writing. Students read a paragraph about U.S. coins and write answers to questions. Teaching suggestions are provided in the Skills Journal annotation.

LIFE SKILLS Planning ways to save. Have students decide what they would like to save money for and how they might earn the money. Circulate and help students come up with a plan for how long it will take them to reach their goal. Then have students write about their plans.

Sequencing. Make a strip story of the directions, one step per strip. Ask the students to work in pairs to put the strips in the correct order. Pair students of varying ability to promote cooperative learning. Ask students to read the directions aloud. (CALLA: Sequencing)

Using TPR. Do a TPR review of the verbs in the directions. Pantomime the actions; have students say what you are doing. Do a detailed check quiz of the directions: *Where do we put the orange to dry? How many layers of paper do we use?*, etc. Students scan for the information. Have students each write a question; have partners continue.

ONGOING ASSESSMENT

SELF-EVALUATION Writing directions. With books closed, have students write a letter to a friend in which they describe in their own words how to make a piggy bank. Then have them check their instructions with the instructions in the book and make corrections as needed. To assess students' work, use the **Writing Checklist** in the *Amazing Assessment Package.*

MULTICULTURAL AWARENESS

Invite the students to share with the class some of the ways to earn money in their home cultures. At what age do students try to start earning money? What kinds of jobs can they do? How much might they earn for each type of job?

STAFF DEVELOPMENT

See the *Amazing How-To Handbook* for additional ways to integrate CALLA strategies into the curriculum.

DO THE DOG WALK

THEME 5 • • • • • • • •

Animals Wild and Tame

LEVEL C, PAGE 89

KEY EXPERIENCES

- Learning/comparing animal sounds
- Identifying baby and grown animals
- Singing a TPR song
- Creating new verses

KEY LANGUAGE

- duckling, frog, kitten, puppy, tadpole

1 INTRODUCE

MULTI-LEVEL TEACHING STRATEGIES

Building background: Playing *What's Missing?* Display pictures or small models of the following animals: *dog, cat, duck, frog, cow, sheep.* Teacher or review the names. Work **T-C**. Prepare word labels for the animals. Help students use phonetic clues to read the words. Have students place each word card by the correct animal. Then ask the students to close their eyes. Remove one animal picture or model. Have students open their eyes. Ask, *What's missing?* Repeat the game, letting different students remove an animal and ask a classmate *What's missing?* Include all students in the activity by asking questions appropriate to each student's language stage. Here are some sample questions:

Speech Emergence: (Point to an animal picture/model.) *What is this? What is missing? Is the cow missing?*

Developing Fluency: *What's missing? Which animal was missing before?*

Playing a guessing game. Make several sets of animal outlines traced from stencils or from pictures in books: *dog, cat, duck, frog.* Include one animal for each student, a matching word card for each animal, and safety pins. Model the game by having a student pin an animal on your back. Ask, *Is it a cow? Is it a dog?* When you have discovered the animal, go to the stack of word cards and find the correct word label. Pin animal pictures to the backs of the students and let them play the game. When all of the students hold the correct word labels, give **TPR** directions to form groups: *All dogs line up at the door, All frogs line up under the flag,* etc. (CALLA: Guessing)

2 EXPLORE

Activating prior knowledge. Open to page 89 of the Student Book. Ask students how they know "Do the Dog Walk" is a song. Encourage students to comment about the page, *What is the dog doing?* Allow time for **independent reading.**

Exploring new vocabulary. Ask a volunteer to read the words of the song aloud, or read them aloud yourself. Ask, *What do you call a baby dog?* Write *dog/puppy* on the board. Model **T-C**. Introduce the words for the other three baby animals: *cat/kitten, duck/duckling, frog/tadpole.* If possible, show a picture, sketch, or ask a student to sketch a tadpole. Ask, *What is a baby (cat)?*

🎵 **MUSIC** "Do the Dog Walk." Play the tape or sing the song as the students listen. Present the song again as the students sing along, following the words in their books. Teach the names of other baby animals, writing the word pairs on the board: *cow/calf, sheep/lamb, goat/kid, horse/foal.* Talk about the sound each animal makes. Sing the song again.

SKILLS JOURNAL PAGE 80

Writing new poetry verses. Students write and illustrate new verses for "Do the Dog Walk." Teaching suggestions are provided in the Skills Journal annotation.

Home-School Connection. Have the students ask at home about the names of animals and animal sounds in the primary language. Students can write down the names and sounds for each animal and bring the list to class to share.

ART Illustrating a class book. Have students draw pictures of animals for a class book. Have each student select one or more different animals to draw: *a dog, a cat, a duck, a frog, a cow, a sheep.* Depending on the number of students, you may want to suggest other animals to illustrate: *a horse, a bird, a goat, a bee.* Have each student copy on a separate piece of paper the names of all the animals illustrated.

Making a multi-lingual class book. Help students mount their art work and bind the book. Write the English word for the animal in the upper left corner. Underneath, write the name in the other languages represented in your class. Have students vote on a title for the book and design a cover. Shelve the book in the class library.

● ONGOING ASSESSMENT

PERFORMANCE Oral language. Provide pictures of the adult/baby animal pairs taught in this lesson. Provide matching word card labels. Observe pairs of students as they work with the pictures and word cards. One student chooses a picture and names the animals (*cat, kitten*). The other finds the matching word cards. Both students say the animal sound, *meow, meow.* Students switch roles and repeat the activity. Observe different students' levels of participation. Use the **Oral Language Checklist** in the *Amazing Assessment Package*.

PORTFOLIO Save **Skills Journal** page 80 as an example of creative writing.

MULTICULTURAL AWARENESS

Ask students to have their families or friends help them translate a verse of "Do the Dog Walk!" into their primary languages. Encourage them to translate only the animal sound part if the whole verse is too difficult. Copy onto a piece of chart paper. Help the class sing the song in different languages.

TEACHER TO TEACHER

If your students work with other teachers, you may want to suggest that they encourage English learners to listen for rhyming pairs in songs and poems they hear in class.

COMMUNICATION 2A

Animals Wild and Tame

LEVEL C, PAGE 90

KEY EXPERIENCES

- Comparing past and present
- Reading about a dream
- Talking about circus life/circus animals
- Writing about an occupation that has to do with animals

KEY LANGUAGE

- Past tense verbs: clapped, dreamed, lived, traveled, stayed, loved, cheered, whistled, stamped
- animal trainer, fans

••• 1 INTRODUCE •••

MULTI-LEVEL TEACHING STRATEGIES

Building background: Comparing past and present. On the board draw a picture of a hill with a little door at the bottom. Students look at the picture as you teach this Mother Goose rhyme: *There was an old woman Who lived under a hill, And if she's not gone, She lives there still.*

Teach students the difference between *lived* and *lives* by using the context to help them understand the meaning. Include all students in the discussion by asking questions appropriate to each student's language stage. Here are some sample questions:

Speech Emergence: *Was the woman young or old? Where did the woman live? Does she live there now? Do we know?*

Developing Fluency: *If she's not gone, does she live there now? How do we now? What word tells us that?* (still)

Roleplaying. Make a bed out of a shoe box and place a puppet with an *I* pronoun label attached to it in the bed. Roleplay a monologue such as this: *Last night I dreamed I was a doctor. I helped people. I lived a great life. Sick people loved me. They listened when I said they would feel better soon. They cheered when they felt better. I didn't get famous but I was happy.* Check comprehension by asking **multi-level questions** such as *What did she dream? Did she get famous? What was the story mostly about?*

Practicing pronunciation. Ask students to say the sound /-d/ as they hold their hands about an inch in front of their mouths. Ask them if they feel anything. Repeat with the sound /-t/. (The /-t/ sound is aspirated and students should feel a puff of air on their hands.) Have students practice saying sounds with both endings: *rushed, promised, closed, moved, dreamed, crossed,* etc.

••• 2 EXPLORE •••

Activating prior knowledge. Open to page 90 of the Student Book. Encourage students to comment on the page. Ask, *What do you see? What clues tell you this is a dream?*

Exploring key vocabulary. Students point to these words as you demonstrate, pantomime, or have volunteers explain each one: *dreamed, clapped, lived, traveled, stayed, loved, cheered, whistled, stamped.* Introduce additional unfamiliar vocabulary items such as *animal trainer, fans, hoops.*

 **GUIDED READING** Have students follow along in their books as you read the text or play the tape. Ask, *What did he dream?* Encourage students to respond, *He dreamed he was an animal trainer.* Briefly discuss what an animal trainer does. Continue with **multi-level questions** to suit your class. *What animals did he train? Where did he stay?* Read the text or play the tape again and have students read along in their books **chorally.**

Practicing the conversation. Read or play the tape for the conversation at the bottom of the page. Have students point to the lines as they listen. Read the conversation again, pausing for students to repeat.

Help students substitute other phrases for "*...dream he was a doctor*" so that all the past tense verbs are practiced in context. Example: *Did he live a bad life? Did he travel to Canada?*

SKILLS JOURNAL PAGE 81 **Matching written language to pictures.** Students work with a partner to write answers to the questions. Teaching suggestions are provided in the Skills Journal annotation.

SOCIAL STUDIES **Writing about animal-related occupations.** Have the students write "I dreamed I was ..." paragraphs about different occupations that have to do with animals. First, brainstorm possible occupations: *an animal researcher, a zoo keeper, a kennel operator, a veterinarian, a software engineer who creates animal animation, a sound technician who creates animal sound effects,* etc. Help students find resource materials as needed. Ask students to exchange paragraphs and help each other make corrections. (CALLA: Cooperation)

ONGOING ASSESSMENT

PERFORMANCE **Reading; oral language.** Rewrite the sentences from the story on page 90 out of order. Duplicate a copy for each student. Students work in small groups for cooperative learning. They read the sentences, cut them out, put the sentences in correct order, and then paste the sentences in correct order on paper. Observe different students' levels of participation. Use the **Oral Language Checklist** in the *Amazing Assessment Package.*

COMMUNICATION 2B

Animals Wild and Tame

LEVEL C, PAGE 91

KEY EXPERIENCES

- Touring the school library
- Roleplaying checking out books
- Creating new conversations using a Data Bank
- Using the local library

KEY LANGUAGE

- *Can I help you?*
- *I want to (borrow a book).*
- *How many can I take out?*
- *See you next week!*
- CD, cassette tape, library card, magazine, painting, stories, videotape
- borrow, check out, take out

1 INTRODUCE

MULTI-LEVEL TEACHING STRATEGIES

Building background: Touring the school library. Plan a visit to your school library. Before going, find out what students already know about the library and about checking out books. Write relevant vocabulary, such as *library, librarian, library card, check out* , on the board. When you visit the library, point out any signs and have volunteers try to read them. Introduce students to the librarian. Then have the librarian show the students around. Afterward ask students about their experiences visiting the library. Include all the students by asking questions appropriate to each student's language stage Here are some sample questions:

Speech Emergence: *Do you go to the library? Do you like the library? What do you give the librarian?*

Developing Fluency: *What kinds of books do you like to borrow? How often do you go to the library?*

Reading. Print the following sentences on strips: *Can I help you? / Yes, please. I want to borrow a book. / Do you have a library card? / Yes, I do. / Here are some good books. / How many can I take out? / You can check out three. / I want these please.* Help the students read the strips **chorally.** Write *Librarian* and *Student* on chart paper. Give a sentence strip to a volunteer to read aloud, for example, *How many can I take out?* Ask students to tell you who might have said that. Have the volunteer tape the strip under *Student.* Continue with the other sentences.

2 EXPLORE

Activating prior knowledge. Open to page 91 of the Student Book. Encourage students to comment about the page. Include all students in the discussion by asking **multi-level questions,** such as *Who do you see? Are they at the bank? Where are they?*

Exploring key vocabulary. Point to each vocabulary item in the Data Bank as you introduce it: *a CD, a cassette tape, a video tape,* etc. Ask students to repeat these words **chorally.** Elicit that libraries carry many things besides books.

Checking understanding. Have students listen and point to the appropriate pictures as you describe the situation. *She is at the library. She is looking for some books about animals. The librarian finds some good books for her. She checks out three books. She needs to bring the books back next week.* Check understanding, *What is she looking for?*

Encourage them to respond, *She is looking for books about animals.* Expand your questions to meet the capabilities of your students.

 **GUIDED READING** Have the students follow along as you read the text or play the tape. Divide the class into groups. One group is the librarian, the other is the girl. Have the students read the conversational bubbles in groups, switching roles. Then have partners practice the conversation, substituting words from the Data Bank. Circulate and help as needed.

SKILLS JOURNAL PAGE 82 **Asking/answering questions.** Students write answers to questions independently and ask interview questions. Teaching suggestions are provided in the Skills Journal annotation.

MULTICULTURAL AWARENESS

Invite students to tell you about libraries in their home cultures. Did they have a library near their home? Could they check out books? How long could they keep them? You may want to suggest that students ask parents or older family members if they do not recall themselves.

Roleplaying checking out books. Have students work in pairs to roleplay checking out books on different topics, modeling their conversation after that on Student Book page 91. First, brainstorm ideas on topics students might be interested in. Make a list on the board. Circulate and help as needed. Encourage students to switch roles and continue. You may want to set up a class library where students can check out books during free time. Make classroom library cards for the students to use. Students can make a schedule of when books are due.

MATH Word problems. Explain to the students that a library usually charges a fine for late books. Give students examples based on the procedure at your local library. Ask students word problems, for example, *Tina borrowed one book from the library. The fine was a nickel a day. She returned the book three days late. How much did she have to pay?* You may also want to substitute videotapes or CDs with larger fines ($.25 or $1 per day).

ONGOING ASSESSMENT

PERFORMANCE Oral language. Ask students to roleplay the conversation in the Student Book. Observe different students' participation. Use the **Oral Language Checklist** in the *Amazing Assessment Package.*

PORTFOLIO Writing. Save **Skills Journal** page 82 as an example of interviewing skills.

CHECK THIS OUT!

Animals Wild and Tame

LEVEL C, PAGES 92–93

KEY EXPERIENCES

- Using titles to predict content
- Reading short selections
- Recalling details
- Scanning
- Reading "Amazing Facts"
- Discussing animals

KEY LANGUAGE

- cicada, cricket, grasshopper, grip

1 INTRODUCE

MULTI-LEVEL TEACHING STRATEGIES

Building background: Recalling details. Open to pages 92–93 of the Student Book. Ask students to read the titles and look carefully at the pictures. After one minute, have them close their books. Engage students in a discussion of what the selections are about. Include all the students in the discussion by asking questions appropriate to each student's language stage. Here are some sample questions:

Speech Emergence: *What sound does a cat make? What sound does a dog make? What are you going to read about in the box titled "Animal Talk"?*

Developing Fluency: *What did you see? What was strange about the birds? What do you think the selection "The Year of the Dragon" is about?*

Playing a rhyme game. Have each child make two cards. On one card students should print the word *rhyme* and on the other the words *don't rhyme*. Then say pairs of words that rhyme as well as words that don't rhyme. Have students hold up the correct card. You might begin with these examples of rhyming words: *grow/toe, goes/clothes, eyes/size*.

Previewing vocabulary. Show the students pictures of an elephant, a grasshopper, a beetle, and a cicada, if available. Also include pictures of some of the animals on Student Book page 27 from the Chinese calendar (rat, tiger, ox, hare, snake, horse, sheep, monkey, rooster, pig). Name each animal with the students. Make word cards for the animals. Help students match the word cards and the picture cards.

2 EXPLORE

Activating prior knowledge. Open to pages 92–93 again. Call on volunteers to read the titles aloud. Ask students to predict what the readings will be about. For "The Year of the Dragon—2000," ask students where they have seen something like this before. (page 27)

GUIDED READING Scanning. Direct students' attention to "The Year of the Dragon—2000." Read the introduction or play the tape. Ask students to **scan** for the following information: *What animal is (1998) named for? What animal comes after Snake? Before Tiger? Is (1997) the year of the (Ox) or the year of the (Pig)?* Tailor the questions to the capabilities of your students; maintain a rapid pace.

Predicting. Direct students' attention to "Don't Lose That Grip!" Read the first line, *Have you ever wondered how birds sleep?* Elicit ideas. Do a **choral reading** of the text. Check comprehension, *How do birds sleep? Why don't they fall off?* (CALLA: Predicting)

SCIENCE Reading for information: Amazing Facts. Ask a prereading question: *How do insects hear?* Have students read **independently.** Ask about each insect: *How does a cicada hear?* Encourage students to respond, *A cicada hears with its stomach.* Ask students to make comparisons: *A cicada hears with its stomach, but a cricket hears with its front legs.*

Reading a poem. Have students listen to the rhyme and rhythm as you read the poem "Way Down South." Have students follow along as you present the poem again. Do a **choral reading** of the poem. Ask for volunteers to read different lines of the poem. Ask literal and inferential questions tailored to your students, for example, *What did the grasshopper do? How did the elephant feel?*

Scanning. Direct students' attention to "Animal Talk." Ask, *What three animals do you see in the box?* Ask the students to **scan** for the answers. *What does a (dog) say in (Japanese)?* Continue asking questions, pausing only briefly for students to scan for the answers.

SKILLS JOURNAL
PAGES 83–84

Reading for a purpose. Students read a paragraph about insects and write answers to questions. **Writing new poetry verses.** Students write and illustrate their own poems. Teaching suggestions are provided in the Skills Journal annotation.

• • • **3 EXTEND** • • •

ART Making animal puppets. Bring books about different animals to class. Have students look through the books and select their favorite animal. Have students make paper bag puppets of their favorite animals. Ask volunteers to present their animals to the class and demonstrate some of the sounds the animal makes.

- - - - **ONGOING ASSESSMENT** - - - -

PORTFOLIO Save **Skills Journal** page 83 as an example of reading comprehension.

STAFF DEVELOPMENT
See the *Amazing How-To Handbook* for additional information on developing reading strategies.

LANGUAGE POWER A

Animals Wild and Tame

LEVEL C, PAGE 94

KEY EXPERIENCES

- Guided reading
- Identifying a sequence
- Using map skills
- Retelling a story
- Learning about seeing-eye dogs

KEY LANGUAGE

- Past tense verbs: traveled, waited, loaded, collected, patted, boarded, counted, started up, shouted
- passengers, seeing-eye dog

••• 1 INTRODUCE •••

MULTI-LEVEL TEACHING STRATEGIES

Building background. Ask the students to open their books to page 94 and cover the text. Give them time to look carefully at the pictures. Say, *The story is about a girl named Mary. She takes a trip.* Ask students to predict what happens in the story. Include all students by asking questions appropriate to each student's language stage. Here are some sample questions:

Speech Emergence: (Point to each picture.) *Who do you see? Is she waiting for the bus? Where is she going?*

Developing Fluency: *Who is with Mary? Why do you think she has her dog with her? Who does Mary visit?*

Identifying a sequence. After you have discussed each picture, review the sequence. Write *first, second, next,* and *then* on the board. Point to the first square, *First Mary waited for the bus.* Continue with the other pictures. Work **T-C** or **S-S.**

GEOGRAPHY Using map skills. Use a map of the U.S. or of California. Explain that Mary traveled to Los Angeles to visit her grandmother. It took her four hours to get there. Have students look at the map and brainstorm where Mary might live. Consider the speed of the bus, for example, *If the bus goes 60 mph, where does she live?* Encourage students to also use a mileage chart of California, if one is available. (CALLA: Problem solving)

Previewing vocabulary. Print the following words on the board: *traveled, waited, loaded, collected, patted, boarded, counted, started up, shouted.* Help students read the verbs. As you read each word, clap on *-ed* to emphasize the separate syllable. Then ask the students to spell each word **chorally.** Have students copy the words on paper.

••• 2 EXPLORE •••

Activating prior knowledge. Have students uncover the text at the top of page 94. Ask students to scan for the verbs ending in *-ed.* Students point to the verbs as you demonstrate, pantomime, explain or have a student explain each one: *traveled, waited, loaded, collected, patted, boarded, counted, started up, shouted.*

 **GUIDED READING** Ask students to point to each picture as you read the text or play the tape. Then have students do **independent reading.** Check comprehension, *What did Mary do in the first picture?* Encourage students to respond, *She waited for the bus.* Continue

with other **multi-level questions** tailored to the capabilities of your students. Read the text or play the tape again and have students follow along **chorally.**

Practicing the conversation. Read or play the tape for the conversation at the bottom of the page. Have students point to the lines as they listen. Read the conversation again, pausing for students to repeat.

Help students substitute other phrases for "...*travel to Chicago*" so that all the past tense verbs are practiced. For example, ask, *Did Mary's cat travel with her? Did they wait at the bus stop?*

Completing a crossword puzzle using past tense verbs. Students fill in the blanks with the past tense of verbs in the Data Bank and write them in the crossword puzzle. Teaching suggestions are provided in the Skills Journal annotation.

Spelling practice. Print the base form of the verbs used in the story: *travel, wait,* etc. Ask students to write the past tense form of each verb (*traveled,* etc.). Circulate and check spelling. Ask the students to read the words aloud, emphasizing the pronunciation.

Retelling the story. Have students work in groups of four. Assign parts: Mary, the driver, the narrator, the prompter. Group the students so that the stronger students are the narrator and prompter. The narrator covers the text and retells the story using the illustrations. The prompter listens and uses the text to help the narrator as needed. The students who are Mary and the driver listen and pantomime the actions.

SCIENCE Learning about seeing-eye dogs. Help students use resource materials to find out how seeing-eye dogs are trained. If there is a training facility in your community, invite someone to speak to the class. Help students make a list of questions to ask, for example, *How long does it take to train a dog? How old is the dog when the training starts? What do the trainers do to train the dogs? What kinds of dogs are used?* (CALLA: Resourcing)

Building vocabulary. Use *Amazing English!* Word Attack 3 Interactive Vocabulary Games for practice with vocabulary.

ONGOING ASSESSMENT

PERFORMANCE Oral Language. Circulate as the students retell the story. Observe different levels of participation. Use the **Oral Language Checklist** in the *Amazing Assessment Package.*

STAFF DEVELOPMENT

See the *Amazing How-To Handbook* for additional ways to develop problem-solving strategies.

BACKGROUND INFORMATION

If students seem interested, you may want to expand the discussion to include other types of companion animals. These include dogs trained to be the "ears" for people who are hearing impaired and dogs trained to help quadriplegics. In a few instances, small monkeys have also been trained to assist quadriplegics.

LANGUAGE POWER B

Animals Wild and Tame

LEVEL C, PAGE 95

KEY EXPERIENCES

- Expressing ownership
- Talking about pets
- Reviewing pet vocabulary

KEY LANGUAGE

- *This is my/his dog.*
- *That is your/her cat /parrot.*
- *these are our gerbils.*
- *Those are their turtles.*
- *pets*

●●● 1 INTRODUCE ●●●

MULTI-LEVEL TEACHING STRATEGIES

Activating prior knowledge. Open the Student Book to page 55. Review the sentences at the bottom of the page, *I am looking for my hat*, etc. Say, *The students are going home now. Let's help them find their things.* Point to the picture and ask, *Where is (her skate)?* Point to her other roller skate and say, *This is her skate.* Continue. Ask a variety of questions to prompt responses that include, *That is his, These are his, These are their*, etc. Include all the students by asking questions appropriate to each student's language stage. Here are some sample questions:

Speech Emergence: *Is this her skate? Where is her other skate?*

Developing Fluency: *What are these?* Encourage the long utterance, *Those are their sweaters.*

Expressing ownership. Print the following sentences on the board: *This is my jacket. That is your pen. This is his book. That is her book. These are our papers. Those are their papers.* Help students read the sentences. Say, *"This" and "these" are close; "that" and "those" are far away.*

Using TPR. Circulate around the room, indicating items: *This is my desk.* Alternate pointing to items that are close and far away as you model the sentences: *This is his jacket. That is her jacket.* Gesture as you model the sentences. Cue individual students to point to an item in the classroom and make sentence; work **T-S.**

MUSIC Playing a game. Students march in a circle around the room as you play music. When you stop the music, the students stop. Cue students with *close* and *far away.*, for example, *Tina, close.* Tina identifies something near her: *This is Tony's desk.* Continue, *Adam, far away.* Adam identifies something far away: *That is her book.*

●●● 2 EXPLORE ●●●

Activating prior knowledge. Open to page 95. Encourage students to comment about the page. Have a volunteer read the title, "Pet Show." What do students think a pet show is? Has anyone ever been to a pet show?

Exploring new vocabulary. Point to and name each pronoun and noun, *my dog, your cat, his goat, her parrot, our gerbils, their turtles.* Students repeat. Ask, *Who has a (dog) as a pet?* Ask the students to point to the correct picture.

 **Look, listen, and talk.** Have students look, listen, and point to the appropriate pictures as you read the text or play the tape. Check comprehension, *Whose goat is that?* Encourage students to respond, *That is his goat.* Then have students read the text **chorally.** For the sentences beginning *This/These*, have students point at their desks as they read the sentence. For the sentences beginning *That/Those*, have them point toward the front of the room as they read.

Paired reading. Have students practice reading with a partner. One student points to a picture; the other student reads the text. Students switch roles and repeat. Ask them to gesture as they read to reinforce the idea of close vs. far away.

SKILLS JOURNAL PAGE 86 **Expressing ownership.** Students work independently to complete the cloze exercise using a Data Bank, then they share their responses with the class. Teaching suggestions are provided in the Skills Journal annotation.

LIFE SKILLS Writing about pet care. Have students choose a pet and find out how to take care of it. Brainstorm a list of questions to ask about. They can interview another student who has the same pet or talk to someone at a pet shop. Have students write up daily instructions as well as special weekly or monthly tasks. Have students exchange papers and make corrections. Pair students of varying abilities to promote cooperative learning. (CALLA: Brainstorming)

SCIENCE Caring for a pet. Make arrangements to have a small classroom pet, such as a gerbil, guinea pig, or hamster. With the students, print a set of instructions for caring for the pet. Assign students to take care of the pet on a daily basis. Post a schedule next to the pet's cage. Encourage students to ask questions whenever they are not sure what to do, whose turn it is, etc. (CALLA: Questioning for clarification)

STAFF DEVELOPMENT

See the *Amazing How-To Handbook* for other ways to implement TPR in the classroom.

WRITING PROJECT

Writing Project 5A, *How to Take Care of a Pet,* is directly linked to this lesson. See the Process Writing Portfolio Program Teachers' Handbook, pages 24-25, for the Lesson Plan.

Students will find instructions and a Prewriting Sheet in the Writing Projects booklet inside the Portfolio.

153

HANDS-ON SCIENCE

Animals Wild and Tame

LEVEL C, PAGES 96–97

KEY EXPERIENCES

- Identifying animals
- Learning about animal habitats
- Reading/following directions
- Making a chart
- Comparing habitats

KEY LANGUAGE

- names of animals
- habitats

1 INTRODUCE

MULTI-LEVEL TEACHING STRATEGIES

Building background: Identifying animals. Show the students photographs of wild and tame animals: *tiger, giraffe, elephant, zebra, cow, pig,* etc. Print the names on the board under the word *Animals.* Help the students read each name. Then brainstorm the names of some habitats: *forest, jungle, plains, river, ocean, farm.* List them on the board under *Habitats.* Help the students identify each animal and say where it lives. Include all students in the discussion by asking questions appropriate to each student's language stage. Here are some sample questions:

Speech Emergence: (Point to a picture.) *Is this a cow or a horse? Does a cow live on a farm or in the jungle?*

Developing Fluency: (Point to a picture.) *This is a lion. On which continent do lions live? Have you ever seen a lion at a zoo?*

Using TPR. Ask student volunteers to pantomime each of the animals. The rest of the class guesses the animal.

2 EXPLORE

Activating prior knowledge. Direct the students' attention to pages 96–97 of the Student Book. Read the title, "Animal Habitats," aloud. Ask for examples of what a habitat is.

GUIDED READING Reading directions. Have students look and listen as you read the directions. Remind students that directions often start with simple verbs. Ask the students to read the directions carefully, paying attention to the verbs, *find out, choose, draw,* etc. Then ask students to read the directions **independently.** Check understanding with **multi-level questions** such as *What are we going to make? What do you do first? Then what do you choose? In step 2, what two things do you do? In step 3?* Prompt as needed.

Following directions. Have students follow the steps and create an animal habitat chart. First help students decide which animals they will research in order to have a variety of animals on the chart. In small groups, have students share the interesting facts they learned about the animals they researched. Encourage them to make comparisons, for example, *Monkeys live in forests, but whales live in the ocean.* (CALLA: Cooperation)

SKILLS JOURNAL PAGE 87

Reading for a purpose; writing. Students read a paragraph about elephants and write answers to questions. Teaching suggestions are provided in the Skills Journal annotation.

SCIENCE Learning about the Amazon rain forest. Help students find out what animals live in the Amazon rain forest. Help them learn about how the rain forest is being reduced by economic development and the impact this is having on the animals that live there. Encourage students to use resource materials at the library to get information. (CALLA: Resourcing)

SCIENCE Comparing habitats. Have students choose the habitats of two animals to compare. Students can make comparisons regarding rainfall, temperature, vegetation, location, etc. Students can work in pairs, then share their information in small groups to promote cooperative learning. (CALLA: Cooperation)

Developing critical thinking skills. Ask students to use the information they have learned about different animal habitats to consider the task of designing a zoo. In small groups, have students design exhibits; for example, one group can design an elephant exhibit, one can design a polar bear exhibit, etc. Have students use the information from the habitat chart as they consider the temperature, vegetation, water, etc. needed at each exhibit. Ask students to make drawings of their exhibits. Encourage groups to help each other. (CALLA: Organizational planning)

ONGOING ASSESSMENT

PORTFOLIO Writing. Ask students to use the animal habitat chart to write four sentences about different animals. Have students exchange writing and make corrections. Use the **Writing Checklist** in the *Amazing Assessment Package.*

STAFF DEVELOPMENT

See *The CALLA Handbook* for more on using science in the ESL classroom and on CALLA strategies.

TEACHER TO TEACHER

If your students work with other teachers, you may want to mention to them that the students have been learning about animal habitats. Suggest that teachers look for opportunities to discuss this topic in other classes.

KOKO'S COMPUTER

Animals Wild and Tame

LEVEL C, PAGES 98–101

KEY EXPERIENCES

- Reading a nonfiction selection
- Learning about gorillas
- Relating Koko's language learning to students' experiences

KEY LANGUAGE

- American Sign Language, mad, mittens, icon, symbol

1 INTRODUCE

MULTI-LEVEL TEACHING STRATEGIES

Building background: Previewing the selection. Open to page 98 of the Student Book. Read the title, "Koko's Computer," aloud or call on a volunteer to do so. Ask, *What is this animal?* Then have students look at the other photographs on pages 99–101 and predict what the story is about. Encourage the students to use their imaginations. Include all students in the discussion by asking questions appropriate to each student's language stage.

Speech Emergence: (Point to a picture.) *Is this (a baby gorilla)? What is Koko doing here?*

Developing Fluency: (Point to the picture on page 99.) *Why is Koko covering her eyes? How does she feel? What does Koko use the computer for? What does Koko like to eat?*

SCIENCE Learning about gorillas. In the Learning Center display pictures and books about gorillas in the wild and in zoos. Help students gather information from the pictures by asking questions: *Are grown-up gorillas bigger or smaller than people? Do gorillas have tails? What do gorillas eat?*

SOCIAL STUDIES Learning about American Sign Language. Tell students that gorillas are very intelligent. Koko's trainer taught Koko to talk. One way she talks is with sign language. Say, *I'm going to teach you some of the signs Koko knows.* Write the words on the board and teach the students the following ASL signs:

cat (move thumb and index fingers out from nose, drawing whiskers)
good (stroke right hand out over left palm)
mad (spread fingers and jerk thumbs up over shoulders; look angry)
love (hug self)

2 EXPLORE

Activating prior knowledge. Have students look at the pictures on 98–101 again. Ask, *What do you want to know about Koko?* Write students' questions on the board.

GUIDED READING Have students close their books. Read or play the tape for "Koko's Computer" as the students listen. As you present the story, point to the illustrations and comment on the scene. Encourage comments from the students as well. On page 101, point out the *icons* or *symbols* on the computer. Pause for students to read Koko's sentence and try to correct it.

Developing comprehension skills. Check understanding and help students develop critical thinking skills by asking **multi-level questions** such as the following:

Page 98: *Is Koko a baby or a grown-up in this picture? What is Koko doing? Is Koko in a zoo?* Page 99: *Who is in this picture? What is Dr. Patterson reading? Does Koko like the story? In the story, the mother cat is mad at her kittens. Show me the sign for "mad."*

Page 100–101: *Is Koko a baby or a grown-up in this picture? What is Koko doing? What icons does Koko have on her computer? How does Koko use the computer? Can she hear what she types in? What does Koko do for fun? What does she like to eat? What are her favorite foods?*

Paired reading. Have partners reread the story, alternating paragraphs. To promote cooperative learning, encourage students to ask each other about unfamiliar words or parts of the story they don't understand.

Reading for a purpose; completing a cloze exercise. Students work independently to complete sentences about Koko. **Communicating through American Sign Language; socializing.** Students identify signs and make up their own message to sign to their friends. Teaching suggestions are provided in the Skills Journal annotations.

Koko's address. For more information about Koko, have the students write to The Gorilla Foundation, PO Box 620530, Woodside, CA 94062.

Writing questions for Koko. Ask students, *Would you like to be Koko's teacher? What questions would you ask her on the computer?* Ask students to complete the sentence starter, *I'd ask Koko ...* Encourage students to write a list of questions. In pairs, have students take turns reading their questions. Ask their partners to point to the icons Koko might use to answer them. (CALLA: Deduction)

· · · ONGOING ASSESSMENT · · ·

PORTFOLIO Reading comprehension. Save **Skills Journal** page 88 as an example of reading comprehension.

BACKGROUND INFORMATION
Gorillas live in central and west central Africa. They live in family groups of 5–30 members with one adult male leader. Gorillas eat plants. They spend about half of the day looking for food and eating and the rest of the day taking it easy in the sun. Gorillas are the largest of the great apes. Adult gorillas are often over 6 feet tall and weigh 300–400 pounds. Despite their size and great strength, gorillas are shy and peace loving. They are an endangered species.

TEACHER TO TEACHER
Display a copy of the manual alphabet used in American Sign Language (ASL). Encourage students to look at the alphabet and try to learn more signs. Invite a resource person to teach the students, if possible.

WRITING PROJECT
Writing Project 5B, *Animal Talk,* is directly linked to this lesson. See the Process Writing Portfolio Program Teachers' Handbook, pages 26-27, for the Lesson Plan.

Students will find instructions and a Prewriting Sheet in the Writing Projects booklet inside the Portfolio.

HOLISTIC ASSESSMENT

Animals Wild and Tame

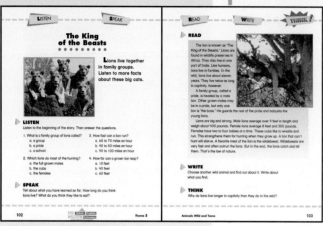

LEVEL C, PAGES 102–103

KEY EXPERIENCES

- Learning about lions
- Listening for information
- Reading factual information
- Predicting outcome
- Expressing opinions

KEY LANGUAGE

- captivity, cubs, hunting, leap,
- outrun, preserves, pride

• • • 1 INTRODUCE • • •

MULTI-LEVEL TEACHING STRATEGIES

These two pages offer a variety of assessment opportunities. The left-hand page consists of listening and speaking activities that follow a taped presentation. In the speaking activity, students are asked to summarize the story and make predictions based on what they have heard. The right-hand page consists of writing and critical thinking activities. These follow a reading passage that completes the listening component. You can use the activities to assess listening, speaking, reading, writing, and critical thinking skills. Have children work as a class or in small groups. Record your observations as appropriate on the **Anecdotal Record Form,** the **Reading Checklist,** and the **Writing Checklist** in the *Amazing Assessment Package.*

Building background: Introducing the topic. Begin by asking students if anyone has seen a lion in a zoo. Tell students that most lions in the wild live in Africa. Ask if anyone knows where Africa is. Have volunteers point it out on a map. Tell students that lions are members of the cat family. If possible, bring in pictures of lions. Then ask questions appropriate to each student's language stage. Here are some sample questions:

Speech Emergence: *Have you ever seen a lion? Was it in a zoo? Where do lions in the wild live?*

Developing Fluency: *Are lions in the zoo tame or wild? Where is Africa? What domestic animals do lions look like? (cats)*

• • • 2 EXPLORE • • •

Previewing the topic. Open the Student Book to page 102 and let the students (child) comment on the picture. Say, *Today we are going to learn about lions.* Ask, *What are lions like?*

Preparing to listen. Tell the students they will listen to the tape and learn some facts about lions. Do **choral reading** of the listening questions. Give students time to read the questions independently.

▓ Listening to the story. Read or play the tape for the first part of "The King of the Beasts." You will find the tapescript in the Appendix.

Have students work independently to answer the listening questions. Read or play the tape again in segments; pause for students to check their work and make corrections.

Speaking. Ask **multi-level questions** as you encourage the students to talk about what they have learned in the story so far, *What is a family of lions called? Do the cubs do most of the hunting? Who does the hunting?*

GUIDED READING Read the story on Student Book page 103 as the students listen and follow along in their books. Have the students do **partner reading,** alternating paragraphs. Ask **multi-level** questions, such as *Where do lions live? How long do they live in the wild?*

Observing the students. As you discuss the story, notice the level of participation and the particular abilities of each child. What new words have they learned? What language structures do they use? Which students use only single word responses? Which students can speak in long utterances? You may want to add progress notes to students' **portfolios** at this time. Use the **Anecdotal Record Form** in the *Amazing Assessment Package.*

Reading comprehension. Students work independently to complete cloze sentences, using words from a Data Bank. Teaching suggestions are provided in the Skills Journal annotation. Save this page in the student's **Assessment Portfolio.**

SCIENCE Researching other cats. Help students use resource materials to find out about another member of the cat family. Provide photos of other cats and help students with names: *tiger, cheetah, leopard, cougar.* Then have students use the story on lions as a guide for questions they might research about another cat. (CALLA: Resourcing)

Critical thinking. Ask the students to consider why lions live longer in captivity than in the wild. Encourage them to discuss their ideas in small groups. Give students time to write one or two sentences. Ask volunteers to share their ideas with the class. To assess students' work, use the **Writing Checklist** in the *Amazing Assessment Package.*

STAFF DEVELOPMENT
See the *Amazing How-To Handbook* and *Authentic Assessment* for more on holistic assessment and other assessment topics.

AMAZING FACTS

Animals Wild and Tame

LEVEL C, PAGE 104

KEY EXPERIENCES

- Predicting questions
- Recalling details
- Playing a game
- Creating a game

KEY LANGUAGE

- Review

MULTI-LEVEL TEACHING STRATEGIES

Activating prior knowledge. Use the animal habitat chart from Student Book pages 96–97. Engage the students in a review of wild and tame animals and animal habitats. Include all students in the activity by asking questions appropriate to each student's language stage. Here are some sample questions:

Speech Emergence: (Point to a picture on the chart.) *What animal lives here? Is this a tiger or a lion? Tell me the names of two wild animals.*

Developing Fluency: *What animal lives here? Where do monkeys live? Tell me two tame animals people like to have for pets.*

🎵🎶

📻 **MUSIC "Do the Dog Walk."** Play the tape or sing the song as the students use their books to sing along (page 89). During the animal sound verses, have the students walk in a circle like each animal as they sing. Continue, singing several verses the students wrote.

Retelling a story. Print on the board: *rushed, kissed, opened, asked, answered, washed, dried, brushed, trimmed, tied, looked.* Help the students read the words. Ask, *How do you spell (rushed)?* Work **T-C.** Open to page 87. Point to the pictures as you ask students questions to help them retell the story. For example, ask, *What did she do when she got home from school?* Encourage students to respond, using the sequence words, *first, second, then, next,* for example, *First she kissed her mom.*

2 EXPLORE

Activating prior knowledge. Open to page 104. Have students cover the questions. Ask, *How do you play the Amazing Facts game?* Continue, *What do we need to do first?* (Divide into teams.) Group students of varying abilities.

Predicting the questions. Ask, *What did you learn about Koko the gorilla?* Encourage students to share what they remember. Continue, *What animals are in the Chinese calendar?* See how many animals the class can remember without looking at the Student Book. (CALLA: Predicting)

Playing the game. Set the time limit and have the teams work together to answer the questions. Circulate and help as needed. At the end of the time period, have the teams compete for the correct answers orally. Read the questions in random order. The first team to raise their hands and answer the question correctly wins a point. The team with the most points at the end of play wins the game.

Challenge. For extra fluency practice, ask the students to answer the questions in complete sentences: *Koko makes sentences with her computer.*

Creating a game. Students create their own Amazing Facts games, researching answers if necessary. Teaching suggestions are provided in the Skills Journal annotation.

Amazing Facts Games revisited. Divide the students into new teams. Ask students Amazing Facts questions from Themes 1–4. Students answer orally. On the board, keep track of the score. The team with the most points at the end of play is the winner. Talk about the facts. Encourage students to help each other remember what they have read.

ART Making a comic strip. Have students create a few comic book frames of a story about animals. Have them use the habitat chart for information and ideas. Encourage them to draw speech bubbles and add animal sounds. Students can work in pairs or small groups to write and illustrate their work. Display in the classroom.

Playing *What Year Was I Born?* Some people believe a person's personality is influenced by the year in which the person is born. For example, someone born in the year of the rooster might like to wake up early and make some noise. On index cards, write the names of the twelve animals in the Chinese calendar. Give each student a card. Ask the student to do an activity in the manner of his or her animal. The rest of the class guesses, *Were you born in the Year of the Rooster?* or *Are you a rooster?* depending on the language capabilities of your students.

Home-School Connection. Have the students take home the Amazing Facts game they made in their Skills Journal. Encourage them to play it with their families and explain the facts.

- - - - - - **ONGOING ASSESSMENT** - - - - - -

PERFORMANCE Listening comprehension; oral language. Ask students to exchange the Amazing Facts games they created and play them in small groups. Circulate and observe student participation. Use the **Oral Language Checklist** in the *Amazing Assessment Package.*

TEACHER TO TEACHER

If your students work with other teachers, you may want to encourage them to remind students to add to their Learning Logs any new vocabulary they learn in their textbooks and in their reading for pleasure.

ASSESSMENT

You will find background information on the latest thinking in assessment as well as the assessment instruments for this theme in the *Amazing Assessment Package*.

You have been collecting assessment data through the ongoing and holistic assessment options (Oral Language Checklist, Reading Checklist, Writing Checklist, Anecdotal Record Form) in this theme. The following are specific end-of-theme assessment strategies that will help you evaluate your students' progress as well as adapt your instruction to meet their needs.

Student Self-Assessment. Self-assessment surveys are a means for students to have input into their own learning process. Students can use them to **reflect** on the work they have done and the learning strategies they have used during this theme.

Interpreting and Applying Assessment Data. As teachers, you collect assessment data in order to inform your instruction. Assessment information is a tool that helps you tailor your program to better meet the needs and interests of your students.

Evaluate the checklists, anecdotal records, portfolio collections, and test results from this theme as a means of informing your instruction.

- In which areas are students showing confidence and enthusiasm?
- In which areas are they hesitant or confused?
- Should you provide more classroom opportunities for oral language or writing?
- Would certain students (or the whole class) benefit from a focused mini-lesson on a certain area or skill?
- Remember to recycle skills as you teach the next theme and provide students with many opportunities to improve their competence.

Review the results of the **Student Self-Assessment** survey and incorporate students' interests as you plan your instruction for the next theme. What do they want to learn next? Which activities did they enjoy most? If your students particularly enjoyed choral reading, roleplaying, or working in partners, try to emphasize those kinds of activities in the next theme.

THEME CELEBRATION

The end of a theme study is a good time for students to share some of their accomplishments with others. Suggest to students that you hold a celebration to spotlight their work. This celebration can be an excellent opportunity to build stronger connections with other students and teachers in the school. Your students can show their piggy banks and give a demonstration of how to make them. Students can perform new verses of "Do the Dog Walk," teach the American Sign Language alphabet, and share the Amazing Facts games they have researched and played. If possible, invite family members to the theme celebration.

END-OF-THEME READ-ALOUD BOOK

I Am the Dog, I Am the Cat

by Donald Hall

illustrated by Barry Moser

New York: Dial Books, 1994

A dog and a cat take turns telling about themselves—what they do, what they like, and essentially, who they are. This insightful dialogue illuminates animals' motivations behind their behavior. Toward the end, the cat and dog list the qualities that give them the most pride.

It's important to get students excited about independent reading. Remember to distribute the Literature Links Bibliography for the next theme to your students and encourage them to use the *Amazing Book Bytes* CD-ROM to respond to their reading.

Changing Seasons

THEME 6

PREVIEW

In Theme 6, students explore work and recreation in the world outdoors. Through literature, articles, poetry, and language activity pages in the **Student Book**, students will learn about the seasons and the weather. They will compare snowfall in several cities, make an accordion book from Asian tradition, and read two folktales, one from Japan and one from Africa. The **Skills Journal** offers opportunities for further language practice, reading, writing, and research on a variety of theme-related topics.

Multi-Level Teaching Strategies integrated into each lesson plan insure that all students can participate in these class activities, each at his or her own level of language proficiency. **Home-School Connection** activities provide enjoyable extension activities for students and family members to do together.

The **Ongoing Assessment** suggestions in the lesson plans will help you keep track of your students' progress. On **Student Book** pages 124-125, the "Listen, Speak, Read, Write, Think" selection offers an opportunity for **holistic assessment**. The end-of-theme **Wrap-Up** page includes guidelines for implementing the full range of assessment tools and interpreting the results.

PLANNING TIPS

The **At-a-Glance Lesson Planner** on the next two pages provides an overview of the Key Experiences and Key Language presented in each lesson of the theme. Quickly scan the lesson plan Materials lists to see if there are materials to gather or prepare. Check the **Wrap-Up** page in case you want to plan ahead for the Theme Celebration.

The following **Read-Aloud Books** are recommended with this theme. Gather these titles and your own theme-related favorites. We encourage you to read aloud to your students every day. If possible, record the stories on tape and let students reread the books as they listen to the tapes.

- *Alligators and Others All Year Long* by Crescent Dragonwagon
- *Where the Sidewalk Ends* by Shel Silverstein
- *Frederick's Fables* by Leo Lionni
- *The Giving Tree* by Shel Silverstein
- *Weather Report* by Jane Yolen
- *The Seasons of Arnold's Apple Tree* by Gail Gibbons (Wrap-Up page)

READING CORNER

Encourage independent reading for information and pleasure. If possible, set up a reading corner—a quiet, comfortable place that is just for reading (and perhaps listening to any books on tape you've collected). Make a bulletin board on which you can post book covers, students' BookBytes reviews and the Literature Links Bibliographies that support each theme. See the Appendix for the complete Literature Links Bibliography for this theme. It offers a variety of fiction and non-fiction choices **in English and in other languages.**

163

LESSON PLAN

KEY EXPERIENCES

1 **Student Book p. 105**
Theme Opener

Talking about seasons • Describing one's favorite season • Predicting meaning of theme titles • Brainstorming ideas

2 **Student Book p. 106**
Communication 1A

Talking about seasonal activities • Roleplaying conversations • Following conversational sequence • Reading "Amazing Facts" • Making a graph

3 **Student Book p. 107**
Communication 1B

Discussing the growth cycle of plants • Interpreting visual images • Talking about seasonal chores • Drawing seed germination

4 **Student Book p. 108**
Read and Do

Discussing kites and kite-flying • Reading/following directions • Making a kite • Talking about air pressure and lift

5 **Student Book p. 109**
Dreams

Guided reading of a poem • Discussing metaphors • Discussing dreams and their importance • Enjoying other poems

6 **Student Book p. 110**
Communication 2A

Telling a story in question-and-answer form • Following a sequence • Describing past actions • Asking for/giving information

7 **Student Book p. 111**
Communication 2B

Talking about/describing the weather • Roleplaying conversations • Creating new conversations • Keeping a weather log

8 **Student Book pp. 112-113**
Check This Out!

Talking about geography and climate • Reading short selections • Summarizing • Reading "Amazing Facts" • Making comparisons

9 **Student Book p. 114**
Language Power A

Talking about seasons/plants • Reading • Expressing obligation • Relating reading to own experience • Learning about plants

10 **Student Book p. 115**
Language Power B

Asking for/giving information • Describing past actions • Describing sequence • Talking about responsibilities • Roleplaying conversations

11 **Student Book pp. 116-117**
Hands-On Social Studies

Reading/following directions • Making an accordion book • Learning about holidays in other countries • Planning a treasure hunt

12 **Student Book pp. 118-123**
The Grateful Statues

Reading and enjoying a multicultural folktale • Talking about characters and setting • Learning about festivals and customs in Japan

13 **Student Book pp. 124-125**
Holistic Assessment

Listening for information • Reading and enjoying a folktale from Africa • Predicting outcomes • Expressing opinions

14 **Student Book p. 126**
Amazing Facts Game

Recalling details • Reading for information • Playing a game • Creating a game • Critical thinking: Synthesizing information

KEY LANGUAGE

spring, summer, fall, winter • pumpkins, seasons, weather

What's your favorite season? • What do you do in the (winter)? • cold, snowy, ice skating, fishing, sledding, swimming, kites

What does she have to do in the (spring)? • She has to (dig). • ground, have to, hose, leaves, rake, seeds, shovel, snow, tree, yard

kite, paper bag, roll of string

barren, dreams, hold fast

Where did he . . .? • What did he . . .? • Irregular verbs: eat/ate, drink/drank, go/went, ride/rode, catch/caught

What's the weather like? • It's (very cold and snowy). • What's the weather forecast for tomorrow? • It's going to be (cloudy and rainy).

gust of wind, desert, poles, tropics, sea gull • Abbreviations: ME, AK, NY, VT, NH, CO

weeds, water, sweep, scrape off

Did you (play) after school yesterday? • No, I didn't. I had to (study). • deliver, practice, watch, dentist, papers, piano

China, Japan, Korea • accordion book, lightweight, scroll

New Year, rice cakes, statue, straw hat

delicious, garbage, gifts, starve, stuffed, waste

Review

CONTENT AREAS

Social Studies • Language Arts

Art • Math • Language Arts

Art • Science • Language Arts

Art • Language Arts

Art • Music • Language Arts

Social Studies • Language Arts

Science • Language Arts

Science • Social Studies • Language Arts

Music • Science • Language Arts

Social Studies • Language Arts

Art • Social Studies • Language Arts

Art • Language Arts

Assessment

Assessment

THEME OPENER

Changing Seasons

LEVEL C, PAGE 105

KEY EXPERIENCES

- Talking about seasons
- Describing one's favorite season
- Predicting meaning of theme titles
- Brainstorming ideas

KEY LANGUAGE

- spring, summer, fall, winter
- pumpkins, seasons, weather

1 INTRODUCE

MULTI-LEVEL TEACHING STRATEGIES

Building background: Discussing seasons. Discuss the photograph on page 105 of the Student Book. Call on a volunteer to read the unit title, "Changing Seasons," aloud. Find out if anyone knows what the four seasons are. Write the words *spring, summer, fall,* and *winter* on the board. Show students photographs of scenes during different seasons of the year. Talk about the weather and the seasons. Include all the students by asking questions appropriate to each student's language stage. Here are some sample questions:

Speech Emergence: (Point to a picture.) *Is it winter or summer? Is it spring or fall? Is it warm? Do you like winter?*

Developing Fluency: *What season is it? Name two things in the picture that tell you it is fall. Do you like fall? Why?*

Talking about the weather. Ask, *What is the weather like today?* Prompt with vocabulary as needed. Continue, *What was the weather like yesterday? Last weekend?* Work **Teacher-Class; Teacher-Student.** Ask, *How can we find out what the weather might be tomorrow?* Brainstorm ideas: *Listen to the TV or radio; Look in the newspaper.* If possible, show students the weather page from the local newspaper. Read the forecast. Ask, *Will it be cold? Will it rain?*, etc.

ART Drawing the weather. Ask students to draw a picture showing their favorite weather. Encourage them to draw themselves doing an activity they enjoy, such as sledding, swimming, or playing in the leaves.

2 EXPLORE

Activating prior knowledge. Direct students' attention to the first title, "Dreams." Tell the students one of your dreams, for example, *When I was young, I dreamed of becoming an astronaut. One of my dreams was to go to the moon.* Open the Student Book to page 70. Point to a picture: *When she was a girl, she dreamed of being a doctor. Now she helps sick people. When he was a boy, he dreamed of being a chef. Now he cooks food at a restaurant.* Continue with other examples to make sure students understand the difference between a dream we have while sleeping, and a wish or hope for the future.

SCIENCE Talking about weather facts. Say, *Let's talk about the weather. Let's see what we know.* On the board make a **word web.** Write *weather* in the center of the circle. Brainstorm ideas. Prompt by asking what the weather is like during different seasons, as well as what causes different weather. For example, *Who knows what makes the wind blow? Who knows why it rains?* (CALLA: Brainstorming)

Previewing. Explain that "The Grateful Statues" is a folktale. It is a story about an old man and woman who do something good. Ask students to guess what the story is about. Encourage students to use their imaginations. *Where do the man and woman live? What season is it? What is the weather like? What do they do?* (CALLA: Predicting)

 **Writing about a photograph; expressing ideas through art.** Students write a description of the photograph on the theme opener page and draw and write about their favorite season. Teaching suggestions are provided in the Skills Journal annotation.

Using TPR. Have students take turns pantomiming an activity they enjoy during their favorite season. The rest of the class identifies the activity, *swimming, jumping in leaves, playing soccer,* etc.

SCIENCE Making a weather chart. Help students make a chart, *Weather Facts.* Make two columns. In the left column write at least five questions that students want to learn the answers to during this unit, for example, *Why does it rain?* Encourage students to fill in the answers as they learn them, as well as add new questions as they work through the unit.

ART Illustrating predictions. Ask students to illustrate what they think "The Grateful Statues" is about. Encourage students to use their imaginations about what happens. Emphasize that this is only their best guess; they will read the story later.

ONGOING ASSESSMENT

PERFORMANCE Oral language. Ask the students to describe for you their drawings for "The Grateful Statues." Observe different students' levels of description. Use the **Oral Language Checklist** in the *Amazing Assessment Package*.

PORTFOLIO Independent writing. Save **Skills Journal** page 43 as an example of independent writing.

STAFF DEVELOPMENT
See *The CALLA Handbook* for suggestions on implementing CALLA in the classroom.

167

COMMUNICATION 1A

THEME 6 • • • • • • • •

Changing Seasons

LEVEL C, PAGE 106

KEY EXPERIENCES

- Talking about seasonal activities
- Roleplaying conversations
- Following conversational sequence
- Reading "Amazing Facts"
- Making a graph

KEY LANGUAGE

- *What's your favorite season?*
- *What do you do in the (winter)?*
- *I (go sledding and ice skating).*
- *cold, snowy*
- *ice skating, fishing, sledding, swimming*
- *kites*

MULTI-LEVEL TEACHING STRATEGIES

Building background. Ask students what they like to do with their friends during each season. As students name activities, keep a list on the board. List *-ing* forms wherever possible. Include all students in the discussion by asking questions appropriate to each student's language stage. Here are some sample questions:

Speech Emergence: *Do you like to go swimming? What is your favorite activity in the winter? Do you go ice skating with your friend?*

Developing Fluency: *Do you go fishing in the summer? What else do you do with friends?*

Playing a matching game. Mount photographs of different activities on cards. Create a second set with names of the activities. Use *-ing* forms wherever possible: *swimming, golfing, fishing, playing soccer, jogging,* etc. Have students work in teams or with partners to match words with the appropriate activities. Afterward have students brainstorm and classify activities in various ways, for example, by season, team vs. individual activities, indoor vs. outdoor. (CALLA: Classifying)

Activating prior knowledge. Open to page 106 of the Student Book. Ask students to comment about the page. *Who do you see? What are they doing?*

Exploring new vocabulary. Introduce and review vocabulary items *sledding, ice skating*. On the board, write, *I ice skate. I go ice skating. I swim. I go swimming. I fish. I go ...* Have students fill in the blank. Model the sentences **Teacher-Class.**

Look, listen, and talk. Have students look and listen as you read the text or play the tape of the text at the top of the page. Check understanding: *What is (his) favorite season? What does (he) do in the winter?*

Practicing the conversation. Read the text or play the tape again, pausing for students to repeat. Divide the class into two groups. One group asks the questions, the other answers. Have groups switch roles and repeat. In pairs, have students practice the conversation, switching roles. Then have students talk about themselves. You can put more able students with those needing extra practice. Circulate and help with vocabulary as needed.

Reading for information: Amazing Facts. Direct students' attention to the bottom of the page. Give students time to read the Amazing Facts **independently.** Then read or play the tape. Ask **multi-level questions,** such as *What do skywriters have to be able to do? Why? What did James Plimpton do? When? What is the world record for kites on a single line? How do you think you could put that many kites together?*

 **Data Collection.** Students conduct interviews, record the information in charts, and use it for paired conversation practice. Teaching suggestions are provided in the Skills Journal annotation.

SKILLS JOURNAL PAGE 94

MATH Making a graph. Have students do a class survey of favorite activities. Begin by having students brainstorm a list of activities and questions. Have students graph the data and compare student interests. (CALLA: Comparing)

ART Making a mural. Have students work in four groups to make a class mural showing their favorite seasonal activities. Have those who prefer winter work together on that section, etc. (CALLA: Cooperation)

Home-School Connection. Invite students to ask parents or older family members about the weather and seasons in their home countries. Later, students can share the information with classmates. Depending on the level of your class, you can use this information to discuss weather in the northern and southern hemispheres.

ONGOING ASSESSMENT

PERFORMANCE Oral language. Go around the class asking students about their favorite seasons and seasonal activities, *What's your favorite season? What do you do in (winter)?* Help students who are having trouble by rephrasing the questions, *Do you like (winter)?* etc. Observe students' responses. Use the **Oral Language Checklist** in the *Amazing Assessment Package.*

STAFF DEVELOPMENT

See the *Amazing How-To Handbook* for more on ways to involve the students' families through Home-School Connection.

TEACHER TO TEACHER

If your students work with other teachers, you may want to suggest that they look for opportunities to ask ESL students what they know about seasons and the weather in other parts of the world.

RELATED RESOURCES

WordStuff CD-ROM, I-Play Mode: Winter, Snow

WRITING PROJECT

Writing Project 6A, *A Great Place to Live,* is directly linked to this lesson. See the Process Writing Portfolio Program Teachers' Handbook, pages 28-29, for the Lesson Plan.

Students will find instructions and a Prewriting Sheet in the Writing Projects booklet inside the Portfolio.

Changing Seasons

LEVEL C, PAGE 107

KEY EXPERIENCES

- Discussing the growth cycle of plants
- Interpreting visual images
- Talking about seasonal chores
- Drawing seed germination

KEY LANGUAGE

- *What does she have to do in the (spring)?*
- *She has to (dig).*
- *What do they have to do?*
- *They have to (dig and plant).*
- spring, summer, fall, winter (R)
- ground, have to, hose, leaves, rake, seeds, shovel, snow, tree, yard

MATERIALS

- seeds, soil, pots

1 INTRODUCE

MULTI-LEVEL TEACHING STRATEGIES

Building background: Discussing the growth cycle. Use a large piece of chart paper divided into fourths. Have students watch as you make simple line drawings with the names of the four seasons. (You can make the drawing ahead of time if you prefer.) In the squares draw a tree with buds *(spring)*, a tree full of leaves *(summer)*, a tree losing brown, yellow, red, and orange leaves *(fall)*, a tree without any leaves *(winter)*. Talk about the seasons. Include all students in the activity by asking questions appropriate to each student's language stage. Here are some sample questions:

Speech Emergence: *Is it winter here or summer? Is it spring here?*

Developing Fluency: *What season is it here? How do you know this is (fall)?*

Interpreting visual images. Show outdoor pictures of your community or a place with similar geography to illustrate the four seasons. As you show students each picture, ask *When was this picture taken? How do you know?* Encourage students to look for clues. You may need to model the language: *This is winter. This is summer.* Students can talk about the things they do each season. Encourage comparisons between the seasons in the U.S. and those in other parts of the world. (CALLA: Deduction)

Relating to the community. Display the pictures you drew of the four seasons. Point to the appropriate season as you talk about events in your own community. Model conversations such as: *I'm so glad it is spring. Every year in May I go to the parade for "Cinco de mayo."* or *I love summer. I love the fireworks on the Fourth of July.* Ask students to name other community events. List the events on the board under each season.

2 EXPLORE

Activating prior knowledge. Open to page 107 of the Student Book. Ask students to comment about the page and compare the seasons in the pictures with the seasons in your own community.

 **Look, listen, and talk.** Students look and listen as you describe the page. Explain that the pictures show seasonal *chores*. Write the word on the board; elicit that it means *work* or *jobs*. Have students look at the pictures as you describe what is happening in each. Then ask **multi-level**

questions, such as *What do they have to do in the spring? What does she have to do in the winter?* Encourage students to respond, *He has to plant seeds. She has to dig. They have to rake leaves.*

Following conversational sequence. Read or play the tape for the conversation at the bottom of the page. Have students point to the lines as they listen. Read the conversation again, pausing for students to repeat. Check comprehension, *What does she have to do in the spring? What do they have to do in the spring?* Work **T-C**.

Help students substitute the other seasons and activities in the conversation: *What does he have to do in the summer?* etc.

Identifying seasons and weather. Students mark the things that don't belong in each season picture and compare their work with their classmates'. Teaching suggestions are provided in the Skills Journal annotation.

SCIENCE How plants grow. Help students use resource materials to learn about how plants grow. Talk about what is needed: light, moisture, heat, nutrients, etc. If possible, set up the following experiment: Divide the class into groups. Have each group plant the same type of seed in the same type of soil and pot. Vary the amount of light, water, or nutrients each plant gets. Compare the plants at regular intervals. Ask students to record and discuss the differences they observe. (CALLA: Comparing)

ART Drawing seed germination. Use a resource book to show students the stages of seed germination. Ask the students to draw a sequence of four frames illustrating the germination process: in the first frame, the seed has not germinated; in the last, it has sprouted through the soil. Help students label the steps. Display in the classroom.

Reapply. Have students use other photographs in the book to continue describing seasonal activities. You may want to use pages 3 and 16–18 for this purpose. For additional practice with *has to/have to*, students can return to the Hands-On Science pages to describe the steps in the experiments. For example, *First you have to … Then you have to ….*

STAFF DEVELOPMENT
See *The Amazing How-To Handbook* for suggestions on implementing CALLA in the classroom.

TEACHER TO TEACHER
If your students work with other teachers, you may want to suggest that they ask students to describe the plant growth experiment that they are doing.

RELATED RESOURCES
WordStuff CD-ROM, I-Play Mode: Spring, Gardens

READ AND DO

Changing Seasons

LEVEL C, PAGE 108

KEY EXPERIENCES

- Discussing kites and kite-flying
- Reading/following directions
- Making a kite
- Talking about air pressure and lift

KEY LANGUAGE

- kite, paper bag, roll of string

MATERIALS

- paper bags (or large pieces of mylar), markers, rulers, 16-inch sticks, tape, scissors, pencils, a roll of string, strips of cloth or mylar for tails

1 INTRODUCE

MULTI-LEVEL TEACHING STRATEGIES

Building background: Discussing kites. Bring to class pictures of kites. If possible, show students examples of different types of kites from various countries. Talk about kite-flying and have students describe the kites. Review shape words as needed. Encourage students to share their own experiences flying kites. Include all of the students by asking questions appropriate to each student's language stage. Here are some sample questions:

Speech Emergence: *What color is this kite? What shape is it? What does it look like? Do you like kites?*

Developing Fluency: *Which kite is bigger, this kite or that one? Which kite do you think is easier to fly? Why? Which country is this kite from?*

Talking about flying a kite. Show students two pictures: one of a windy day, one of a calm day. Ask, *On which day is it easier to fly a kite? Why?* Elicit that it is easier on a windy day because the wind lifts the kite. Continue, *On a day that is not windy, you can run to get your kite to fly.* Ask, *Do you know why this works?* Explain that as you run, the air gets pushed into the kite and this lifts it up. You can demonstrate this with a plastic bag. First, just hold the bag up in front of you. Nothing happens Then pull the bag quickly. It will fill with air and move. (CALLA: Deduction)

2 EXPLORE

Activating prior knowledge. Open to page 108 of the Student Book. Have students look at the drawings and skim the page. Ask, *What are we going to do? How many steps are there?*

Exploring new vocabulary. On the board, write the vocabulary words for the things needed to make the kite. Hold up each item, point to the word, model it and have students repeat. Work **T-C; T-S.** Distribute the things the students need.

GUIDED READING: Following directions. Read the directions aloud, using pantomime to demonstrate the verbs. Then have the students take turns reading the directions to each other. As one partner reads, the other pantomimes the steps.

Cooperative learning. In pairs, students help each other make their kites, rereading the directions as needed. Circulate and help them.

Encourage students to ask questions of you or of classmates if they are not sure what to do. Note: Make sure students measure the string correctly, or measure and cut it before class. (CALLA: Questioning for clarification)

Reading for a purpose; writing. Students read about the Wright brothers and write answers to questions. Teaching suggestions are provided in the Skills Journal annotation.

ART Making kite tails. Help students make tails to add to their kites. Discuss what the effects of different tails might be. Ask critical thinking questions, such as *Will this material make the kite too heavy? Will a long tail make the kite easier or more difficult to fly?* Provide a variety of lightweight materials for the students to use to make their own kite tails. (CALLA: Deduction/induction)

Flying the kites. Before taking the students outside to fly their kites, discuss kite safety. Remind students to fly kites only in large, open areas away from any power or phone lines. Have students experiment by flying their kites with and without tails. Encourage students to help each other make adjustments so that the kites fly better. Have students take notes on their observations. Back in the classroom, ask them to write up their notes, then share their observations in small groups. (CALLA: Cooperation)

Home-School Connection. Have students take their kites home over a weekend to fly with family and friends. Have students copy the following questions to answer at home in writing: *What was the weather like? What time of day did you fly it? Did anyone help you? Did your kite fly? Did you have fun?* Ask students to report their experiences to the class. If students were unable to fly their kites, discuss possible reasons: *There wasn't enough wind, The string was too short, etc.*

ONGOING ASSESSMENT

PERFORMANCE Oral language. Observe the students as they share their weekend kite-flying experiences. Use the **Oral Language Checklist** in the *Amazing Assessment Package.*

PORTFOLIO Writing. Save **Skills Journal** page 96 as an example of reading comprehension.

STAFF DEVELOPMENT

See the *Amazing How-To Handbook* for additional ways to integrate science into the ESL curriculum.

DREAMS

Changing Seasons

LEVEL C, PAGE 109

KEY EXPERIENCES

- Guided reading of a poem
- Discussing metaphors
- Discussing dreams and their importance
- Enjoying other poems

KEY LANGUAGE

- barren, dreams, hold fast

MULTI-LEVEL TEACHING STRATEGIES

Activating prior knowledge. Open to page 52 of the Student Book. Point to the picture of the child wishing on a star. Reread that short selection with students. Review how we wish on a star for something we dream of having or doing. On the board, write an example, *My dream is to travel all over the world. I dream of doing that with my friend.* Discuss what the child in the picture might be dreaming of. Include all students in the discussion by asking questions appropriate to each student's language stage. Here are some sample questions:

Speech Emergence: *Does she want to go to the moon? Does she want to be a doctor?*

Developing Fluency: *What is she dreaming of doing when she grows up?*

NOTE: Point out the difference between *dream about* vs. *dream of.*

Playing a rhyme game. Have each child make two cards. On one card the students should print: *The words rhyme.* On the other card students should print: *The words don't rhyme.* Say sets of words that rhyme as well as words that don't rhyme. Have students hold up the appropriate card. You may want to begin with these examples: *die/fly, go/snow.* Continue, *we/see, stop/hope, say/snow, stop/mop, class/grass, made/said,* etc.

Activating prior knowledge. Have students open to page 109. Encourage students to comment about the page, *What do you see? Who do you see? What are they doing?*

Exploring new vocabulary. Point to the word *broken-winged.* Ask students to visualize what that means. Also introduce *hold fast* and *barren field.* Tailor your explanations to meet the needs and capabilities of your students.

GUIDED READING Read or play the tape for the poem as the students follow along in their books. Emphasize the rhythm as you read. Ask for volunteers to read different lines of the poem. Reread the poem and ask students to close their eyes and let their imaginations form pictures.

Choral reading. Divide the class into two groups. Try to mix strong and weak readers in each group. Have each group practice reading one verse. Encourage students to read with expression. Bring the class back together. Have each group read their verse.

 **MUSIC "In a Child's Heart."** Play the tape or sing the song. (See the Tapescript in the Appendix.) Encourage students to join in.

SKILLS JOURNAL PAGE 97 **Brainstorming; finishing a poem.** Students brainstorm about dreams then finish a poem about dreams with their own words. Teaching suggestions are provided in the Skills Journal annotation.

Language experience writing: Writing a poem about dreams. As a prewriting activity, ask students to talk about things they would like to do. Have them talk about occupations as well as things people can do to make this a better world. Have students write their own poems about dreams.

ART Illustrating dreams. Have students draw a vision of their own dreams with a caption. Display with their poems in the classroom or hallway.

Creating a Poetry Corner. Designate a bulletin board or a corner of your classroom for poetry. Display poetry for students as well as poetry by the students. Print the poems on tag board or construction paper. Poems provide an effective context for practicing the rhythm and intonation patterns of natural language. Encourage choral and independent reading of poetry.

ONGOING ASSESSMENT

PERFORMANCE Oral language. Print the poem "Dreams" on a piece of paper. Cut the lines into strips and put them in a pile in random order. Ask the students to put the lines into the correct order, then read the poem again. Observe different students' levels of participation. Use the **Oral Language Checklist** in the *Amazing Assessment Package.*

PORTFOLIO Writing. Save **Skills Journal** page 97 as an example of brainstorming and completing a poem.

BACKGROUND INFORMATION
Langston Hughes (1902–1967) was an African American poet and writer. During his lifetime he lived in many cities and traveled extensively, even journeying to Africa as a steward on a freighter. His writings have provided generations with a window on the black experience in the U.S.

MULTICULTURAL AWARENESS
Ask students to share their favorite poems in their native languages. Encourage students to bring a book of poetry to class to place in the Poetry Corner for a few days. Those students who are able may also want to read for the class a short poem in their primary language.

175

COMMUNICATION 2A

Changing Seasons

LEVEL C, PAGE 110

KEY EXPERIENCES

- Telling a story in question-and-answer form
- Following a sequence
- Describing past actions
- Asking for/giving information
- Learning about rivers

KEY LANGUAGE

- *Where did he ...?*
- *What did he ...?*
- Irregular verbs: eat/ate, drink/drank, go/went, ride/rode, catch/caught

MULTI-LEVEL TEACHING STRATEGIES

Building background: Problem solving. Before students arrive, display an empty cup that has obviously had something to drink in it. You can also display a plate with a piece of food. When students arrive, explain that someone was here. Have students look at the evidence and try to guess what the person did, and what the person drank and ate. Encourage students to talk about more than one possibility. Include all students in the activity by asking questions appropriate to each student's language stage. Here are some sample questions:

Speech Emergence: (Point to the cup.) *What is this? Is it clean? What was in it?*

Developing Fluency: *What did the person drink? Do you think the person liked the drink? Why do you think that?*

Roleplaying. Display "he" and "she" puppets with props. Use the puppets to roleplay a conversation about what the two did yesterday. Be sure to talk about what they ate, drank, rode, and where they went. You can begin the conversation with this: P 1: *When did he get up?* P 2: *He got up at eleven.* P 1: *What did she eat?* P 2: *She ate bananas.*

Matching questions and answers. Make sentence strips of the conversation you modeled above, with separate questions and answers. Help students read the strips. Have students read the questions and use the pronoun puppets to pantomime each answer. Spread the questions and answers on a table. Read one of the questions. Have students find the corresponding answer.

2 EXPLORE

Activating prior knowledge. Open to page 110 of the Student Book. Encourage students to comment on the page. Read the introductory sentence, *Here's what Danny did on a sunny, summer day.*

Look, listen, and talk. Introduce nouns that may be unfamiliar to students, *eggs, juice, river, fish.* Point to the pictures as you say, *get up, eat, drink, go to the river, ride a motorcycle, catch fish.* Pantomime or have one of your most able students pantomime *drinking, catching a fish.* Then have students look and listen as you read or play the tape.

Practicing the questions and answers. Divide the students into two groups. One group asks the questions; the other answers. Then have students work with a partner. One student asks the questions; the other answers. Have students switch roles and repeat. I

Spelling check. On the board write the present tense verbs, *get up, eat, drink*, etc. Ask students to tell you the past tense forms, *got up, ate, drank*, etc. Write them on the board Have students copy on a separate piece of paper.

STAFF DEVELOPMENT
For more on self-assessment, see the *Amazing How-to Handbook* and *Authentic Assessment*.

Telling a story in question and answer form; practicing conversations. Students work independently to write answers to questions and then practice conversations. Teaching suggestions are provided in the Skills Journal annotation.

Interviewing a classmate. In pairs, have students find out what their partner did the previous weekend. Have them ask the questions in the Student Book on page 110, changing to the pronoun *you*. Suggest that students change the last question to *Where did you go?* Students record the answers on a piece of paper.

SOCIAL STUDIES Learning about rivers. Have students conduct research about rivers. Encourage students to go to the library and borrow books and other library materials about work and play on rivers. Students may want to investigate types of commercial as well as recreational fishing, or look at some of the environmental issues regarding rivers. Encourage students to draw pictures and write sentences about their research. (CALLA: Resourcing)

Playing Mad Libs. Have students make up their own humorous question-and-answer stories. Encourage students to be silly but to use correct forms in their questions and responses. For example, *What did she catch? She caught a car.*

Home-School Connection. Ask the students to interview someone at home about what that person did the previous weekend, *When did you get up on Saturday?* etc. Ask students to report to the class. **Work T-S.** *When did your brother get up on Saturday, Thomas?*, etc.

ONGOING ASSESSMENT

SELF-EVALUATION Following a sequence. Make sentence strips of the questions and answers in the Student Book. Mix them up. Have the students match the questions with the answers, then check their answers on page 110 and make corrections. Ask students what they found difficult or easy about this lesson.

PORTFOLIO Save **Skills Journal** page 98 as an example of telling a story in question-and-answer form.

COMMUNICATION 2B

Changing Seasons

LEVEL C, PAGE 111

KEY EXPERIENCES

■ Talking about/describing the weather

■ Roleplaying conversations

■ Creating new conversations using a Data Bank

■ Keeping a weather log

KEY LANGUAGE

■ *What's the weather like?*

■ *How's the weather?*

■ *It's (very cold and snowy).*

■ *What's the weather forecast for tomorrow?*

■ *It's going to be (cloudy and rainy).*

■ cloudy, cool, rainy, snowy, sunny, windy

1 INTRODUCE

MULTI-LEVEL TEACHING STRATEGIES

Building background: Discussing the weather. Talk about the weather on different days and at different times of the year. Refer students to the **word web** of weather-related words and ideas they did for Lesson 1 of this theme. Include all the students by asking questions appropriate to each student's language stage. Here are some sample questions:

Speech Emergence: *Is it warm today? Is it raining? Was it warmer on Monday or Tuesday? Is it hot in spring?*

Developing Fluency: *How's the weather today? What's the weather like in December?* Encourage students to answer with a long utterance, *It's cold in December.*

SCIENCE Talking about the weather forecast. Bring to class the local newspaper with the weather forecast for the following day. Ask, *What do you think the weather is going to be tomorrow?* Ask students to predict based on the temperature, the sky, and other conditions they have observed. Read the weather forecast, simplifying as needed. Check comprehension, *Is it going to be rainy tomorrow or sunny? Is it going to be hot or cold?* (CALLA: Predicting)

2 EXPLORE

Activating prior knowledge. Open to page 111 of the Student Book. Talk about the weather in each picture. Ask, *Is it(cold)? Is it windy? Is it sunny?*, etc. Encourage students to comment about the page.

Exploring key vocabulary. Point to each vocabulary item in the Data Bank as you introduce it: *cold, hot,* etc. Contrast *cool* and *cold.* Ask students to repeat the words **chorally** and individually. On the board, write: *It is raining. It's rainy. It is snowing. It's snowy.* Help students read the sentences. Point out how the letter *n* doubles in *sunny.*

Look, listen, and talk. Students listen as you describe the conversation on page 111. *They're talking about the weather. They're talking about the weather now and the forecast for tomorrow.* Then have the students follow along as you read the text or play the tape. Read or play the tape again, pausing for students to repeat **chorally.** Check comprehension with (pointing to the top left picture) *What's the weather like?* Encourage students to respond, *It's very cold and snowy.* Continue in the same way with the other picture.

Practicing the conversations. Divide the class into groups. One group asks the questions, the other answers. Then have partners practice the conversations, substituting words from the Data Bank with different questions.

S1: *How's the weather?*
S2: *It's cool and windy.*

Asking and answering questions using weather vocabulary. Students write answers to questions, then make practice conversations. Teaching suggestions are provided in the Skills Journal annotation.

SCIENCE Keeping a weather log. Ask students to keep a weather log for one week. Have them record the temperature—in Fahrenheit, Celsius, or both—and other conditions they observe. At the end of the week, have them check their information in small groups and make comparisons, *It was warmer on Tuesday than on Wednesday.* etc.

SCIENCE Reading about the weather in other cities. Check the local newspaper for a table of the temperatures and weather conditions in different cities. Show it to the students. Have them scan for information, *What was the temperature in Rio de Janeiro? In Denver? Where was it the warmest?* (CALLA: Comparing)

Roleplaying a weather forecast. Have students roleplay a weather forecast on TV. Encourage them to watch the weather forecast on TV and observe what the forecaster says and does. If possible, take them on a field trip to a TV station to meet a meteorologist. Have students make drawings and maps to use with their roleplays. Ask volunteers to roleplay for the class.

ONGOING ASSESSMENT

PORTFOLIO Oral language. Observe students as they roleplay a TV weather forecast. Use the **Oral Language Checklist** in the *Amazing Assessment Package.*

MULTICULTURAL AWARENESS

Invite volunteers teach the class words for the weather in their native languages. Make a chart for the classroom. You may want to use both Fahrenheit and Celsius when discussing temperatures.

TEACHER TO TEACHER

If your students work with other teachers, you may want to encourage them to use those ESL students who are comfortable measuring temperature in Celsius as resources in the classroom. Suggest that teachers do this when presenting metric measurements as well.

CHECK THIS OUT!

Changing Seasons

LEVEL C, PAGES 112–113

KEY EXPERIENCES

- Talking about geography and climate
- Reading short selections
- Summarizing
- Reading "Amazing Facts"
- Making comparisons

KEY LANGUAGE

- gust of wind, desert, poles, tropics, sea gull
- Abbreviations: ME, AK, NY, VT, NH, CO

1 INTRODUCE

MULTI-LEVEL TEACHING STRATEGIES

Building background: Recalling details. Ask students to open to pages 112–113 of the Student Book and look carefully at the pictures. After one minute, have students close their books. Engage students in a discussion of the illustrations. Include all the students in the discussion by asking questions appropriate to each student's language stage. Here are some sample questions:

Speech Emergence: *What did you see? Did you see a frog? Where was the frog?*

Developing Fluency: *Did you see a man in a car? What was the weather like? Did you see two animals wearing scarves and hats? Do you know the names of those animals? Why do you think they were wearing scarves and hats?*

SCIENCE Talking about geography and climate. Use a world map or globe. Point out the Sahara Desert and the Tropics. Talk about what the weather is like there. Guide the conversation with **multi-level questions,** such as *Where is the Sahara Desert? Is it warm there? Where is it wetter, in the Tropics or in the Sahara Desert?*

SOCIAL STUDIES Learning abbreviations. Print on the board the following abbreviations: *ME, AK, NY, VT, NH, CO.* Next to each abbreviation, write the name of the state: *Maine, Alaska, New York, Vermont, New Hampshire, Colorado.* Help students read the names of the states. Work **T-C.** Ask, *What is the abbreviation for (New York)?* Work **T-C; T-S.** Help students use a map of the U.S. to locate each state. *Where is Vermont? Point to Colorado,* etc. Work **T-S.**

2 EXPLORE

Activating prior knowledge. Open to pages 112–113 again. Have volunteers describe pictures, read the titles, and predict what the selections will be about.

GUIDED READING Summarizing. Direct students' attention to the selections on the Sahara Desert and on the Tropics. Divide the class into two groups. Ask one group to read about the Sahara Desert, the other to read about the Tropics. Have students do **independent reading.**

Next, pair students from the two groups. Have students take turns telling their partners what they read. (CALLA: Summarizing)

Direct students' attention to the selection on Victor. Play the tape or read the selection as the students follow along in their books. Do a **choral reading** of the text.

Reading for information: Amazing Facts. Print on the board prereading questions: *How strong was the wind on Mt. Washington? What is a Komodo dragon? How big can it get?* Have students do **independent reading** of the facts. Check answers.

Reading a chart. Direct students' attention to the list of the snowiest cities in the U.S. Ask the students to **scan** for information, *How much snow is there in (Denver, CO)?* Have students **make comparisons.** *Where is there more snow, (Albany, NY) or (Portland, ME)?* (CALLA: Comparing)

Have students do **independent reading** of the selection about the poles. Have students read to each other in pairs about sea gulls. Then let students read "April Showers" in unison.

Research; filling in a graph. Students find out the highest average temperatures for the cities listed and complete the graph. **Reading for a purpose; writing.** Students read a paragraph about penguins and write answers to questions. Teaching suggestions are provided in the Skills Journal annotations.

Making comparisons. Help students use resource materials to find out annual statistics for snow, rainfall, temperature, etc. in the town or city where you live. Have students make comparisons with the cities they have read about. (CALLA: Comparing)

Home-School Connection: Weather proverbs. Discuss proverbs and sayings about the weather. If possible, share with the class some of the weather expressions used by sailors. Have students ask at home about proverbs or sayings in their home cultures concerning the weather. Ask students to share them with the class. Print the proverbs and sayings on chart paper. Ask the students to illustrate. Display in the classroom.

ONGOING ASSESSMENT

PERFORMANCE Listening; reading comprehension. Ask students to scan for information on the list of snowiest cities. Observe different students' levels of response and the length of utterances. Use the **Anecdotal Record Form** in the Amazing Assessment Package.

PORTFOLIO Save **Skills Journal** page 100 as an example of completing a graph.

MULTICULTURAL AWARENESS

Ask students to scan weather lists of cities from around the world and make comparisons of rainfall, temperature, etc. Weather lists are often available in large city newspapers, in atlases, and in other resource materials.

STAFF DEVELOPMENT

See the *Amazing How-To Handbook* for other suggestions on developing reading strategies.

RELATED RESOURCES

The Cat Came Back CD-ROM, Read Along Mode: Cyclones (pages 17-19)

LANGUAGE POWER A

LEVEL C, PAGE 114

KEY EXPERIENCES

- Talking about seasons/plants
- Reading
- Expressing obligation
- Relating reading to own experience
- Learning about plants

KEY LANGUAGE

- weeds, water, sweep, scrape off

1 INTRODUCE

MULTI-LEVEL TEACHING STRATEGIES

Activating prior knowledge. Open to page 74 of the Student Book. Say, *Remember Ben? He wakes up late. What does he have to do to get to work?* Review his activities, using *has to/have to.* Model the language, *He has to get up,* etc. Include all the students by asking questions appropriate to each student's language stage. Here are some sample questions:

Speech Emergence: *Does he have to brush his teeth? Does he have to wash his face?*

Developing Fluency: *Does he have to rush to catch the bus?* Encourage the students to respond, *He had to rush to catch the bus.*

Previewing. Make the following sentence strips: *She has to dig up the ground. He has to plant the seeds. She has to pull up the weeds. He has to water the plants. She has to rake the leaves. He has to sweep the walk. She has to scrape off the car. He has to shovel the walk.* Help students read the sentences. Open to Student Book page 114. Read a sentence strip. Help students point to the appropriate picture and repeat the sentence, *He has to plant the seeds.*, etc.

2 EXPLORE

Activating prior knowledge. Open to page 114. Encourage students to comment about the page. Ask, *What season is it here?* Encourage students to look back at page 107 and note similarities between the two pages.

Exploring new vocabulary. Students locate the words as you read them, *shovel, scrape, dig,* etc. Ask volunteers to pantomime the verbs.

 **Look, listen, and talk.** Have students look at the pictures. Ask students to describe the activity in each picture and name the season. Have the students name the seasons in order: *spring, summer, fall, winter.* Then have students follow along as you read the text or play the tape. Ask students to describe tasks they have to do each season. Have students follow along as you read the following: *After they work they enjoy their yard. What do you think they do?* Ask students to describe leisure activities for each season and make predictions, *Maybe they go swimming,* etc. (CALLA: Predicting)

Choral reading. Divide the class into four groups. Have each group read and reread one paragraph. Encourage students to read with expression.

 MUSIC "White Coral Bells." Play the tape or sing the song. (See the Tapescript in the Appendix.) Invite students to join in.

Using *has to/have to*; writing about activities. Students look at pictures and write sentences telling what people have to do, as well as write about what the students have to do at home. Teaching suggestions are provided in the Skills Journal annotation.

Using TPR. Put the sentence strips used during **Introduce** in a basket or hat. Ask one student or a pair of students at a time to choose a sentence strip and pantomime the activity. The rest of the class identifies the activity using *has to/have to: She has to dig up the ground. They have to rake the leaves.*, etc.

Home-School Connection. Ask students to keep a log for one week of the tasks they and members of their family had to do. Encourage students to write at least two sentences for each day. Ask them to share their logs in small groups, *On Saturday I had to clean my room. My sister had to clean her room, too.*

SCIENCE Learning about plants. Help students find out information about the growth cycle of one kind of tree, bush, or other plant. Questions to consider are *How do seeds spread and germinate? Does it flower? Need pruning? Shed leaves? What animals use it?* etc. Help students make reports and drawings to share with the class and display. (CALLA: Resourcing)

Building vocabulary. Use *Amazing English!* Word Attack 3 Interactive Vocabulary Games for practice with vocabulary.

ONGOING ASSESSMENT

PERFORMANCE Oral Language. Ask students to match the sentence strips to the appropriate pictures then read the sentences aloud. Observe different levels of participation. Use the **Oral Language Checklist** in the *Amazing Assessment Package.*

PORTFOLIO Writing. Save **Skills Journal** page 102 as an example of mastery of *has to/have to* constructions.

STAFF DEVELOPMENT

See the *Amazing How-To Handbook* for additional suggestions on science and research activities.

TEACHER TO TEACHER

If your students work with other teachers, you may want to suggest that they ask students what they think is needed to become proficient in English or in an activity such as playing the piano or tennis. Encourage students to offer each other suggestions and advice as well.

RELATED RESOURCES

WordStuff CD-ROM, I-Spy Mode: Gardens/Planting

LANGUAGE POWER B

Changing Seasons

LEVEL C, PAGE 115

KEY EXPERIENCES

- Asking for/giving information
- Describing past actions
- Describing sequence
- Talking about responsibilities
- Roleplaying conversations

KEY LANGUAGE

- *Did you (play) after school yesterday?*
- *No, I didn't. I had to (study).*
- deliver, practice, watch
- dentist, papers, piano

1 INTRODUCE

MULTI-LEVEL TEACHING STRATEGIES

Building background: Roleplaying. Print *yesterday* on the board and have the students read it. Ask what day of the week yesterday was. Roleplay a conversation among several puppets about what they did and did not do yesterday. You may want to display appropriate pictures.

P1 : *Did you practice the piano yesterday?*
P2 : *No, I didn't. I had to wash the dishes.*
P2 : *Did you play outside yesterday?*
P3 : *No, I didn't. I had to watch my sister.*

Include all the students by asking questions appropriate to each student's language stage. Here are some sample questions:

Speech Emergence: *Did he practice the piano yesterday? Did he play outside or watch his sister?*

Developing Fluency: *Who did he have to watch yesterday? Who washed dishes?*

Continuing practice. Continue with other examples. Ask students to suggest other activities or chores. Encourage volunteers to use the puppets to roleplay.

2 EXPLORE

Activating prior knowledge. Open to page 107 of the Student Book. Encourage students to comment about the page, *Where are they? What are they doing?*

Exploring new vocabulary. Introduce unfamiliar words: *dentist, piano, papers.* You (or a student) can pantomime: *practice my piano lessons, clean my room, deliver papers, watch my baby sister.*

Look, listen, and talk. Students look and listen as you read the text or play the tape. *Did you play after school yesterday? No, I didn't. I had to study.* Have students look at the text as you and the puppets model:

P1 : *Did you play after school yesterday?*
P2 : *No, I didn't. I had to study.*
P2 : *Did you play after school yesterday?*
P3 : *No, I didn't. I had to go to the dentist.*

Practicing the conversation. Divide the class into groups. One group asks the questions, the other answers. Switch roles and repeat. Then have students practice in pairs, talking about each picture and adding any other chores they want.

 **Using** *had to;* **writing about activities; home-school connection.** Students look at pictures and write sentences telling what people had to do, as well as write about what they had to do at home. Teaching suggestions are provided in the Skills Journal annotation.

Playing a Chain Game. Make cards for a chain game: *go to the dentist; deliver papers; practice my piano lessons; watch my baby sister; clean my room; go shopping.* Place them in a basket. Print on the board and read aloud: *Did you play after school yesterday?* S1 answers by drawing a card from the basket and using it to respond: *No, I didn't. I had to (watch my baby sister).* S1 then reads the question on the board. S2 draws a card and answers. Continue in this way.

SOCIAL STUDIES Talking about responsibilities. Invite students to discuss their own chores and responsibilities. List on the board. Depending on the class, you might ask students to discuss which chores they get paid for (or would like to get paid for when they're older) and how much. Have students do a roleplay featuring true information about their own activities.

Problem solving. Play a variation of Twenty Questions. Tell students that you have to do something very important (choose chores done at home, such as washing the dishes). Children ask yes/no questions to find out what you have to do. Students then make up chores they have to do and play the game with one another. (CALLA: Guessing)

ONGOING ASSESSMENT

PERFORMANCE Oral language Observe the students as they play the chain game. Are they able to understand the instructions? Are they able to ask complete questions and respond in long utterances? Use the **Oral Language Checklist** in the *Amazing Assessment Package.*

MULTICULTURAL AWARENESS

Ask students to tell the class about any special chores they have to do in their home cultures on holidays. Are there special foods or decorations to make? Other household preparations to be done? Expand the conversation to include a discussion about who does what types of chores. As you explore this topic, keep in mind that students may already have relatively set ideas about gender roles.

HANDS-ON SOCIAL STUDIES

Changing Seasons

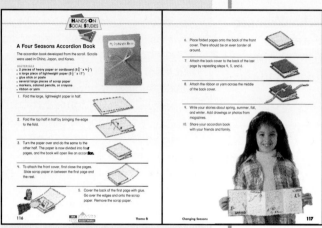

LEVEL C, PAGES 116–117

KEY EXPERIENCES

- Discussing China, Japan, and Korea
- Reading/following directions
- Making an accordion book
- Learning about holidays in other countries
- Planning a treasure hunt

KEY LANGUAGE

- China, Japan, Korea
- accordion book, lightweight, scroll

MATERIALS

- heavy paper or cardboard for covers (5 3/4" x 4 1/2"); lightweight paper (5 1/2" x 17"); glue stick or paste; large pieces of scrap paper; markers, colored pencils, or crayons; ribbon or yarn

1 INTRODUCE

MULTI-LEVEL TEACHING STRATEGIES

Building background. Open the Student Book to pages 116–117. Read the title, "A Four Seasons Accordion Book," aloud and ask students to look at the photo and illustrations. Explain that students are going to make accordion books. Fold a piece of paper into an accordion shape to help facilitate understanding. Engage students in a discussion of the pages. Include all of the students by asking questions appropriate to each student's language stage. Here are some sample questions:

Speech Emergence: *What shape is the book? What do you think it is made from?*

Developing Fluency: *Describe the accordion book. Does it look difficult to make? What do you think the book will be about?*

SOCIAL STUDIES Discussing China, Japan, and Korea. Use a world map or globe. Point out or ask volunteers to locate *China, Japan,* and *Korea.* Ask, *What do you know about (China)?* Make a **word web** on the board for each country. Encourage students to use the word webs to **make comparisons.** *Japan is small, but China is very big. Japan is an island. All three countries are in Asia. All three are very old countries. People speak Korean in Korea. People speak many languages in China.*

ART Appreciating scrolls. Bring to class art books or other resource books that have pictures of scrolls from China, Japan, or Korea. Discuss what a scroll looks like. *What color is it? How big is it?* etc. Explain that scrolls were used to send messages and communicate ideas just as books are.

2 EXPLORE

Activating prior knowledge. Have students skim pages 116–117. Ask, *What are we going to do? How many steps are there?*

Exploring new vocabulary. On the board, write the vocabulary words for the items needed to make an accordion book. Hold up each item, point to the word, model it, and have students repeat. Work **T-C; T-S.** Distribute the things the students need.

Following directions. Read the directions aloud, using pantomime to demonstrate the verbs. Make sure students understand *an even border* in step 6. Have volunteers describe the directions in their own words, using expressions such as *First you have to ...*, *Next*, etc. (CALLA: Sequencing)

Cooperative learning. In pairs, students help each other make the accordion books, rereading the directions as needed. Circulate and help them. Encourage students to ask questions of you or classmates if they do not understand the steps. Provide photos from magazines or drawing paper for students to use in step 9. Ask students to share their accordion books in small groups and help one another make adjustments. (CALLA: Questioning for clarification)

 **Observing weather; completing a chart.** Students observe the weather for a week and fill in a chart. Teaching suggestions are provided in the Skills Journal annotation.

SOCIAL STUDIES Learning about holidays in other countries. Teach the students about a holiday such as the lunar New Year or Children's Day in Japan. Encourage students to use resource materials to learn about other holidays as well. (CALLA: Resourcing)

ART Creating a hall display. Help students make a hallway display of their accordion books. Encourage students to add maps and information about Japan, China, and Korea.

Home-School Connection. Encourage students to take the books home to share with friends and family after you have displayed them for a time.

Planning a treasure hunt. Divide the students into groups to plan treasure hunts in the classroom or outdoors. Have the students write their messages on pieces of paper, then roll them up like scrolls and tie them. Each group can use a different colored string or ribbon to avoid confusion. After students complete the treasure hunt, have them bring the scroll messages to the front of the class and read them.

ONGOING ASSESSMENT

PERFORMANCE Oral language. Ask the students to tell you how to make an accordion book. Observe different students' participation. Use the **Oral Language Checklist** in the *Amazing Assessment Package*.

STAFF DEVELOPMENT

See the *Amazing How-To Handbook* for suggestions on integrating multicultural activities in the classroom and for more about cooperative learning.

TEACHER TO TEACHER

If your students work with other teachers, you may want to suggest that they have students make more accordion books to use to write original stories at home. The ESL students can show their classmates how to make the books.

THE GRATEFUL STATUES

Changing Seasons

LEVEL C, PAGES 118–123

KEY EXPERIENCES

- Reading and enjoying a multicultural folktale
- Talking about characters and setting
- Learning about festivals and customs in Japan
- Appreciating multicultural art

KEY LANGUAGE

- New Year, rice cakes, statue, straw hat

1 INTRODUCE

MULTI-LEVEL TEACHING STRATEGIES

Building background: Discussing Japan. Show the students a world map or globe. Give them clues to locate Japan. Open to page 118 of the Student Book. Explain to the students that you are going to read a folktale from Japan. Ask warm-up questions to help students become interested in the story as you turn the pages. Include all students by asking questions appropriate to each student's language stage. Here are some sample questions:

Speech Emergence: *What season is it? Is it winter? Is it cold? Is it hot?*

Developing Fluency: *Where does the story take place? What is the weather like? Who are these people? Are they husband and wife? What do you think people are getting ready to celebrate?*

Previewing. Ask students to look at the illustrations on pages 118–123 in the Student Book. Based on the illustrations, ask the students to predict what happens in the story. Ask questions that will help all students to join in, *What do you see here? What happens next?* etc. Read the title, "The Grateful Statues," aloud. Tell students that as they read, they should think about the answers to these questions: *What are the statues? Why are they grateful?* (CALLA: Predicting)

2 EXPLORE

 **GUIDED READING** Play the tape once through without stopping, or read and ask a volunteer to serve as a page turner. Read the story with expression. As you read the story (or play the tape), point to the characters and illustrations to clarify meaning. Encourage students to respond to the story by asking: *Did you like the story? Show me the picture you liked best.*

Discuss how people feel when they haven't been able to celebrate a holiday the way they had wanted. Encourage students to talk about their own experiences or disappointments. Ask students to tell you who the **characters** are. Then ask what the **setting** is. Prompt with questions as needed: *Which people are in the story? Are the statues like people? Where does the story take place? What time of year is it?*

Choral reading. If possible, reread the story the day after the first reading. To introduce the second reading, ask the students to remember what the man and woman did not have for the New Year. Review the

characters and **setting.** Then play the tape or read as students follow along **chorally.** Invite comments about the story.

Paired reading. Have partners reread the story, alternating pages or paragraphs. Then ask **multi-level questions** such as *Did the family have money to buy rice? Why did the family want to buy rice? Why did the man give the hats to the statues?* Encourage students to talk about what it feels like to do something for someone else and what it feels like to be grateful. Expand the discussion to meet the needs and capabilities of your students.

SKILLS JOURNAL PAGES 105-106

Matching written language to pictures. Students find the correct pictures and number them, then check answers with the class. **Understanding details.** Students complete questions about "The Grateful Statues," then check answers with the class. Teaching suggestions are provided in the Skills Journal annotations.

3 EXTEND

Language experience writing. Ask students to talk about acts of kindness they have experienced. Ask students how kindness is repaid. Have students draw a picture of a kindness they have experienced. Ask students to write a sentence, poem, or story describing the experience. To assess students' work, use the **Writing Checklist** in the *Amazing Assessment Package.*

Playing Statues. Teach students the traditional game of Statues. Play music or clap and have students walk around the room or dance. When the clapping or the music stops, students freeze and become statues. Everyone stands still until one person moves. The person that moves first is out. The game continues until there is only one "statue."

ART Appreciating multicultural art. Display art prints from a variety of cultures: Japanese, Native American, European, Chinese, etc. Art prints are available from school or public libraries. Encourage students to examine the prints and use them for inspiration in their own art work.

ONGOING ASSESSMENT

SELF-EVALUATION Writing. Ask the students to write down what they remember about the story. Encourage them to retell the story in their own words. Then have students open to the story and check what they wrote. Encourage them to make corrections and expand their original sentences.

PORTFOLIO Save **Skills Journal** page 106 as an example of understanding details.

MULTICULTURAL AWARENESS

Have students talk about the ways they celebrate the New Year. Ask when they celebrate the New Year, who they celebrate with, what special foods they eat, and what activities they do.

STAFF DEVELOPMENT

See the *Amazing How-To Handbook* for suggestions on developing reading strategies.

WRITING PROJECT

Writing Project 6B, *A Haiku Poem,* is directly linked to this lesson. See the Process Writing Portfolio Program Teachers' Handbook, pages 30-31, for the Lesson Plan.

Students will find instructions and a Prewriting Sheet in the Writing Projects booklet inside the Portfolio.

HOLISTIC ASSESSMENT

Changing Seasons

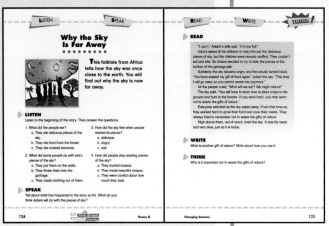

LEVEL C, PAGES 124–125

KEY EXPERIENCES

- Listening for information
- Reading and enjoying a folktale from Africa
- Predicting outcomes
- Expressing opinions
- Writing about gifts of nature

KEY LANGUAGE

- delicious, garbage, gifts, starve, stuffed, waste

1 INTRODUCE

MULTI-LEVEL TEACHING STRATEGIES

These two pages offer a variety of assessment opportunities. The left-hand page consists of listening and speaking activities that follow a taped presentation. In the speaking activity, students are asked to summarize the story and make predictions based on what they have heard. The right-hand page consists of writing and critical thinking activities. These follow a reading passage that completes the listening component. You can use the activities to assess listening, speaking, reading, writing, and critical thinking skills. Have children work as a class or in small groups. Record your observations as appropriate on the **Anecdotal Record Form,** the Reading Checklist, and the **Writing Checklist** in the *Amazing Assessment Package.*

Building background. Invite students to describe the sky. List student ideas on the board. Ask **multi-level questions** to enable students at different proficiency levels to participate.

Speech Emergence: *Does the sky sometimes seem alive? Have you ever seen the sky look angry? When?*

Developing Fluency: *What does the sky look like before a storm? What do you see? What does the sky look like on a sunny day?*

2 EXPLORE

Previewing the story. Open Student Book to page 124 and let the students comment on the picture. Say, *Today we are going to learn a folktale from Africa.* Ask, *What do you think happens in the story?* Write the ideas on the board.

Preparing to listen. Tell the students they are going to hear the first part of the folktale. Direct their attention to the listening questions. Give students time to do **independent reading** of the questions.

Listening to the story. Read or play the tape for the story. You will find the tapescript in the Appendix. Have students work independently to answer the listening questions. Read or play the tape again in segments; pause for students to check their work and make corrections.

Speaking. Ask **multi-level questions** as you encourage the students to talk about what they have learned in the story so far, *What did the people eat? What did some people do with extra pieces of sky?*

Making predictions. Ask students to tell you what they think Adami will do with the pieces of sky. (CALLA: Predicting)

GUIDED READING Read the story on page 125 as the students listen and follow along. Then have the students do **partner reading,** alternating paragraphs. Use the **Reading Checklist** in the *Amazing Assessment Package.*

Drawing conclusions. Ask, *Why did the sky sail away? Why did they have to grow their own food and cook their meals?* Discuss the meaning of *a gift of nature.* Encourage students to share their ideas. (CALLA: Deduction)

Observing the students. As you discuss the story, notice the level of participation and the particular abilities of each child. What new words have they learned? What language structures do they use? Which students use only single word responses? Which students can speak in long utterances? How well can you understand them? Which students can answer *why* questions? You may want to add progress notes to students' **portfolios** at this time. Use the **Anecdotal Record Form** in the *Amazing Assessment Package.*

Reading comprehension; cloze exercise. Students work independently to finish cloze paragraphs about "Why the Sky Is Far Away." using words from the Data Bank. Teaching suggestions are provided in the Skills Journal annotation. Save this page in the student's **Assessment Portfolio.**

Writing about gifts of nature. Ask the students to choose one of the gifts of nature to write a paragraph about. Have them include what the gift is and the reasons it is a gift. Example: *Air is free. It is all around us. Anyone can breathe the air.* Encourage students to exchange paragraphs and help each other make corrections. Use the **Writing Checklist** in the *Amazing Assessment Package.* (CALLA: Cooperation)

Critical thinking. Ask the students to consider why it is important not to waste the gifts of nature. Choose one gift, such as trees. In small groups, have students discuss ways in which they can recycle in order to save trees. Encourage them to use resource materials to find out about the relationship between recycling efforts and forest preservation (How many recycled newspapers does it take to save a tree?). Ask volunteers to report to the class what they learn. (CALLA: Resourcing)

AMAZING FACTS

Changing Seasons

LEVEL C, PAGE 126

KEY EXPERIENCES

- Recalling details
- Reading for information
- Playing a game
- Creating a game
- Critical thinking: synthesizing information

KEY LANGUAGE

- Review

● ● ● 1 INTRODUCE ● ● ●

MULTI-LEVEL TEACHING STRATEGIES

Activating prior knowledge. Engage students in a discussion of the seasons and seasonal activities and tasks. Include all students in the discussion by asking questions appropriate to each student's language stage. Here are some sample questions:

Speech Emergence: *What are the four seasons? What season comes after summer? What is your favorite activity in the winter? Do you have to dig in the spring?*

Developing Fluency: *What is your favorite season? Why? What do you have to do in the (fall)? Tell me one activity you like to do each season.* Encourage the students to respond in long utterances, *I like to plant flowers in the spring.*

Using TPR. Put the sentence strips from Lesson Plan 9 for Student Book page 114 in a basket. Ask one student or a pair of students at a time to choose a sentence strip and pantomime the activity. The rest of the class identifies the season and the activity using *has to/have: It is spring. He has to plant seeds. / It is fall. They have to rake the leaves,* etc.

Reviewing abbreviations. Print on the board the following abbreviations: *ME, AK, NY, VT, NH, CO.* Ask, *What is the abbreviation for (New York)?* Work **T-C; T-S.** Prompt as needed. Ask students to open to page 113. Direct students' attention to the list of the snowiest cities in the United States. Ask, *How much snow is there in (Albany, NY)?* Continue asking questions. Work **T-C; T-S; S-S.**

Retelling a story. Ask students to tell you the story "The Grateful Statues" in their own words. Ask one student to start. Cue students in turn to continue. Tailor the amount each student is expected to retell according to capability.

● ● ● 2 EXPLORE ● ● ●

Activating prior knowledge. Open to page 126 of the Student Book. Have students cover the questions. Ask, *What do we need to do first?* (Divide into teams.) Group students of varying abilities. Continue, *How many points do you get for each correct square?* (5) *How many points do you get for three correct squares in a row?* (10)

Playing the game. Set the time limit and have the teams work together to answer the questions. Circulate and help as needed. At the end of the time period, have the teams compete for the correct answers orally. Read the questions in random order. The first team to raise their hands and answer the question correctly wins a point. The team with the most points at the end of play wins the game.

Challenge. For extra fluency practice, ask the students to answer the questions in complete sentences: *You can go sledding and ice skating in the winter.*

Creating a game. Students create their own Amazing Facts games, researching answers if necessary. Teaching suggestions are provided in the Skills Journal annotation.

Amazing Facts Tournament. Explain to the students that you're going to have an Amazing Facts tournament. Divide the class into four teams. Give students time (about 10 minutes) to review the *Amazing Facts* questions from Themes 1–5. Ask the teams Amazing Facts questions from Themes 1–5 in random order. Students answer orally. On the board, keep track of the score. The team with the most points at the end of play is the winner. You can give an award for the "AMAZING" team.

Telling an original story. Have students create their own stories, using the question and answer format on page 110. For students ready to go beyond a simple repetitive version, have them solicit answers to open-ended slots: something to eat, a place, a thing. Their stories can have a touch of humor when read out loud. For example, *What did she catch? She caught a car.* Students use correct irregulars as they learn to work with humor in English.

SCIENCE Synthesizing information. Have students work individually, with partners, or in small groups to do research on tropical rain forests. Questions to consider are *What animals and plants live there? What is the weather like? What gifts of nature are available in the rain forests?* Students can write a paragraph about why it is important to protect rain forests. (CALLA: Resourcing)

STAFF DEVELOPMENT

See the *Amazing How-To Handbook* for more on "Amazing Facts."

ASSESSMENT

You will find background information on the latest thinking in assessment as well as the assessment instruments for this theme in the *Amazing Assessment Package*.

You have been collecting assessment data through the ongoing and holistic assessment options (Oral Language Checklist, Reading Checklist, Writing Checklist, Anecdotal Record Form) in this theme. The following are specific end-of-theme assessment strategies that will help you evaluate your students' progress as well as adapt your instruction to meet their needs.

Student Self-Assessment. Self-assessment surveys are a means for students to have input into their own learning process. Students can use them to **reflect** on the work they have done and the learning strategies they have used during this theme.

Interpreting and Applying Assessment Data. As teachers, you collect assessment data in order to inform your instruction. Assessment information is a tool that helps you tailor your program to better meet the needs and interests of your students.

Evaluate the checklists, anecdotal records, portfolio collections, and test results from this theme as a means of informing your instruction.

- In which areas are students showing confidence and enthusiasm?
- In which areas are they hesitant or confused?
- Should you provide more classroom opportunities for oral language or writing?
- Would certain students (or the whole class) benefit from a focused mini-lesson on a certain area or skill?
- Remember to recycle skills as you teach the next theme and provide students with many opportunities to improve their competence.

Review the results of the **Student Self-Assessment** survey and incorporate students' interests as you plan your instruction for the next theme. What do they want to learn next? Which activities did they enjoy most? If your students particularly enjoyed choral reading, roleplaying, or working in partners, try to emphasize those kinds of activities in the next theme.

THEME CELEBRATION

The end of a theme study is a good time for students to share some of their accomplishments with others. Suggest to students that you hold a celebration to spotlight their work. This celebration can be an excellent opportunity to build stronger connections with other students and teachers in the school. Your students can demonstrate their kites, display and explain their four seasons accordion books, or dramatize one of the folktales. Students may also want to share the Amazing Facts games they have researched and played. If possible, invite family members to the theme celebration.

END-OF-THEME READ-ALOUD BOOK

The Seasons of Arnold's Apple Tree

by Gail Gibbons

San Diego: Harcourt Brace Jovanovich, 1984

Arnold enjoys his apple tree in different ways each season, from smelling its apple blossoms to building a snow fort around it. This book includes a recipe for apple pie and a description of how an apple cider press works.

APPENDIX

Home-School Connection: Family Involvement Letters **197**
   (English and Spanish)
      Theme 1 Letter
      Theme 2 Letter
      Theme 3 Letter
      Theme 4 Letter
      Theme 5 Letter
      Theme 6 Letter
      Invitation Letter
      Teacher-Parent Conference Letter

Reading Corner: Literature Links Bibliographies **215**

Tapescript **223**

Student Book Index **243**

Process Writing Portfolio Program: Level C Scope and Sequence . . . **246**

Amazing English!

Dear family,

In English class, we are beginning our first unit, "Friend to Friend." The children will be getting to know their classmates and discovering their school. They will be talking, reading, and writing about schedules, calendars, and activities in and out of school.

Here are some activities you can do **in your home language.** These activities will help your child develop skills related to the things we are learning in English.

♦ **Calendar.** Encourage your child to mark events on a home calendar. Play a "Mystery Month" game. You choose the Mystery Month. Your child will figure out the month by asking "before" and "after" questions: "Is it after May?" (yes) "Is it before October? (yes) Then, let your child choose a Mystery Month for you to guess.

♦ **Family Stories.** Tell your child stories about friends you had when you were his or her age. What did you like to do with your friends? Encourage your child to talk about his or her friends and the things they like to do together.

♦ **Video Fun.** At the end of this unit, the children will be reading a selection from *The Wizard of Oz*. You may enjoy watching the movie with your child; borrow the video tape from your local library or video store.

Thanks for your interest in our class!

Sincerely,

_____
(teacher's name)

Amazing English!

Estimada familia:

En la clase de inglés comenzamos nuestra primera unidad, "Friend to Friend" (De amigo a amigo). Los niños van a conocer a sus compañeros de clase y van a descubrir su escuela. Ellos estarán hablando, leyendo y escribiendo acerca de horarios, calendarios, y actividades en la escuela y afuera de la escuela.

He aquí algunas actividades que usted puede hacer en español. Estas actividades ayudarán a su hijo/a a desarrollar destrezas relacionadas con lo que estamos aprendiendo en inglés.

- **Calendarios.** Anímele a su hijo/a a anotar eventos en un calendario en la casa. Jueguen "Mes misterioso". Usted escoge el mes misterioso. Su hijo/a tratará de adivinar el mes haciendo preguntas con "antes" y "después": "Es después de mayo?" (sí) "Es antes de octubre?" (sí) Luego, deje que su hijo/a escoja un mes misterioso para que usted lo adivine.

- **Historias de familia.** Cuéntele a su hijo/a historias de amigos que tuvo cuando tenía la misma edad de su hijo/a. ¿Qué le gustaba hacer con los amigos? Anímele a su hijo/a a hablar acerca de los amigos y qué les gusta hacer juntos.

- **Diversión con videos.** Al final de esta unidad, los niños van a leer una selección del libro *El Mago de Oz.* Usted se divertirá viendo esa película con su hijo/a; preste el video de la biblioteca o arriéndelo en la tienda de videos.

¡Gracias por su interés en nuestra clase!

Atentamente,

_____

(nombre del maestro)

Amazing English!

Dear family,

In English class, we are beginning the unit "Families Around the World." The children will be talking, reading, and writing about different families, things they like to do together, and foods they like to eat.

Here are some activities you can do **in your home language.** These activities will help your child develop skills related to the things we are learning in English.

- ♦ **Family Stories**. Tell your child stories about your own childhood. How was your family life different from your child's? How was it the same? Do you have friends or relatives living in another country? How is family life for children different in that country? If possible, help your child find that country on a world map.

- ♦ **Family Shopping.** Let your child help you shop for groceries. Write a shopping list and gather coupons together. At the store, point out information found on food packages: the price, the expiration date, the ingredients. Compare the cost of different brands and packages by using the unit price information on the shelf stickers.

- ♦ **Video Fun.** At the end of this unit, the children will be reading a selection from *Bambi*. You may enjoy watching the movie with your child; borrow the video tape from your local library or video store.

Thanks for your interest in our class!

Sincerely,

(teacher's name)

Amazing English!

Estimada familia:

En la clase de inglés comenzamos la unidad, "Families Around the World" (Familias a través del mundo). Los niños estarán hablando, leyendo y escribiendo acerca de diferentes familias, de las cosas que les gusta hacer juntos, y de las comidas que les gustan.

He aquí algunas actividades que usted puede hacer en español. Estas actividades ayudarán a su hijo/a a desarrollar destrezas relacionadas con lo que estamos aprendiendo en inglés.

♦ **Historias de familia.** Cuéntele a su hijo/a historias de su propia niñez. ¿En qué forma fue su vida familiar diferente a la de su hijo/a? ¿En qué forma fue similar? ¿Tiene usted amigos o parientes que viven en otro país? ¿Cómo se diferencia la vida familiar de los niños en ese país a la de éste? Si es posible, ayúdele a su hijo/a a buscar ese país en un mapa mundial.

♦ **Compras de familia.** Permita que su hijo/a le ayude a hacer el mercado. Juntos escriban una lista de compras y busquen cupones para productos. En la tienda, muéstrele a su hijo/a la información que se halla en los empaques: el precio, la fecha de expiración, los ingredientes. Comparen el costo de diferentes marcas y tamaños usando el precio por unidad que ponen en las etiquetas en los estantes.

♦ **Diversión con videos.** Al final de esta unidad, los niños van a leer una selección del libro *Bambi.* Usted se divertirá viendo esa película con su hijo/a; preste el video de la biblioteca o arriéndelo en la tienda de videos.

¡Gracias por su interés en nuestra clase!

Atentamente,

_____

(nombre del maestro)

Amazing English!

Dear family,

In English class, we are beginning the unit "Adventures in Space." The children will be talking, reading, and writing about space exploration and space fantasies.

Here are some activities you can do **in your home language.** These activities will help your child develop skills related to the things we are learning in English.

- **Astronaut Survey.** Ask your child, "Would you like to be an astronaut? Why or why not?" Have your child ask at least three other people this question, and let you know what they say. Your child could write people's comments in two lists: *Good Things About Being an Astronaut* and *Bad Things About Being an Astronaut.*

- **Word Game.** You can play this game with the whole family. Each player or team writes the word **SPACE** down the side of a piece of paper. You have three minutes to think up a word beginning with each letter: **S, P, A, C,** and **E.** Each word must have something to do with space.

- **Pack Your Bags.** Imagine that you are going to spend a year on the moon. The moon colony provides food, clothes, and housing. You may bring three personal items. What will you bring? What will your child bring? Compare your choices.

Thanks for your interest in our class!

Sincerely,

_____
(teacher's name)

Amazing English!

Estimada familia:

En la clase de inglés comenzamos la unidad, "Adventures in Space" (Aventuras en el espacio). Los estudiantes van a hablar, leer y escribir acerca de la exploración del espacio y las fantasías espaciales.

He aquí algunas actividades que usted puede hacer en español. Estas actividades ayudarán a su hijo/a a desarrollar destrezas relacionadas con lo que estamos aprendiendo en inglés.

♦ **Encuesta sobre astronautas.** Pregúntele a su hijo/a, "¿Te gustaría ser astronauta? ¿Por qué sí o por qué no?" Pida que su hijo/a les haga esas mismas preguntas a otras tres personas y que le deje a usted saber cuáles son las respuestas. Su hijo/a podría anotar los comentarios que recibe en la encuesta en dos listas: *Puntos buenos de ser astronauta* y *Puntos malos de ser un astronauta.*

♦ **Juego de palabras.** Usted puede jugar esto con toda la familia. Cada jugador o equipo escribe la palabra **ESPACIO** de arriba abajo en una hoja de papel. Tienen tres minutos para pensar en una palabra comenzando con cada letra: **E, S, P, A, C, I** y **O.** Cada palabra debe tener algo que ver con el espacio.

♦ **Empaquen sus bolsas.** Imagínese que va a pasar un año en la luna. La colonia en la luna le proveerá a usted con comida, ropa y vivienda. Usted puede traer tres artículos personales. ¿Qué va a traer usted? ¿Qué va a traer su hijo/a? Comparen lo que eligen para traer.

¡Gracias por su interés en nuestra clase!

Atentamente,

_____
(nombre del maestro)

Amazing English!

Dear family,

In English class, we are beginning the unit "Across the USA." The children will be studying maps and learning about history and life today in various parts of the country .

Here are some activities you can do **in your home language.** These activities will help your child develop skills related to the things we are learning in English.

♦ **Study a Map.** Look at a map of the U.S. with your child. Help your child find the state you live in. Ask, "What states border our state? Which ocean are we closer to?" Plan an imaginary vacation trip to another state. Trace your route. How many miles will you travel? Who will you visit? What will you see and do?

♦ **Write a Letter.** Encourage your child to write a letter to a friend or relative in a different state or town. Help your child write the address and return address on the envelope, and show him or her where to place the stamp.

♦ **Where Was It Grown?** In this unit, the children read a story written by a child whose family picks fruits and vegetables for a living. Help your child find out where the fruits and vegetables your family eats are grown. The information is sometimes on stickers or wrappers or on the boxes in the grocery stores.

Thanks for your interest in our class!

Sincerely,

_____
(teacher's name)

Amazing English!

Estimada familia:

En la clase de inglés comenzamos la unidad, "Across the USA" (A través de los Estados Unidos). Los niños van a estudiar los mapas y van a aprender acerca de la historia y la vida actual en varias partes del país.

He aquí algunas actividades que usted puede hacer en español. Estas actividades ayudarán a su hijo/a a desarrollar destrezas relacionadas con lo que estamos aprendiendo en inglés.

- ♦ **Estudiar un mapa.** Con su hijo/a miren un mapa de los Estados Unidos. Ayúdele a su hijo/a a buscar el estado donde ustedes viven. Pregúntele, "Cuáles estados rodean a nuestro estado? ¿Cuál océano queda mas cerca?" Planeen una vacación imaginaria a otro estado. Tracen su ruta. ¿Cuántas millas viajarán? ¿A quién visitarán? ¿Qué verán y qué harán?

- ♦ **Escribir una carta.** Anímele a su hijo/a a escribir una carta a un amigo o un pariente en otro estado u otra ciudad. Ayúdele a su hijo/a a escribir la dirección y su propia dirección en el sobre, y muéstrele dónde poner la estampilla.

- ♦ **¿Dónde fue cultivado?** En esta unidad, los niños leen un cuento escrito por un niño cuya familia cosecha frutas y verduras para ganarse la vida. Ayúdele a su hijo/a a averiguar en dónde fueron cultivadas las frutas y verduras que consume su familia. A veces esa información se encuentra en la tienda de mercado en las etiquetas y envolturas o en las cajas.

¡Gracias por su interés en nuestra clase!

Atentamente,

_____
(nombre del maestro)

Amazing English!

Dear family,

In English class, we are beginning the unit "Animals Wild and Tame." We will be reading, writing, and talking about pets, seeing-eye dogs, lions, gorillas, and more.

Here are some activities you can do **in your home language.** These activities will help your child develop skills related to the things we are learning in English.

♦ **I'm Thinking of an Animal.** Play a "Twenty Questions" guessing game with your child. One of you thinks of an animal. The other asks questions that can be answered "yes" or "no." For example: "Does it have fur?" "Can it fly?"

♦ **Family Field Trip.** Where can you see wild animals or farm animals nearby? Plan a family visit to a zoo, aquarium, nature center, or petting farm. Public libraries often have free passes available.

♦ **Nature Shows.** There are many popular wildlife programs on TV. Choose a show to watch with your child. Talk about the new information you learned from the show. Then, go to the library to find out more. There are many children's books about animals with wonderful photographs and interesting, easy-to-read information.

Thanks for your interest in our class!

Sincerely,

_____
(teacher's name)

Amazing English!

Estimada familia:

En la clase de inglés comenzamos la unidad, "Animals Wild and Tame" (Animales salvajes y domesticados). Leeremos, escribiremos y hablaremos acerca de animales de casa, perros para ciegos, leones, gorilas y mucho más.

He aquí algunas actividades que usted puede hacer en español. Estas actividades ayudarán a su hijo/a a desarrollar destrezas relacionadas con lo que estamos aprendiendo en inglés.

♦ **Pienso en un animal.** Con su hijo/a jueguen las adivinanzas "Veinte preguntas". Uno de ustedes piensa en un animal. El otro hace preguntas que se pueden contestar con "si" o "no". Por ejemplo: "¿Tiene pelo?" "¿Puede volar?"

♦ **Paseo de familia.** ¿En qué sitio pueden ustedes ver animales salvajes o animales de granja cerca del lugar donde viven? Planee un paseo con la familia al zoológico, acuario, centro de naturaleza, o una granja de mascotas. Muchas bibliotecas públicas prestan pases gratis para que los que viven en la comunidad puedan hacer visitas a sitios como esos.

♦ **Programas sobre la naturaleza.** En la televisión hay muchos programas populares que se tratan de la vida salvaje. Con su hijo/a escojan uno de estos programa para verlo juntos. Hablen sobre lo que aprendan por medio del programa. Vayan a la biblioteca a buscar mas información. Hay muchos libros para niño que se tratan de animales; tienen fotografías maravillosas e interesantes e información que es fácil de leer.

¡Gracias por su interés en nuestra clase!

Atentamente,

_____
(nombre del maestro)

Amazing English!

Dear family,

In English class, we are beginning the unit "Changing Seasons." The children will be reading, writing, and talking about the weather and the seasons in places around the world.

Here are some activities you can do **in your home language.** These activities will help your child develop skills related to the things we are learning in English.

- ◆ **Family Stories.** What different things does your family do in different seasons? Talk about it together. Have you ever lived in a place where the weather was quite different? Do you know someone who does? Tell your child about it and talk about what people in those places do in the different seasons.

- ◆ **Family Brainstorm.** As a family activity, make a list of all the good things about spring, and all the bad things about spring. Which list is longer?

- ◆ **Sky Watch.** Make a point of observing the sky with your child. Notice where the sun rises and where it sets. Now that it is spring, is the sun rising earlier or later every day? Watch the sunset several times a week and note how the colors and the patterns differ. In the evening, look at the moon and notice its changing shape.

Thanks for your interest in our class!

Sincerely,

_____

(teacher's name)

Amazing English!

Estimada familia:

En la clase de inglés comenzamos la unidad, "Changing Seasons" (Los cambios de las estaciones). Los estudiantes van a leer, escribir y hablar acerca del tiempo y de las estaciones en lugares alrededor del mundo.

He aquí algunas actividades que usted puede hacer en español. Estas actividades ayudarán a su hijo/a a desarrollar destrezas relacionadas con lo que estamos aprendiendo en inglés.

♦ **Historias de familia.** ¿Qué cosas distintas hace su familia en las distintas estaciones? Comenten juntos. ¿Ha vivido usted en un lugar donde el tiempo sea completamente diferente al tiempo de aquí? ¿Conoce usted a alguien que vive en un sitio como tal? Cuéntele a su hijo/a acerca de esto y de lo que hace la gente en estos lugares en las diferentes estaciones del año.

♦ **Intercambio de ideas entre familia.** Como una actividad de familia, hagan una lista de todas las cosas buenas de la primavera y todas las cosas malas de la primavera. ¿Cuál lista es más larga?

♦ **Observar el cielo.** Haga el esfuerzo de observar el cielo con su hijo/a. Noten el punto donde el sol aparece y donde desaparece. Ya que ha llegado la primavera, ¿amanece el sol más temprano o más tarde cada día? Observen el atardecer varias veces en una semana y noten como los colores y las figuras cambian. Por las noches, miren la luna y noten sus cambios de forma.

¡Gracias por su interés en nuestra clase!

Atentamente,

_____

(nombre del maestro

Teacher-Parent Conference

Dear, _____

At this time of the year, we set aside time to meet with parents and talk about each child's progress in school. During the conference, we will look at samples of your child's work, talk about your child's learning strengths and interests, and discuss goals for the next part of the year.

I am looking forward to meeting with you and talking about your child. You may want to invite a translator to come with you.

I have scheduled our conference on _____ , at

                                        (date)

_____ , in _____

     (time)   (location)

Please fill out the bottom part of this page and send it back to school with your child.

Sincerely,

_____

--<CUT HERE>--

Your conference has been scheduled on _____ at

                                          (date)

_____ , in _____ .

       (time)   (location)

Please respond.

        Yes, I can come to the conference at that time.

        No, I can't come at that time. I'd like to schedule a conference at a different time.

        I am free on the following days: _____

        at the following times: _____

Your name: _____

Reunión de maestro y padre

Estimado/a: _____

En esta época del año escolar, los maestros fijamos un tiempo con los padres para reunirnos y hablar acerca del progreso en la escuela de cada estudiante. Durante esta reunión miraremos muestras del trabajo de su hijo/a, hablaremos acerca de los intereses y las aptitudes de él o ella, y estableceremos metas para el resto del año.

Espero poder reunirme con usted para hablar acerca de su hijo/a. Tal vez quiera invitar a un traductor a acompañarlo.

He planeado nuestra reunión para el _____ a las
                                            (fecha)

_____ en _____ .
           (hora)   (lugar)

Le pido el favor de llenar la parte baja de esta hoja y mandarla de regreso con su hijo/a.

Atentamente,

_____

---------------------------------- *<corte aquí>* --

Nuestra reunión está planeada para el _____ a las
                                            (fecha)

_____ en _____ .
           (hora)   (lugar)

Favor responder con el siguiente:

        Sí, puedo venir a esa hora.

        No, no puedo venir a esa hora. Prefiero tener la reunión a una hora diferente.

        Puedo venir en los siguientes días: _____

        a las siguientes horas: _____

Su nombre: _____

Come to a Celebration!

Dear family,

We are planning a celebration. We want to share some of the work we have done in English class. We hope you can join us!

Date: _____

Time: _____

Place: _____

Teacher(s): _____

¡Vengan a celebrar!

Estimada familia:

Estamos planeando una celebración. Queremos compartir parte del trabajo que hemos hecho en nuestra clase de inglés. ¡Esperamos que nos pueda acompañar!

Fecha: _____

Hora: _____

Lugar: _____

Maestro(s): _____

LITERATURE LINKS
BIBLIOGRAPHIES

THEME 1

All About You, by Catherine & John Anholt. Viking Penguin. Encourages children to talk about themselves; good for vocabulary.

An Alphabet of Rotten Kids!, by David Elliot. Philomel. A distinctive alphabet book children will find funny. *ER*

Angel Child, Dragon Child, by Michele Maria Surat . Scholastic. An immigrant child from Vietnam tries to adjust to new life in America—very highly recommended.

Enemies, by Robert Klein. Scholastic. Sworn enemies become friends.

Halloween Echo, by Susan Clymer. Scholastic. Friendship between two girls is tested when a new neighbor moves in.

I Hate English! by Ellen Levine. Scholastic. A multicultural book that encourages self-esteem as it explores learning a new language. *ER*

L. Frank Baum: Royal Historian of Oz, by Carpenter & Shirley. Lerner. Good biography of Baum.

Maria Teresa, by Mary Atkinson. Lollipop Power A young Chicano girl faces discrimination in a small American town.

Postman Pat, To the Rescue, by John Cunliffe. Scholastic. One of a series about Pat, everyone's friend. *ER*

School Friends series, by Bernice Chardiet and Grace Maccarone. Scholastic. Wonderful illustrations and simple stories kids can relate to. *ER*

Soccer: A Heads Up Guide to Super Soccer, by Richard Brenner. Sports Illustrated for Kids Books.

The Wind in the Willows, by Kenneth Grahame. Scribner. Never out of date, the story of three great friends.

The Wizard of Oz, by Frank L. Baum. Holt.

Titles in Languages Other than English

Margaret y Margarita by Lynn Reiser. New York: Lectorum Publications, Inc.

Querido Sebastián by Luz María Chapela. México: SEP.

The Runaway Riceball by Hiroko Quackenbush **(English/Japanese)**. Los Angeles, CA: Jeong-Eum-Sa Imports, Inc. (The Korea Book Center).

The Son of the Cinnamon Tree; The Donkey's Egg adapted by D. Vorhees, M. Mueller **(Korean)**. Los Angeles, CA: Jeong-Eum-Sa Imports, Inc. (The Korea Book Center).

Torta de cumpleaños by Ivar Da Coll. Bogotá, Colombia: Carlos Valencia.

ER = Easy Reading

Abuela, by Arthur Dorros. Dutton Children's Books. In a wonderful blend of fantasy and fact, a little girl flies over New York City with her grandmother.

Bambi: A Life in the Woods, by Felix Salten. Simon & Schuster. Read the whole classic aloud.

Brothers and Sisters, by Ellen Sensi. Scholastic. A multicultural celebration of family love. *ER*

Eating Fractions, by Bruce McMillan. Scholastic. Wonderful math concept book that uses food.

I Love My Family, by Wade Hudson. Scholastic. An African-American boy describes his annual family reunion. *ER*

Is Your Mama a Llama?, by Deborah Guardino. Scholastic. Enchanting classic about animals and families. *ER*

Isla, by Arthur Dorros. Dutton. A sequel to *Abuela* in which a girl and her grandmother have wonderful adventures.

It Takes a Village, by Jane Cowen-Fletcher. Scholastic. Beautiful picture book based on a West African proverb. *ER*

Loving, by Ann Morris. Lothrop, Lee & Shepard Books. Classic multicultural book about families around the world. *ER*

Mama Zooms, by Jane Cowen-Fletcher. Scholastic. Wonderful picture book about a boy and a wheelchair-bound mother. *ER*

Rap Tales, by Bernice and John Chardiet. Scholastic. Rap retellings of traditional folktales offer read-aloud fun.

Space Travelers, by Margaret Wild. Scholastic. A homeless family seeks shelter in a playground rocket.

This is the Place for Me, by Joanna Cole. Scholastic. A bear named Morty searches for a home. *ER*

Vejigante Masquerader, by Lulu Delacre. Scholastic. A Puerto Rican boy's story told bilingually and with instructions on how to make the masquerader's mask. *ER*

Year Walk, by Ann Nolan Clark. Viking. A Basque boy moves to Idaho and helps his grandfather herd sheep across the frontier.

Titles in Languages Other than English

Celebrating New Year Miss Yuan-Shian by Wonder Kids **(English/Khmer; English/Vietnamese).** Arcadia, CA: Shen's Books and Supplies.

Ciudades de hormigas by Arthur Dorros. New York: Harper Arco Ir*ld* by Jan Yolen **(Multilingual).** Los Angeles, CA: Jeong-Eum-Sa Imports, Inc. (The Korea Book Center).

Grandmother's Tale by Moi McCrory and Eleni Michael **(Turkish/English).** Covina, CA: Multicultural Distributing Center.

Somos un arcoiris/We Are a Rainbow (Bilingual) by Nancy María Grande Tabor. Watertown, MA: Charlesbridge Publishing.

Voy a cocinar (apetitosas recetas para niños) by Maite Lasa. México: SITESA.

ER = Easy Reading

THEME 3

Aligay Saves the Stars, Kazuko G. Stone. Scholastic. An alligator's antics in space! *ER*

Guys from Space, by Daniel Pinkwater. Macmillan. What if a spaceship landed in your back yard?

Harry Newberry and the Raiders of the Red Drink, by Mel Gilden. Henry Holt. A comic book character comes alive.

Judith Resnik: Challenger Astronaut. Lodestar Books. The story of Judith Resnik's life.

The Magic School Bus Lost in the Solar System, by Joanna Cole. Scholastic. Ms. Fizzle's fantastic journey delights and teaches. *ER*

Moog, Moog, Space Barber, by Mark Teague. Scholastic. A boy and his cat have space adventures. *ER*

My Picture Book of the Planets, by Nancy Krulik. Scholastic. Good drawings and NASA photos. *ER*

The Neighbor from Outer Space, by Maureen George. Scholastic. A science fiction fantasy with humor.

Norby and Yobo's Great Adventure, by Issac and Janet Simov. Walker. One of eight entertaining fantasies about Jeff and his robot Norby.

Wilbur's Space Machine, by Morna Balian. Holiday House. Easy to read fantasy. *ER*

A Wrinkle in Time, Madeleine L'Engle. Farrar. A science fiction fantasy about a loving family.

Titles in Languages Other than English

El autobús mágico en el sistema solar by Joanna Cole. New York: Scholastic.

Narara Sut' A Eisu (Fantastical Adventures of a Space Robot) **(Korean).** Los Angeles, CA: Jeong-Eum-Sa Imports, Inc. (The Korea Book Center).

Nuestro sistema solar by Isaac Asimov. Madrid, España: edíciones sm.

The Bridge of Reunion and Other Stories (folktales about the Milky Way) **(Vietnamese).** Arcadia, CA: Shen's Books and Supplies.

ER = Easy Reading

THEME 4

Across a Great River, by Irene Beltran Hernandez. Arte Publico Press. A family's journey across the Rio Grande.

Alvin Josephy's Biography Series of American Indians. Silver Burdett. All the leaders, conflicts, and resolutions.

And It is Still That Way, by Byrd Baylor. Scribner. A collection of legends told by Arizona Indian children.

Children of the Earth and Sky, by Stephen Krensky. Five beautifully illustrated Native American tales. *ER*

Christopher Columbus: Voyager to the Unknown, by Nancy S. Levinson. Lodestar Books. Good biography with lots of interesting archival documents.

Farewell to Manzanar, by Jeanne and James Houston. Houghton. The true story of a Japanese-American family forced into a detention camp.

The Girl Who Married a Ghost and other Tales of the North American Indians , by John Bierhorst. Four Winds.

The Little Island, by Golden McDonald. Scholastic. A Caldecott winner told in rhythmic prose. *ER*

My Side of the Mountain, by Jean George. Dutton. A winter alone in the mountains.

Reach out, Ricardo, by Mary Collins Dunne. Abelhard Schuman. The life of a Mexican American boy gets even harder when his father joins a grape worker's strike.

Stringbean's Trip to the Shining Sea, by Vera B. Williams and Jennifer Williams. A boy's cross-country trip is illustrated with postcards and photos. *ER*

This Is My House, Arthur Dorros. Scholastic. Multicultural tour of dwellings around the world. *ER*

Working Cotton, by Shirley Anne Williams. Harcourt. A migrant family's story with outstanding illustrations by Carole Byard. (Caldecott Honor Book) *ER*

Your Best Friend, Kate, by Pat Brisson. Bradbury Press. A girl travels across the U.S. but stays in touch with her best friend.

Titles in Languages Other than English

The Dancer by Fred Burstein **(English/ Japanese/Spanish)**. Arcadia, CA: Shen's Books and Supplies.

El viaje de Jenny by Sheila White Samton. New York: Viking/Penguin.

Mira Cómo salen las estrellas by Riki Levinson. New York: Dutton Children's Books.

Siempre puede ser peor by Margot Zemach. New York: Farrar, Straus and Giroux/Mirasol/libros juveniles.

The Trek by Ann Jonas **(Chinese)**. Arcadia, CA: Shen's Books and Supplies.

ER = Easy Reading

The Baby Zoo, by Bruce McMillan. Scholastic. Wonderful photo essays.

Bear, by John Schoenberg. Philomel Books. An orphan bear tries to survive the Alaskan wilderness; Caldecott-winner art.

Box Turtle at Long Pond, by William T. George. Greenwillow Books. Wonderful illustrations of a pond habitat teaches science and tells a story, too. *ER*

The Clifford Series, by Norman Bridwell. Scholastic. Everybody's favorite red dog has great appeal. *ER*

Henry & Midge Get the Cold Shivers, by Cynthia Rylant. The 7th book in the series about Henry and his huge dog, Midge.

I'm the Best! by Marjorie W. Sharmat. Holiday House. A dog is shuffled from owner to owner until he finds a home with Robert.

Koko's Kitten, by Francine Patterson. Scholastic. The classic about the gorilla as a "baby." *ER*

Momo's Kitten, by Mitsu Yashima. Viking. A Japanese-American girl finds a stray kitten. *ER*

The Mud Pony, by Caron Lee Cohen. Scholastic. A native American tale about a boy and a magical pony.

My Life with the Chimpanzees, by Jane Goodall. Simon & Schuster. Very interesting autobiography.

Quail Song: A Pueblo Indian Tale, by Valarie S. Carey. G.P. Putnam's Sons. Quail must outsmart trickster Coyote.

The Story of Nim: The Chimp Who Learned Language, by Anna Michel. Random House. True story about the chimp who could use sign language.

Why Ducks Sleep on One Leg, by Sherry Garland. Scholastic. A charming Vietnamese creation tale. *ER*

Wild Animal Stories, by Margaret Davidson. Scholastic. Nature book about animal families. *ER*

With Love from Koko, by Faith McNulty. Scholastic. Nice account of author's meeting with Koko.

Titles in Languages Other than English

El bosque tropical by Helen Cowcher. New York: Farrar, Straus and Giroux/Mirasol/libros juveniles.

El Manchas by Marinés Medero. México: Coedición-SEP/Ediciones Samara.

El perro del cerro y la rana de la sabana by Ana María Machado. Carácas, Venezuela: Ediciones Ekaré - Banco del Libro.

The Grateful Crane by Hiroko Quakenbush **(English/Japanese).** Arcadia, CA: Shen's Books and Supplies.

The Tiger and the Dried Persimmons (traditional) **(Korean).** Los Angeles, CA: Jeong-Eum-Sa Imports, Inc. (The Korea Book Center).

ER = Easy Reading

THEME 6

Chinese Mother Goose Rhymes, by Robert Wyndham. Philomel Books. Traditional rhymes told over hundreds of years.

Cricket Songs: Japanese Haiku, by Harry Behn. Harcourt. Poems celebrating nature; great models for student innovations.

Dragonfly's Tale, by Kristina Rodanas. Clarion Books. Respect for nature's gifts in a Zuni folktale.

The Dream Keeper, by Langston Hughes. Knopf. A collection of poems by the noted African-American poet.

The Funny Little Woman, by Arlene Mosel. Dutton. A tale set in medieval Japan.

King of Another Country, by Fiona French. Scholastic. Fabulous paintings portray African culture. *ER*

The Magic School Bus Inside the Earth, by Joanna Cole. Scholastic. Ms. Fizzle goes to the center of the earth. *ER*

Ming Lo Moves the Mountain, by Arnold Lobel. Scholastic. Beautiful paintings of rural China tell a folktale. *ER*

Moon Rope: A Peruvian Folktale, by Lois Ehlert. Harcourt. Fox talks mole into climbing to the moon on a grass rope.

Momataro: Peach Boy, by George Suyeoka. Island Heritage. A Japanese fantasy. *ER*

The Princess and the Beggar, by Anne Sibley O'Brien. Retelling of a 6th century Korean folktale.

Shining Princess and Other Japanese Legends, The, by Eric Quayle. Arcade. Ten legends from an ancient land.

The Tale of the Mandarin Ducks, by Katherine Paterson. Lodestar Books. Highly acclaimed version of a Japanese folktale.

Titles in Languages Other than English

Doña Piñones by María de la Luz Uribe. Carácas, Venezuela: Ediciones Ekaré - Banco del Libro.

Le Quang Vinh (Moon Festival) by Tet Trung Thu **(Vietnamese)**. Covina, CA: Multicultural Distributing Center.

Pedro y su roble by Claude Levert and Carme Solé Vendrell. Madrid, España: Susaeta Ediciones.

Pyol Kwa Ttonanun Iyagi Yohaeng (Winter, Spring, Summer, Fall) by Mew-young Park **(Korean)**. Los Angeles, CA: Jeong-Eum-Sa Imports, Inc. (The Korea Book Center).

Sapo en el invierno by Max Velthuijs. Carácas, Venezuela: Ediciones Ekaré-Banco del Libro.

ER = Easy Reading

TAPESCRIPTS

AMAZING ENGLISH
LEVEL C STUDENT BOOK

AMAZING ENGLISH Theme Song

(Round 1)
Amazing English is such fun,
Lots of fun for everyone.
Amazing English is such fun,
Amazing every day.

(Round 2)
Read amazing stories,
Read amazing stories,
Read amazing stories,
Amazing every day.

(Round 3)
Amazing English is my favorite,
Amazing English is my favorite,
Amazing English is my favorite,
Amazing every day.

(Round 4)
A-A-A-A-A-A-mazing,
A-A-A-A-A-A-mazing,
A-A-A-A-A-A-mazing,
Amazing every day.

THEME ONE — FRIEND TO FRIEND

I Know Everyone's Name
Listen to the song. Then sing along and make up
your own song.

(Chorus)
This is a nice song,
This is a nice song,
I know everyone's name;
We will get along,
We will get along,
I hope you feel the same.

(1st verse)
My name is Alice (child stands up and sings)
Her name is Alice (class stands up and sings)
I know everyone's name; (class sings,
moves/dances to music)
We will get along,
We will get along,
I hope you feel the same. (class sits)

(2nd verse)
My name is Carlos (class stands up and sings)

His name is Carlos (class stands up and sings)
I know everyone's name; (class sings,
moves/dances)
We will get along,
We will get along,
I hope you feel the same. (class sits)

(3rd verse)
My name is Sun-Mi (child stands up and sings)
Her name is Sun-Mi (class stands up and sings)
I know everyone's name; (class sings,
moves/dances)
We will get along,
We will get along,
I hope you feel the same. (class sits)

(Chorus)

My name is Alice (stands, then sits)
Her name is Alice (class stands, then sits)
My name is Carlos (stands and sits)
His name is Carlos (class stands and sits)
My name is Sun-Mi (stands and remains standing)
Her name is Sun-Mi (class stands, moves to music)
I know everyone's name;
We will get along,
We will get along,
I hope you feel the same!

Communication 1, Page 4
Listen to the conversation. Then make a conversation of your own with a friend.

Is your best friend a boy or a girl?
A girl.
What's her first name?
Her first name is Rosita.
What's her last name?
Her last name is Perez.
Is she older or younger than you?
She's older.
How old <u>is</u> she?
She's eleven.
What do you like to do together?
We like to play soccer and we like to dance.

Amazing Facts, Page 4
Listen and look, please.

Soccer games in England long ago were *really*
big! One team could have more than 100 people.

Don't be surprised if you have a friend named Smith — at least 3.3 million Smiths live in the U.S.!

You share your birthday with about *10,000,000* people around the world!

Communication 1, Page 5
Listen to the conversation. Then make conversations of your own.

Where's Julie?
She's in the library.
What's she doing?
She's reading a book.
Where's the library?
It's next to the 4th grade classroom.

Bingo
Listen to the song. Then sing along.

(1st verse)
There was a man who had a dog,
and Bingo was his name, Oh,
B I N-G-O. B I N-G-O, B I N-G-O,
And Bingo was his name, Oh.

(2nd verse)
There was a man who had a dog,
And Bingo was his name, Oh.
(clap) I N-G-O, (clap) I N-G-O. (clap) I N-G-O,
And Bingo was his name, Oh.

(3rd verse)
(clap clap) N-G-O, (clap clap) N-G-O, (clap clap) N-G-O,

(4th verse)
(clap clap clap) G-O, (clap clap clap) G-O, (clap clap clap) G-O,

(5th verse)
(clap clap clap-clap) O, (clap clap clap-clap) O, clap clap clap-clap) O,

(6th verse)
(clap clap clap-clap-clap-), (three times)

The Weekend, Page 7
Listen to the song. Then sing along.

(1st verse)
Well, the weekend comes every week,
We love it, we love it; Oh, we really love it!
Saturday, Sunday, Oh, what a treat!
We love it, we love it; Oh, we really love it!
Now the weekend makes you feel so fine,
We love it, we love it; Oh, we really love it!

Saturday, Sunday, when you're all mine, all mine...Oh

(Chorus)
Playing on the weekend,
Playing with my friends,
Playing on the weekend,
Hope it never ends.
Playing on the weekend,
Morning, noon or night.

Monday, it is gone,
Tuesday, it is gone,
Wednesday, it is gone,
Thursday, it is gone,
Friday, it is gone.

Monday, Tuesday, Wednesday, Thursday, Friday they're all gone
And it's the weekend!

(2nd verse)
Now the weekend makes you feel all right,
We love it, we love it; Oh, we really love it.
Saturday, Sunday, even Friday night.
We love it, we love it; Oh, we really love it!
Now the weekend makes you feel so fine,
We love it, we love it; Oh, we really love it!
Saturday, Sunday, when you're mine...Oh

(Chorus repeated)

Communication 2, Page 8
Listen to the conversation and the names of the months of the year and the days of the week. Then make conversations of your own.

Is your birthday in July?
No, it isn't. It's in August.
What day of the week is it on this year?
It's on Saturday.

January	April	July	October
February	May	August	November
March	June	September	December

Sunday	Thursday
Monday	Friday
Tuesday	Saturday
Wednesday	

Communication 2, Page 9
Listen to the conversation and the words in the Data Bank. Then make conversations of your own.

Happy Birthday! How old are you today?
I'm eleven.

Here's a present for you.
Oh, thank you! What is it?
Open it and find out.

A T-shirt!
I hope you like it.

Oh, I do. Thank you very much.
You're welcome.

Data Bank

baseball cap	tape	bracelet
pin	sweater	ring
scarf	book	

Check This Out! Page 10
I'll Be Your Friend
Listen and look, please.

I'll be your friend
For as long as you like
I'll share all my candy
I'll lend you my bike

We'll go to the movies
We'll play in the park
I'll hold your hand tightly
When we walk in the dark

I'll hug you hard
If you ever cry
And give you half
Of my Mile High Pie

Together we'll be
Together we'll be
Very best friends
Just you and me.

Amazing Facts, Page 10
Listen and look, please.

It takes 72 muscles to speak one word to a friend.

Do you eat bananas and cereal for breakfast? A banana is about 75 percent water!

Millions of Monarch butterflies fly to a special forest in Mexico every year. They come from as far away as Canada, just to be with their friends!

Check This Out, Page 11
Listen and look, please.

We asked some kids, What makes a good friend?

"A friend is someone you share secrets with."

Annie Choung, age 8
Brooklyn, NY

"Good friends talk on the phone with you. They come over to your house and play with your toys, too."

Pedro Ramirez, age 10
Los Angeles, CA

"A good friend trusts you!"

Jess Romer, age 8
Miami, FL

Can you make up a funny way to say good-bye to your friends?

See you later, Alligator.
In a while, Crocodile.
If you wish, Jelly-fish.
Not so soon, Big Baboon!
Toodle-loo, Kangaroo!
Bye-bye, Butterfly.

Every day is somebody's birthday. This chart shows you how many babies are born in an average week in the U.S. Make a chart like this for your class.

Language Power, Page 12
Listen to the conversation at the top of page 12.

Do you like to sing?
Yes, I do.
No, I don't.

Now listen to the questions and answer for yourself.

1. Dance. Do you like to dance?
2. Draw. Do you like to draw?
3. Swim. Do you like to swim?
4. Read. Do you like to read?

Listen to the conversation, page 12

Do you like animals?
Yes, I do.
No, I don't.

Now listen to the questions and answer for yourself.

1. Games. Do you like games?
2. Vegetables. Do you like vegetables?
3. Soccer. Do you like soccer?
4. Pizza. Do you like pizza?

Language Power, Page 13
Listen to the times and the conversations. Then make conversations of your own.

Number 1. It's a quarter after one. It's one fifteen.
Number 2. It's half past one. It's one-thirty.
Number 3. It's a quarter to two. It's one forty-five.

Let's go to the movies on Saturday.
What time do you want to go?
How about two-thirty?
Half past two? Okay. I can take you then.

Roll Over
Listen to the song. Then sing along.

There were ten in the bed and the little one said,
"Roll over, roll over."
So they all rolled over, and one fell out.

There were nine in the bed and the little one said,
"Roll over, roll over."
So they all rolled over, and one fell out.

There were eight in the bed (etc.)....

There was one in the bed and the little one said,
"Good night."

A New Friend Named Charlie, Page 16
Listen to the letter from Roberto.

Dear Auntie,
Guess what happened last week. A kid named
Charlie picked me for his soccer team! Charlie
says I play better than anybody in our grade. I
can't wait for the first game next week.

I am studying very hard. My English is not very
good. And the kids speak so fast. But Charlie is
helping me.

Here is a photo of Charlie and me. I feel better
with a new friend. But I still love you and miss
you very much.

Your nephew,

Roberto

A New Friend Named Charlie, Page 17
Listen to the letter from Roberto's Auntie Blanca.

Dear Roberto,
I was so happy to hear you have a new friend.
Charlie sounds like a really nice boy. I am happy
that you're on a soccer team, too. Keep practic-
ing! Maybe someday you will play in the World
Cup!

Don't worry so much about your English. You can
do it; you're a smart boy. And now you have
Charlie to help you!

Your Uncle and I and all your cousins miss you.
Here is a photo of all of us for you. Please write
again soon.

Love and kisses,

Auntie Blanca

Let's Play Soccer! Pages 18 and 19
Listen and look, please.

First, you need two teams of 11 people. Each
team tries to get the ball across the field to the
opposite goal. To score a point, you must kick the
ball past the goalkeeper and into the net. It's that
easy! Boys and girls can run, pass, kick, and have
a great time.

Soccer Talk—Words to know

Dribble— Kick the ball along the ground while
running.
Tackle— Use your feet to take the ball away
from an opponent.
Pass— Kick or nudge the ball to your team
members. Remember—no hands!
Mark— Guard the ball and make it hard for an
opponent to get it.
Foul— When a player breaks a rule.
Fake— Pretend to kick or pass the ball—then
do something different.

All Day Long
Listen to the song. Then sing along.

(Verse 1)
Oh, did you ever want to—play in the park?
And did you ever want to—stay there all day, till
the dark?
And did you ever want to—dance to the music?
And did you ever want to—do it, do it, do it, never
lose it?

(Chorus)
All day long, you can do it in the nighttime.
All day long, you can do it, it's the right time.
All day long, oh, there's really nothing to it,
All day long, anyone can do it,
All day long, all day long, all day long, I say, all
day long.

(Verse 2)
Did you ever want to—swim in the pool?
And did you ever want to—stay in all day and be
cool?
And did you ever want to—sing a song?

And did you ever want to—sing it, sing it, all day long?

(Chorus, instrumental, and spoken words)

Verse 1 (2 last lines only)

(Chorus)

Dorothy and Her Friends, Page 20

You may know the story of *The Wizard of Oz*. Here is a story about one of Dorothy's adventures. You will hear about the friends she makes.

Dorothy lived in Kansas. One day, a cyclone carried her house far, far up in the sky. Her house finally landed in the Land of Oz. It also landed right on the Wicked Witch of the East!

Strange little people called Munchkins greeted Dorothy. Their friend, the Good Witch of the North, was also there.

"Welcome! We are so grateful. You have killed the Wicked Witch of the East," said the Good Witch.

"Oh no, there must be some mistake," said Dorothy. "I have not killed anything."

"Your house did, anyway. See? These are her toes!"

"But where am I?"

"In the Land of Oz, of course."

"Oh dear. Can you help me find my way back to Kansas?"

The Munchkins and the Good Witch told Dorothy to ask the Wizard of Oz for help. The Wizard lived in the City of Emeralds.

"Follow the yellow brick road," they said. "You can't miss it."

So Dorothy and her little dog Toto started along the yellow brick road. Soon, Dorothy saw a Scarecrow.

THEME TWO — FAMILIES AROUND THE WORLD

Communication 1, Page 24
Listen to the conversation. Then make a conversation of your own with a friend.

Is your family big or small?
My family is big.
How many brothers do you have?

I have two brothers.
What are their names?
Dan and Mike.
How many sisters do you have?
I have three sisters.
What are their names?
Susan, Judy, and Ellen.
Do you have a pet?
No, I don't. But I'd like a hamster for my birthday.

Amazing Facts, Page 24
Listen and look, please.

Musical talent runs in families. Johann Sebastian Bach had 52 relatives that were musicians!

Baby ducks learn how to swim and dive as soon as they hatch. Their mothers make them do it!

You change positions when you sleep about every 10 minutes.

Communication 1, Page 25
Listen to the conversation. Then make conversations of your own.

Where's your baby brother?
He's in the kitchen.
What's he doing?
He's eating cheese.

My Family, Page 27
Listen to the poem.

I was born
in the year of the rooster
so I wake up early.
My brother was born
in the year of the monkey
so he likes to climb trees.
My father was born
in the year of the dragon
so he likes to eat spicy food
and breathe fire.
My mother was born
in the year of the sheep—
but she doesn't really
seem like one.

Ueda Akie, Age 9

Communication 2, Page 28
Listen and look, please.

<u>He</u> is hiding. But I can see <u>him.</u>
<u>She</u> is hiding. But I can see <u>her</u>.

<u>You</u> are hiding. But I can see <u>you.</u>

<u>They</u> are hiding. But I can see <u>them</u>.

<u>I</u> am hiding. Can you see <u>me</u>?
<u>We</u> are hiding. Can you see <u>us</u>?

There's a Hole in the Bottom of the Sea
Listen to the song. Then sing along.

(1st verse)
There's a hole in the bottom of the sea.
There's a hole in the bottom of the sea.
There's a hole, there's a hole,
There's a hole in the bottom of the sea.

(2nd verse)
There's a log in the hole in the bottom of the sea.

(repeat)
There's a log, there's a log,
There's a log in the hole in the bottom of the sea.

(3rd verse)
There's a bump on the log....(etc.)

(4th verse)
There's a frog on the bump...(etc.)

(5th verse)
There's a fly on the frog...(etc.)

Communication 2, Page 29
Listen to the conversation and the words in the Data Bank. Then make new conversations of your own.

May I help you?
Yes, I need a pound of potatoes, please.
I'll have a jar of peanut butter, please.
May I have a gallon of milk?

Data Bank

a pound of	a jar of	a gallon of
onions	jelly	ice cream
carrots	pickles	juice
tomatoes	spaghetti sauce	soft drink

Check This Out! Page 30
Listen and look, please.

Movie Time

Does your family like to go to the movies? It can be very expensive. Long ago, theaters were called "nickelodeons." Can you guess why? Because it was only a nickel to get in!

Just Joking

A cat and her and her kittens are walking down the street. Suddenly a dog jumps from behind a bush. The kittens are terrified! So the mother cat begins to bark wildly, and she scares the dog away. The cat says to her kittens, "You see how important it is to speak another language!"

Giant Mom

The giant ocean sunfish is a record-breaking, Big Mom. It can grow to about 13 feet and weigh more than 1,000 pounds. Big Mom can lay about three *million* eggs!

Amazing Facts, Page 30
Listen and look, please.

Are you an average kid in an average family? Then you will eat 1,500 peanut butter sandwiches by the time you're 18!

On Mother's Day, more than 103 million people make phone calls—most of them to a mom!

Check This Out! Page 31
Listen and look, please.

Unfriendly Families

Did you know that ants live in "families" called colonies?

The colonies can be big, with many thousands of ants. The colonies can be small, with only a dozen ants. Ant homes can be under the ground, in wood, or in high mounds.

Ants are social insects. That means they live and work together. There is a queen ant for every colony of worker ants. Some ants have wings and some don't.

Ants aren't very friendly to ants in other colonies. They make war on smaller ants. They drive the smaller ants out of their nests and steal their eggs. When the eggs hatch, the unfriendly ants make the new ants work as slaves in their colony.

Driver ants are really unfriendly. Driver ants live in parts of South America and Asia. Even the biggest and strongest animals are afraid of driver ants. These ants march in long columns, like an army, and attack anything in their way. Any animal in the ants' way will be covered with millions of bites! One way to fight off an attack is to find water and drown the driver ants.

The best way to survive driver ants is to just stay out of their way!

Language Power, Page 32
Listen to the conversation and the words. Then make conversations of your own.

What are they eating?
They're eating cereal and bananas.

1. rice
2. fish
3. meat
4. soup
5. eggs
6. beans
7. apples
8. sandwiches
9. oranges
10. peaches
11. ice cream
12. cheese

Language Power, Page 33
Listen to the conversations.

How many brothers does she have?
She has two brothers.

How many sisters does she have?
She has one sister.

Do they have a pet?
Yes, they have a bird.

How many aunts does he have?
He has three aunts.

How many cousins does he have?
He has four cousins.

Do they have a pet?
Yes, they have a hamster.

Hands on Myself, Page 35
Listen to the song. Then sing along and make up your own song.

(Verse 1)
Hands on myself, what is this here?
This is my head-thinker, my mama dear.
Head-thinker, head-thinker, nicky, nicky, nicky, noo,
That's what we learned in school.

(Verse 2)
Hands on myself, what is this here?
This is my eye-blinker, my mama dear,
Eye-blinker, head-thinker, nicky, nicky, nicky, noo,
That's what we learned in school.

(Verse 3)
Hands on myself, what is this here?
This is my nose-sniffer, my mama dear,
Nose-sniffer, eye-blinker, head-thinker, nicky, nicky, nicky, noo,
That's what we learned in school.

(Verse 4)
tongue-taster

(Verse 5)
lip-kisser

(Verse 6)
arm-holder

(Verse 7)
hand-shaker

(Verse 8)
lap-sitter

(Verse 9)
knee-bender

(Verse 10)
foot-kicker

The Squeaky Door, Pages 36 through 41
A Play from Puerto Rico
Listen and look, please.

This is a story about a boy named Sonny. Sonny loved to visit his Grandma's house in the daytime. But he didn't like to spend the night. At night, the old house made scary noises. The door to Sonny's room made the scariest noise of all. It squeaked. Sonny was really scared of that squeaky door. Well, one night, Sonny's Grandma tucked him in bed, kissed him good night, and turned off the light. But before long, that squeaky door began to squeak.

Squeak......squeak.

"Waaaah! Grandma!"

Sonny jumped right out of bed. Grandma came running.

"What to do, what to do? Sonny boy, I'll tell you what. You can sleep with the cat. Then you won't be scared, will you?"

"No, not me!"

So Grandma tucked the cat in bed with Sonny, kissed them goodnight, and turned off the light. But before long...

Squeak...squeak!

"Waaah! Grandma!"

That scared the cat, and they both jumped right out of bed.

"Meow-OW!"

Grandma came running.

"What to do, what to do? Sonny boy, I'll tell you what. You can sleep with the cat AND the dog. Then you won't be scared, will you?"

"No, not me!"

So Grandma tucked the dog in with Sonny and the cat, kissed them all goodnight, and turned off the light. But before long...

Squeak...squeak!

"Waah! Grandma!"

That scared the cat and the dog, and all three jumped out of bed.

"Meow-OW!"

"Bow-WOW!"

Grandma came running.

"What to do, what to do? Sonny boy, I'll tell you what. You can sleep with the cat, the dog, AND the rooster. Then you won't be scared, will you?"

"No, not me!"

So Grandma tucked the rooster in with Sonny, the cat, and the dog, kissed them all goodnight, and turned off the light. But before long...

Squeak....squeak!

"Waaah! Grandma!"

That scared the cat, the dog, and the rooster, and all four jumped out of bed.

"Meow-OW!"

"Bow-WOW!"

"Ki-ki-ri-KEE!"

Grandma came running.

"What to do, what to do? Sonny boy, I'll tell you what. You can sleep with the cat, the dog, the rooster, AND the horse. Then you won't be scared, will you?"

"No, not me!"

So Grandma tucked the horse in with Sonny, the cat, the dog, and the rooster, kissed them all

goodnight, and turned off the light. But before long, **THUMP, BUMP, CRASH!** Sonny's bed fell apart, and Sonny, the cat, the dog, the rooster, and the horse fell onto the floor.

"Waah! Grandma!"

"Meow-OW!"

"Bow-WOW!"

"Ki-ki-ri-KEE!"

"Neigh-HEY!"

Grandma came running. She saw Sonny, the cat, the dog, the rooster, the horse and the broken bed. She got out her tool kit and nailed the bed back together. Then she noticed a little can of oil in her tool kit. Grandma smiled. She finally knew what to do.

"Sonny boy, I'll tell you what. Let's put oil on all the hinges of that squeaky door. Then you won't be scared, will you?"

"No, not me!"

And he wasn't. Sonny fell asleep right away. So did the cat, the dog, the rooster, and the horse. And finally, so did Grandma.

Bambi and the Butterfly, Page 42

"Bambi and the Butterfly" tells how Bambi lived with his mother in the forest. Listen to Bambi's questions and find out what he learned about the world.

Bambi was a few days old. He loved to ask his mother questions.
"Who does this path belong to?" asked Bambi.
"To us deer," answered his mother.
"What are deer?" Bambi asked.
"You are a deer," his mother laughed. "I am a deer. We are both deer. Do you understand?"
"Yes, I understand. I am a little deer, and you are a big deer!"
They came to a sunny, open space.
"What is it?" asked Bambi.
"It is the meadow," answered his mother.
The meadow was full of new things.
"Look, Mother! There is a flower flying!"
"That's not a flower. That's a butterfly."
Bambi crept closer. "Please sit still," he said to the butterfly.

Over in a Meadow, Page 42
Listen to the song. Then sing along.

(Verse 1)
Over in the meadow, in the field, in the sun,
Lived an old mother sheep and her little lamb-ie
one;
"Baa," said the mother; "I baa," said the one,
So they baa-ed and were glad in the field, in the
sun.

(Verse 2)
Over in the meadow, where the river runs blue,
Live an old mother fish and her little fish-ies two;
"Swim," said the mother; "We swim," said the two,
So they swam and were glad where the river runs
blue.

(Verse 3)
Over in the meadow, in a nest in a tree,
Lived an old mother bird and her little bird-ies
three;
"Sing," said the mother; "We sing," said the three,
So they sang and were glad in a nest in a tree.

(Verse 4)
Over in the meadow, by the old barn door,
Lived an old mother mouse and her little mouse-
ies four;
"Squeak," said the mother; "We squeak," said the
four,
So they squeaked and were glad by the old barn
door.

(Verse 5)
Over in the meadow, in a big beehive,
Lived an old mother bee and her little bees five;
"Buzz," said the mother; "We buzz," said the five,
So they buzzed and were glad in a big beehive.

THEME THREE—ADVENTURES IN SPACE

Communication 1, Page 46
Listen to the conversation. Then make a conversation of your own with a friend.

Do you like comic books?
Yes, I do.
Who's your favorite hero?
Superman. Who's yours?
Batman. What's your favorite TV show?
I like the *X-Men.*
I do, too. But I like *Star Trek* the best. I'd like to
travel in space.
Me, too. Where would you go?
To Venus.
I'd go to the moon.

Amazing Facts, Page 46

The Great Wall of China is the only human-made
object that can be seen from space without a tele-
scope.

Male astronauts use shavers with tiny vacuums in
space. (Otherwise, what would happen to all
those whiskers?)

Astronauts wear underwear that is cooled by
water tubes!

Communication 1, Page 47
Listen to the conversation.

Do you want to explore the moon?

No, I don't. I'd rather explore Mars.

The Spaceship, Page 49
Listen to the poem.

I dreamed I built a spaceship
Just big enough for me;
I flew around the planets,
To see what I could see.

I set my course for Saturn,
And zoomed around its rings;
I landed on a moonbeam,
And got some rocks and things.

I said hello to Venus,
And flashed around the sun;
I floated in my spacesuit,
It was a lot of fun.

I rested in the Milky Way,
And had myself a snack;
I waved to planet Jupiter,
And then I came right back!

Communication 2, Page 50
It is the year 2050. Mrs. Stone and her son are
busy with errands.
Listen to the conversation and the words. Then
make your own conversations

Where are you going?
I'm going to the library.

What are you going to do there?
I'm going to return a book.

1. supermarket   buy groceries
2. post office   mail a package
3. mall   shop for shoes
4. bank   cash a check

The Street Beat, Page 50
Listen to the song. Then sing along.

(Verse 1)
Kids playing on the sidewalk,
It's the street beat!
All the neighbors just a-talk, talk, talk,
It's the street beat!
Cars and buses make their sound,
And the policeman he comes a-dancing around,
Everybody just a-walking downtown,
It's the street beat! The *street beat!*

(Chorus)
And it's the street beat; Yes, it's the street beat,
Oh, it's the street beat; And it's the street beat.
The street beat!

(Verse 2)
Playing ball in the alleyway, oh, it's the street
beat!
The sirens ringing all night and day, it's the street
beat!
the song playing on the radio,
And the crowds of people just a-go-go-go,
If you've got the time come on and join the show,
'Cause it's the street beat!

(Chorus)

(Bridge)
Now, street beat makes you feel all right,
Feel it every day, feel it in the night;
Street beat is all around,
You can feel it every day in the big, city sound.

(Verse 3)
All the boys try to act so cool, it's the street beat!
Oh, when the girls come a-strutting out of school,
it's the street beat!
Hanging out at the corner store,
And the grocery man, he comes a-bopping
through the door,
Everybody wanting more, more, more,
'Cause it's the street beat!
(Chorus)

Communication 2, Page 51
Listen to the conversation and the words in the
Data Bank. Then make new conversations of your
own.

May I help you?
Yes, how much is this action figure?
It's $4.99.
And how much is this game about space travel?

It's on sale. It's only $8.50.
Here's a twenty dollar bill.
Thank you. And here's the change.

Data Bank

a penny	one cent
a nickel	five cents
a dime	ten cents
a quarter	twenty-five cents

a dollar bill
a five dollar bill
a ten dollar bill

Check This Out! Page 52
Listen and look, please.

Can You Hear Me?

There is no sound on the moon. The moon has no
air, and air carries sound waves. So don't wander
too far from your spaceship and get lost. No one
will hear you when you call for help!

Have you ever wished on a star at night?

Did you know that you can also wish on a star
during the day? That's because the sun is really a
star!

The sun is the brightest star you see because it is
the star nearest the earth.

Just for Laughs

Where do astronauts park their spaceships? At
parking meteors!

Amazing Facts, Page 52
Listen and look, please.

Astronauts can "grow" up to 2 inches when they
travel in space. When they come back to Earth,
they return to their normal height. What makes
them shrink? Gravity!

Stars look white to us, but they're not! The hottest
stars are really blue, and the coolest stars are
really red!

Check This Out! Page 53
Listen and look, please.

UFO Alert!

An airplane pilot in Washington state looked up in
surprise on June 24, 1947. He saw strange-looking
things in the sky. He said they were moving like
saucers skipping over the water. That's why we
call UFOs "flying saucers"!

Ring Around Saturn

Thousands of rings orbit Saturn. They might be made of dust and rocks or pieces of a moon that broke apart. Some chunks are as small as a button—and some are bigger than a house!

A Big Hit!

A meteor is a chunk of rock flying through space. When a meteor hits the earth, it's called a meteorite. A huge meteorite hit the earth and exploded about 20 to 40 thousand years ago. Where did it land? Near what is now Winslow, Arizona. It blasted a hole, called a crater, about 1.2 kilometers wide and 170 meters deep.

Language Power, Page 54
Listen to the conversation. Then make your own conversations.

What were you doing on the moon?
I was driving a moon buggy.

1. driving a moon buggy
2. growing plants
3. playing basketball
4. collecting rocks
5. checking the stars
6. repairing a rocket
7. building a space station

Language Power, Page 55
Listen and look, please.

Back on Earth, help these kids find their belongings.

I am looking for my hat.
You are looking for your dog.
He is looking for his bat.
She is looking for her skate.

It is looking for its bone.
We are looking for our shoes.
You are looking for your socks.
They are looking for their sweaters.

Tip Top Adventures, Pages 58 and 59
Listen and look, please.

Tip and Top discovered a planet covered with water.
They put their spaceship in orbit just above the water.
They checked out their submarine.
Splash! They dove into the water.
They saw strange fish and plants.

Wow! Look at that one!
Suddenly, Top saw a huge hairy space octopus.
EEeek!
It lifted the sub with its eight arms.
Top pushed a button. Eight boxing gloves knocked the octopus out.
Tip pushed another button. The sub went on sonic power.
The octopus chased them through the water.
Top headed for the surface. Pop! The sub flashed into the air.
Hurry! Here comes the spaceship!
Tip grabbed onto the ladder. Top grabbed onto Tip. It was another close call.

More Tip Top Adventures, Pages 60 and 61
Listen and look, please.

Tip and Top arrived at a new planet. It was covered by ice and snow.
It glistened like a huge snowball in space.
Tip and Top dressed in their arctic suits.
They slid down the ladder and put on their space skis.
Icicles froze on Top's nose.
Tip discovered huge footprints in the snow.
They followed the footprints to a big hill of snow.
Suddenly the snow moved!
Uh-oh!
The giant beast roared.
Tip and Top headed for the ship.
Top slipped and fell off his skis. He jumped onto Tip's back.
They reached the ladder just in time. Top slammed the hatch shut, and they blasted off.

Mae Jemison, Astronaut, Page 62

Mae Jemison was the first black woman astronaut. Listen to the story to find out about her amazing life and her adventures in space.

Imagine growing up with a dream—a dream to be an astronaut. Mae Jemison had that dream, and she made it come true. As a child growing up in Chicago, she would look up at the stars and wonder what was up there. She believed she would travel into space some day, but she didn't know how.

Mae got a good education. Her teachers helped her read about the subjects she was interested in, and her parents encouraged her, too. She studied hard. She spent many hours in science museums.

When she was older, Mae studied medicine. In fact, before she was an astronaut, she was a doctor! While she was studying to be a doctor, she also played football and worked with dancers in the theater. Mae was good at many things.

Mae joined the Peace Corps. She was a doctor in West Africa. She especially liked seeing how people live in different places.

But Mae never stopped wanting to be an astronaut. In 1985, she applied to the NASA space program.

THEME FOUR — ACROSS THE USA

Communication 1, Page 66
Listen to the conversation. Then make a conversation of your own with a friend.

Where were you born?
I was born in Chicago.
When did you move here?
When I was six.
What's your address now?
It's 416 Green St.
Los Angeles, California.
What's your phone number?
My phone number is 465-2139.
And the area code?
It's 310.

Amazing Facts, Page 66

Americans use more than two billion pencils a year.

California condors can fly more than 10 miles without flapping their wings.

Temperatures in the deserts of the Southwest drop as much as 80 degrees Fahrenheit at night.

Communication 1, Page 67
Listen to the conversation. Then make new conversations of your own.

Guess which way I'm crossing the U.S.A!
Is it by bus?
No, it isn't. Guess again!

This Land Is Your Land, Page 69
Listen to the song. Then sing along.

This land is your land,
This land is my land,
From California
To the New York island

From the redwood forest
To the Gulf Stream waters;
This land was made for you and me.

As I was walking
That ribbon of highway
I saw above me
That endless skyway
I saw below me,
That golden valley,
This land was made for you and me.
This land is your land (etc.)

When the sun was shining
And I was strolling
And the wheat field waving
And the dust clouds rolling
As the fog was lifting
A voice was chanting
This land was made for you and me.

This land is your land (etc.)

Communication 2, Page 70
Listen and look, please. Then make new conversations of your own.

1. She's a doctor.
   She helps sick people.
2. He's a chef.
   He cooks food.
3. He's a mail carrier.
   He delivers the mail.
4. She's a farmer.
   She grows corn.
5. She's a writer.
   She writes books.
6. He's a truck driver.
   He drives a truck.

   What is her job?
   She's a doctor.
   What does she do?
   She helps sick people.

Communication 2, Page 71
Listen and look, please. Then make new conversations of your own.

1. He works in a restaurant.
   After work, he likes to play hockey.
   He has his skates and a helmet.

2. She works in a bank.
   After work, she likes to jog.
   She has her running shoes and a towel.

3. He works in a factory.
   After work, he likes to play baseball.
   He has his glove and a baseball.

4. She works in a gas station.
   After work, she likes to dance.
   She has her tapes and a tape recorder.

Does he work in a grocery store?
No he doesn't.
Where does he work?
He works in a restaurant.

The Workers Song, Page 71
Listen to the song. Then sing along.

(1st Verse)
Well, I'm a doctor,
I work all day;
I help the sick,
I work all day.

Well, she's a doctor,
She works all day;
She helps the sick,
She works all day.

(Chorus)
Work, work,
Work all day,
We do our work,
And then we play.
(Repeat)

Well, I'm a chef,
I work all day
I cook the food,
I work all day (etc.)

(Chorus)

Well, I'm a mail carrier,
I work all day;
I deliver the mail,
I work all day. (etc.)

(Chorus repeated)

Check This Out! Page 72

Houses
Listen and look please.

There are houses
Made of wood,
And houses made of sticks;
There are houses
Made of mud,

And houses made of bricks.

There are houses
That are high,
And houses that are low;
There are houses
That are single,
And houses in a row.

There are houses
In the east,
And houses in the west;
There are houses
All around me—
But my house is the best!

Where do little American cows go to eat?
To the calf-eteria!

Amazing Facts, Page 72
Listen and look, please.

Most Americans eat about 40 tons of food in their lifetime!

In the U.S.A., people own over 50 millions dogs and 58 millions cats!

Check This Out! Page 73
Listen and look, please.

Truckers and Students Are Pen Pals!

Gary King is a professional truck driver from Elkhorn, Wisconsin. He is the pen pal of a fourth grade class in Williams Bay, Wisconsin.

Writing to each other is lots of fun for both Gary and the kids. So Gary organized a "Trucker Buddy" program for the whole country! This pen pal program lets students take a real-life look at the whole U.S.A. Gary says, "We tell our pen pals about places they may never get to visit themselves."

A teacher from Lake Geneva thinks the program is great. She says, "Our Trucker Buddy sends postcards, short stories, and photographs from all over the nation. The kids love the program."

Want to join, too? Call 1-800-MY BUDDY, or write Trucker Buddy, P.O. Box 1020, Elkhorn, WI 53121

Mount Rushmore

This is Mount Rushmore. It's in the Black Hills of South Dakota.

Four sculptures are carved in stone on the side of the mountain. The men are four famous presidents of the United States. Do you know their names?

America the Beautiful, Page 73
Listen to the song. Then sing along.

(Verse 1)
Oh beautiful, for spacious skies,
For amber waves of grain,
For purple mountain majesties,
Above the fruited plain!
America, America, God shed his grace on thee,
And crown thy good with brotherhood,
From sea to shining sea.

(Verse 2)
Oh beautiful for pilgrim feet,
Whose stern impassioned stress,
A thoroughfare for freedom beat,
Across the wilderness!
America, America, God mend thine every flaw,
Confirm thy soul in self control,
Thy liberty in law.

(Verse 3)
Oh beautiful for heroes proved,
In liberating strife,
Who more than self their country loved,
And mercy more than life!
American, America, God shed his grace on thee,
And crown thy good with brotherhood,
From sea to shining sea.

Language Power, Page 74
Listen and look, please.

Ben is late. He brushes his teeth and washes his face in a hurry. He dresses quickly. He rushes to the bus stop. He misses the bus. He chases the bus down the street. He catches the bus at the next stop. He dashes into the office, but the office is empty! Oh no! It's Saturday! Poor Ben. He wishes he was back in bed.

Does he get up early?
No, he doesn't. He gets up late.

Now make new conversations of your own.

Language Power, Page 75
Listen and look, please.

I belong to a Pen Pal Club. It's lots of fun. My friends and I write to kids in other countries. They write back to us. We save the stamps from their letters. We collect them in a book. We go to the post office to buy special stamps for *our* let-

ters. We like the stamps we get from our pals overseas.

Here are some stamps from our book. Do you know where they are from?

Do they belong to a Music Club?
No, they don't. They belong to a Pen Pal Club

Now make new conversations of your own.

My Home, A story about Manuel Araiza, Excerpted from *Voices from the Fields* Interviews and Photographs by S. Beth Atkin, Pages 78-81

I used to live in Agua Calientes, Mexico. When I was five, my whole family came here, over the hills, across the border.

We first lived in a trailer with two rooms. Then we moved to this house. They are both smaller than our house in Mexico. That house was pink and it had two floors. Our house here is one room with a kitchen. I liked the house in Mexico better because it had bunk beds. Now I sleep with my brother, Juan, and my father in one bed. My mother and my sisters, Bertha, Fatima, Christina, and Carla sleep in the other one.

My parents work hard in the lettuce, strawberries, raspberries, and flowers. Juan and Fatima go also, but Bertha stays home to watch my little sisters. We help my parents in the fields. I like to arrange the strawberries in the box after I pick them.

I'd like to live in a bigger house with gardens in back. I'd like that when I get older. I want to work in the fields and pick raspberries and take them in a truck to the store and drive my truck all over America.

The Amazing Anasazi, Page 82
Listen and look, please.

The Anasazi Indians made their home in the Southwest. In this story, you will hear about the way they lived long ago.

The Anasazi Indians lived long ago in the Southwest. Look at a map. Find the place where New Mexico, Colorado, Arizona, and Utah meet. Then find Mesa Verde, Colorado. Now listen and try to imagine what life was like for the Anasazi people in the year 1250.

The Anasazi live in an amazing kind of "apartment house." They built this house on the side of a steep mountain. The mountain rose more than 700 feet in the air. That's about how tall a 70-story building is! In this amazing cliff house, there were more than 200 rooms, or apartments.

When the Anasazi built the house, they dug little toe holds in the side for their feet. These holes helped people climb up and down the steep sides. Imagine how the Anasazi must have looked on the side of the tall house — like spiders on a wall!

The Anasazi dug special rooms in the ground at the bottom of the house. The rooms were called *kivas*, which means *round rooms*. Here, the men gathered to make laws for all the people. They performed religious ceremonies in the kiva, too.

THEME 5—ANIMALS WILD AND TAME

Communication 1, Page 86
Listen the conversation. Then make a conversation of your own with a friend.

What's your favorite wild animal?
Lions.
What's your favorite pet?
My dog.
What's his name?
Her name is Lady.
What's your favorite animal movie?
The Lion King.
Is there a good book about animals?
Sure. There are lots.
Well, name one!
Charlotte's Web.

Amazing Facts, Page 86

Caterpillars have more than 2,000 muscles in their bodies.

A gorilla's favorite food is bananas. Second favorite food? Celery!

The ostrich is the world's largest bird. Its eggs can weigh three pounds—or more!

Communication 1, Page 87
Listen and look, please.

Yesterday, I rushed home from school. I kissed my mom hello, and opened the refrigerator door. "What's your hurry?" my mom asked.

"Tomorrow is the Pet Show, remember? I have to get Flash ready," I answered. Flash was waiting for me in the back yard. I washed him from head to tail. I dried him off and brushed him. I trimmed the hair around his eyes, and tied a beautiful ribbon around his neck. Flash looked great!

Did she rush home from the library?
No, she didn't. She rushed home from school.

Now make new conversations of your own.

Do The Dog Walk, Page 89
Listen and look, please. Then sing along and make up your own song.

When I was a little puppy,
I'd play and play and play;
Now I am a big, big, dog,
And this is what I say.
Arf, arf, do the dog talk!
Arf, arf, do the dog walk!
Arf, arf, do the dog talk!
Arf, arf, do the dog walk!

When I was a little kitten,
I'd play and play and play;
Now I am a big, big cat,
And this is what I say.
Meow, do the cat talk!
Meow, do the cat walk!
Meow, do the cat talk!
Meow, do the cat walk!

When I was a little duckling,
I'd play and play and play;
Now I am a big, big duck,
And this is what I say.
Quack, quack, do the duck talk!
Quack, quack, do the duck walk!
Quack, quack, do the duck talk!
Quack, quack, do the duck walk!

When I was a little tadpole,
I'd play and play and play;
Now I am a big, big frog,
And this is what I say.
Ribbet, ribbet, do the frog talk!
Ribbet, ribbet, do the frog walk!
Ribbet, ribbet, do the frog talk!
Ribbet, ribbet, do the frog walk!

Now, let's do them all together. (spoken)
Ready...here we go.
Arf, Arf, do the dog talk!
Meow, do the cat walk!

Quack, quack, do the duck talk!
Ribbet, ribbet, do the frog walk!

Communication 2, Page 90
Listen and look, please.

I dreamed I was an animal trainer in the circus. I lived a great life. I traveled across the country. I stayed in the best hotels. My fans loved me and my animals. They cheered when the lions danced. They clapped when the tigers jumped through hoops. They whistled and stamped their feet when the act was over. It was a great dream. I wonder what being an animal trainer is really like.

Did he dream he was a doctor?
No, he didn't.
What did he dream?
He dreamed he was an animal trainer.

Now make new conversations of your own.

Communication 2, Page 91
Listen to the conversation and the words in the Data Bank. Then make new conversations of your own.

Can I help you?
Yes, please. I want to borrow a book.

Do you have a library card?
Yes, I do.

What are you interested in?
Stories about animals.

Here are some good books.
How many can I take out?

You can check out three.
I want these, please.

Here you are.
Thank you. See you next week!

Data Bank

a CD	a cassette tape
a videotape	a painting
a magazine	

Check This Out!, Page 92
Listen and look, please.

The Year of the Dragon—2000!
The Chinese name the years as well as days and months. Each year is named for an animal:

Rat	Ox	Tiger	Hare	Dragon	Snake
1996	1997	1998	1999	2000	2001
2008	2009	2010	2011	2012	2013
Horse	Sheep	Monkey	Rooster	Dog	Pig
2002	2003	2004	2005	2006	2007
2014	2015	2016	2017	2018	2019

Don't Lose That Grip!
Have you ever wondered how birds sleep? They sit up on branches. Birds have special leg muscles that help them hold on. Nothing can knock them off—not even a strong wind!

Amazing Facts, Page 92
Listen and look, please.

A bug called a cicada hears with its stomach.

A water beetle hears with its chest.

Crickets and grasshoppers hear with their front legs.

Check This Out! Page 93
Listen and look, please.

Way Down South
Way down South where bananas grow,
A grasshopper stepped on an elephant's toe.
The elephant said, with tears in his eyes,
"Pick on somebody your own size."

What is smarter than a talking horse?
A Spelling Bee!

Animal Talk
In English, dogs say "arf-arf." But does a dog bark the same way in other languages? Here's how people around the world think dogs sound when they bark.

dog:	Chinese: wang-wang	Italian: bow-bow
	Japanese: wan-wan	Korean: mong-mong
mouse:	English: squeak-squeak	Spanish: cui-cui
	Japanese: chu-chu	Chinese: chee-chee
bird:	English: tweet-tweet	Chinese: ji-ji
	Russian: chic-chiric	Japanese: peechiko-pachiko

Language Power, Page 94
Listen and look, please.

Mary traveled to Los Angeles to visit her grandmother. Mary's seeing-eye dog named Spot traveled with her. They waited for the bus at the bus station. The driver loaded Mary's bags on the bus.

He collected her ticket and patted Spot on the head.

"You can board first, and sit in the row behind me," the driver said.

So Spot and Mary boarded the bus and waited for the rest of the passengers to get on. The driver counted the passengers and the tickets. Then he started up the bus and said, "Here we go!"

Four hours later, Mary and Spot were in Los Angeles.

"Mary, Mary," shouted her grandmother.

"We're right here, and so glad to see you."

Did she travel to Chicago?
No, she didn't. She traveled to Los Angeles.

Pet Show, Page 95
Listen and look, please.

This is my dog.
That is your cat.

This is his goat.
That is her parrot.

These are our gerbils.

Those are their turtles.

Koko's Computer, Pages 98 through 101
Listen and look, please.

Koko the gorilla was born in a zoo. When she was very young, she moved to The Gorilla Foundation in Woodside, California. Dr. Francine Patterson is Koko's trainer and teacher. Dr. Patterson taught Koko ASL—American Sign Language. ASL uses movements of the hands, face, and body to express words. Koko learned more than a thousand words in ASL.

When Koko was a baby, her favorite story was "The Three Little Kittens." The three kittens had lost their mittens, and their mother was mad. Koko understood. She signed, "mad."

Now Koko is all grown up She has her own computer! It has a voice and a special screen with pictures. Koko plays games and answers questions from her trainer. Dr. Patterson asks, "Where's the orange?" Koko touches the icon—the symbol for orange—on the computer screen. The word appears in the box at the top. A computer voice says the word. Koko can make sentences of her

own. What does the sentence in the box say? Can you correct Koko's sentence?

What does Koko do when she's not working on her computer? She likes to run and climb and swing in her play yard with two other gorillas. She also loves to eat—seven times a day! Her favorite foods are apples, nuts, and corn. If you want to learn more about Koko, your teacher has her address!

The King of the Beasts, Page 102
Lions live together in family groups. Listen to more facts about these big cats.

Lions, like gorillas, live in family groups. A group of lions is called a pride. A pride can be quite small, or quite large. It can have as few as four lions, or as many as forty. One full-grown male is the head of the pride. But he doesn't really do much. All the hunting is done by the females. They hunt alone and in teams.

A lion can run very fast for a short period of time. It can reach speeds of 60 to 70 miles an hour. A lion is also a good jumper. It can leap 40 feet in a single bound. Lions are the only members of the cat family that roar.

THEME 6 — CHANGING SEASONS

Communication 1, Page 106
Listen to the conversation. Then make a conversation of your own with a friend.

What's your favorite season?
My favorite season is winter.
Why?
I like cold, snowy weather.
What do you do in the winter?
I go sledding and ice skating.
My favorite season is summer.
What do you do in the summer?
I go swimming and fishing.

Amazing Facts, Page 106
Listen and look, please.

Skywriters have to be able to read upside down and backwards. A single, mile-high letter requires 15 minutes of fancy flying.

James Pimpton invented the first steerable roller skate in 1863.

The world's record for the most kites attached to a single line: 11,284!

Communication 1, Page 107
Listen and look, please.

Spring   Summer   Fall   Winter

What does she have to do in the spring?
She has to dig.
What do they have to do in the spring?
They have to dig and plant.

Dreams, by Langston Hughes, Page 109
Listen and look, please.

Hold fast to dreams
For if dreams die
Life is a broken-winged bird
That cannot fly.

Hold fast to dreams
For when dreams go
Life is a barren field
Frozen with snow.

In a Child's Heart, Page 109
Listen to the song. Then sing along.

(Intro)
I can feel it, I can see it,
I can feel it, I can dream it.

(Verse 1)
I can feel, I can feel the sun a-rising,
I can see, I can see it in the sky;
I can feel, I can feel a new horizon,
I can dream, I can dream that I can fly!

(Chorus)
And I know, it will be forever,
I know it from the start,
And I know, it's a lasting treasure,
When I look in a child's heart.

(Verse 2)
(*I can feel) I can feel, I can feel a light a-glowing,
(*I can see) I can see, I can see it in your eyes,
(*I can feel) I can feel, I can feel that love is growing,
(*I can dream) I can dream, I can dream it in my mind.

(Second Chorus)
And I know, (*And I know) it will be forever,
I know, (*I know) it from the start,
* know, (*And I know) it's a lasting treasure
When I look in a child's heart.

(Instrumental Music)
I can feel it, I can see it,
I can feel it, I can dream it.

(Repeat second chorus with echoes, then repeat both verses.)

Communication 2, Page 110
Listen and look, please.
Here's what Danny did on a sunny, summer day.

1. When did he get up?
   He got up at nine.

2. What did he eat?
   He ate some eggs.

3. What did he drink?
   He drank some juice.

4. Where did he go?
   He went to the river.

5. What did he ride?
   He rode a motorcycle.

6. What did he catch?
   He caught a fish.

Communication 2, Page 111
Listen to the conversation and the words in the Data Bank. Then make new conversations of your own.

What's the weather like?
It's very cold and snowy.

What's the weather forecast for tomorrow?
It's going to be cloudy and rainy

How's the weather?
It's hot and sunny.

What's the weather like?
It's cool and windy.

Data Bank

cold	snowy	cloudy	rainy
hot	sunny	cool	windy

Check This Out! Page 112
Listen and look, please.

Where is one of the sunniest places in the world?

The eastern Sahara Desert in North Africa. The sun shines there almost eleven hours a day—that's more than 4,000 hours of sunshine a year!

Where can you hear the most thunder?

In the Tropics. More than 3,000 thunderstorms happen there every night. Because of so much rain, the Tropics are the wettest region of the world, too.

Victor was a weatherman. He worked for WXYZ, a television station in Alaska. Unfortunately, Victor was the worst weatherman in the world. His forecasts were always wrong. If he said it was going to rain, it was warm and sunny all day. If he forecast a sunny weekend, it was wet and windy all Saturday and Sunday. The local newspaper reported that Victor had been wrong 360 days out of 365. The television company fired him. Victor moved to California where he got a job with a new TV station. "Why did you leave Alaska?" they asked. "The climate did not agree with me," answered Victor.

Amazing Facts, Page 112

The strongest gust of wind ever recorded blew across the top of Mt. Washington in New Hampshire in 1934—at 231 miles an hour!

The Komodo dragon is the world's largest lizard. It can stretch out the length of a compact car!

Check This Out! Page 113
Listen and look, please.

You'd be freezing if you were at either of the two poles.

They're the coldest places in the world. Antarctica surrounds the South Pole, and Greenland and Siberia are around the North Pole.

Here's a list of the snowiest cities in the U.S.

How does your town or city compare with these?

114.9 inches	Sault St. Marie, Michigan
99.9 inches	Juneau, Alaska
92.3 inches	Buffalo, New York
77.9 inches	Burlington, Vermont
71.5 inches	Portland, Maine
65.5 inches	Albany, New York
64.3 inches	Concord, New Hampshire
60.3 inches	Denver, Colorado

April Showers

Sea gull, sea gull, sitting on sand.
It's never good weather when you're on land.

Did you know that birds don't fly out to sea when bad weather is near? So, if you see lots of sea gulls sitting on the beach, watch out for a storm!

Language Power, Page 114
Listen and look, please.

In the spring, they have to work. She has to dig up the ground. He has to plant the seeds.

In the summer, they have to work. She has to pull up the weeds. He has to water the plants.

In the fall, they have to work. She has to rake the leaves. He has to sweep the walk.

In the winter. She has to scrape off the car. He has to shovel the walk.

After they work, they enjoy their yard. What do you think they do?

White Coral Bells, Page 114
Listen to the song and sing along.

(1st Verse)
White coral bells upon a slender stalk,
Lilies of the valley by my garden walk.

(2nd Verse)
Oh, don't you wish that you could hear them ring,
That will happen only when the fairies sing.

Language Power, Page 115
Listen to the conversation and the words. Then make new conversations of your own.

Did you play after school yesterday?

No, I didn't. I had to study.

1. go to the dentist
2. deliver papers
3. practice my piano lessons
4. watch my baby sister
5. clean my room
6. go shopping

The Grateful Statues, Pages 118 through 123
Look and listen, please.

Long ago in Japan, a poor man and his wife lived in a small village. She made straw hats. Her husband sold the hats by the roadside.

One day the man said, "It's the last day of the year. We must make some rice cakes. We must celebrate the New Year tomorrow."

"But we have no rice," said the wife. "And we have no money to buy rice. What shall we do?"

He felt very sad. He and his wife could not celebrate the New Year without rice cakes. Without rice cakes, the New Year would be filled with bad fortune.

"I will sell these five hats," said the man.

"But it is so cold outside," said the woman. "Don't go."

But the man went out to try to sell the hats. It was very cold. No one was out on the road. Everybody was home, making rice cakes. It started to snow. The old man decided to return home.

He came to six statues. They were statues of Jizo, the protector of children. The man thought, "The statues must be cold, even though they are made of stone."

He gave each statue a hat. He gave the sixth statue his own hat. The man was almost frozen when he got home.

He told his wife the bad news. "No one was out on the road. I gave the hats to the statues of Jizo. I gave away my hat, too."

"Don't feel so sad," his wife said. "Let's just go to bed. At least we can keep warm there."

While the cold couple slept, something magical happened. A song floated out of the woods.

> A kind, good man,
> Poor and old,
> Gave us hats to save us
> From the cold.
>
> That kindness we
> Will now repay,
> And give him rice cakes
> On New Year's Day.

What a surprise the old couple had in the morning!

Outside their door, they found two huge rice cakes. They were the freshest, richest rice cakes they had ever seen. Now they could celebrate the New Year. And the year would be filled with happiness and good fortune.

And in the distance, you could see six statues. They were walking back to the snowy woods, protected by their straw hats.

Why the Sky Is Far Away, Page 124

This folktale from Africa tells how the sky was once close to the earth. You will find out why the sky is now far away.

Long ago, the sky was close to the earth. Men and women did not have to plant their own food. They didn't have to cook. When they were hungry, they just reached up and broke off a piece of the sky to eat! Sometimes the sky tasted like ripe bananas. Other times it tasted like roasted potatoes. The sky was always delicious.

People spent their time making beautiful cloth. They painted beautiful pictures and sang songs at night. The grand king Oba had a wonderful palace. His servants made beautiful shapes out of pieces of sky.

Many people in the kingdom did not use the gift of the sky wisely. When they took more than they could eat, the sky became angry. Some people threw the extra pieces into the garbage.

Early one morning, the angry sky turned dark. Black clouds hung over the land, and a great sky voice said to all the people,

"You are wasting my gift of food. Do not take more than you can eat. I don't want to see pieces of me in the garbage anymore or I will take my gift away."

The king and the people trembled with fear. King Oba said,

"Let's be careful about how much food we take."

One mother said, "I won't let my children put pieces of the sky in the garbage anymore."

For a long time, all the people were careful.

But one man named Adami wasn't careful. At festival time, he took so many delicious pieces of sky that he couldn't eat them all. He knew he must not throw them away.

He tried to give the pieces to his wife.

"Here, wife," Adami said. "You eat the rest."

Script for Skills Journal
Page 111

1. He's wearing gloves.
   Color them blue.

2. She's wearing a big hat.
   Color it green.

3. They're eating oranges.
   Color them orange.

4. My grandmother is tall and thin.
   Color her blouse red.

5. She has two uncles.
   Color their shirts blue.

STUDENT BOOK

INDEX

TOPICS

Amazing facts (throughout)
Animals 30, 86-87, 90, 92-93, 95, 96-97, 98-101, 102-103
Astronauts 62-63
Birthdays 8-9, 11
Body parts 34-35
Calendars 8, 92
Cooking 26
Community 50-51, 71
Coping with a disability 94
Cultural diversity 16-17, 26, 27, 36-41, 76-77, 78-81, 82-83, 92, 93, 116-117, 118-123, 124-125
Days of the week 7-8
Descriptions 4
Families 16-17, 24-25, 27, 30-31, 33, 36-41
Feelings 16-17
Food 26, 29, 32
Friends 4, 10-11, 16-17, 73, 75
Insects 31
Jokes 30, 52, 72, 93, 112
Money 51
Months of the year 8
Music 7
Occupations 62-63, 70-71
Personal history 2, 66, 86
Personal preferences 12, 46, 86, 106
Real-life kids 11, 73
Seasons 106-107, 114
Sharing / working together 6
Shopping 29, 51
Soccer 18-19
Space 46, 47, 48, 49, 52-53, 62-63
Time 13
Transportation 67
Weather 111, 112-113, 114

LANGUAGE ACTIVITIES
Oral Communication

Asking for / giving
    information (throughout)
    personal information 4, 5, 8, 12, 24
    preferences 12, 46-47, 86, 106
Creating conversations (throughout)
Describing a scene 67, 107
Discussing
    literature (throughout)
    point of view 78-81
    unit theme 3, 23, 45, 65, 85, 105
Expressing
    feelings 7, 74
    likes 46, 86, 106
    needs / wants / requests 29, 91
    obligations 107, 114

opinions 21, 125
ownership 55, 95
thanks 9
Identifying
    family members / relationships 16-17, 24, 33
    leisure activities 71
    occupations 70-71
    possessions 55, 71, 95
Making plans 13
Playing Amazing Facts game 22, 44, 64, 84, 104, 126
Talking about self 4, 24, 46, 66, 86, 106

LISTENING

Listening for specific information 20, 42, 62, 82, 102, 124
Listening to / discussing a story 20, 36-41, 42, 62, 78-81, 83, 102, 118-123, 124
Listening to / reciting a poem 10, 27, 49, 72, 109
Listening to a rhyme or chant 11, 93, 113
Listening to a song 7, 69, 89

READING

Developing comprehension skills (throughout)
Drawing conclusions 43, 56-57, 83, 103
Following written directions 6, 26, 48, 68, 76-77, 88, 108, 116-117
Identifying the main idea 7, 21, 43, 63, 83, 101, 103, 125
Inferring 63, 83, 103, 125
Learning language through poems 10, 27, 49, 72, 109
Predicting 3, 20-21, 23, 42-43, 45, 62, 65, 82, 85, 102, 105, 114, 124
Reading grammar in context 58-59, 60-61
Recalling details 21-22, 43-44, 63-64, 83-84, 103-104, 125-126
Recognizing rhyme, rhythm 7, 10, 27, 49, 69, 72, 89, 93
Relating information to own experience 7
Shared reading and discussion: literature 36-41, 118-123
Shared reading and discussion: non-fiction 16-17, 18-19, 78-81, 98-101
Understanding humor 30, 36-41, 52, 72, 112

WRITING

Creative writing 21, 43, 63, 125
Descriptive / narrative 43
Letter writing 16-17
Research 83, 96-97, 103
Writing away to get information about a topic 73, 101
Using poems as models for own poems 10, 27, 49, 72, 93, 109

LEARNING IN THE CONTENT AREAS
Learning Strategies / Study Skills
Activating prior knowledge 4, 20, 24, 46, 66, 86, 106
Applying logic to solve problems 6
Comparing 14-15, 35, 56, 113
Cooperating with classmates 6, 14-15, 68
Creating graphic organizers 11, 96-97, 113
Doing research 83, 96-97, 103
Interpreting a map 67
Problem solving 56-57
Summarizing 20, 42, 62, 82, 102, 124
Test-taking skills 22, 44, 64, 84, 104, 126
Using imagery 96-97, 116-117

LITERATURE
Autobiography 78-81
Classic fiction 20-21, 42-43
Fantasy 58-61
Multicultural folktales 36-41, 118-123, 124-125
Non-fiction essays 31, 78-81, 83, 103
Photo essays 18-19, 62, 98-101
Play 36-41
Poetry 10, 27, 49, 72, 109
Songs, rhymes, and chants 7, 69, 89, 93

MATH
Creating graphs/charts 11
Describing
   cost 51
   quantity 29
Interpreting graphs/charts 11, 113
Making a secret number code 6
Measuring
   ingredients 26
   weight 15
   with a ruler 14

SCIENCE
Animal life
   behavior 98-101
   lions 102-103
Experiments
   air 57
   counting heartbeats 35
   ice 56
Hands-on projects
   making an animal habitat chart 96-97
   making magnetic sailboats 68
   making a rocket launcher 48
   making a scale 15
Human body 34-35
Solar system 52-53, 54
Space travel 62-63
Temperature 56-57

Using graphic organizers 96-97
Weather 112-113

SOCIAL STUDIES
Climate 112-113
Geography 67, 69, 73, 76-77, 78-81, 92-93
Hands-on projects
   making a Chippewa dream-catcher 76-77
   making a four-seasons accordion book 116-118
   making fried bananas 26
   making a kite 108
   making a piggy bank 88
Learning about
   Anasazi Indians 82-83
   Chinese calendars 92
   Koko the Gorilla 98-101
   Meteors 53
   Mount Rushmore 73
   Stamps 75
Transportation 67

LINGUISTICS SKILLS
Structures
Adjectives
   comparatives 4
   demonstrative 95
   possessive 4, 8, 55, 66, 71
Count / non-count nouns 32
did questions 87, 90, 94, 100, 115
do-does questions 12, 33, 46-47, 74-75, 107
or questions 4, 24
Prepositions of place 5, 25, 28
Subject pronouns 28, 55, 70-71
wh- questions (throughout)

VERBS
Future with *going to* 50
Habitual present 12, 66, 70-71, 74, 106, 114-115
have to / *had to* + verb 107, 114-115
let's + verb 13
like to + verb 4, 12, 71
Modals
   can / *can't* 28, 51
   may 51
Past progressive 54, 87
Present progressive 25, 28, 32, 50, 55, 106
Simple past
   irregular 83, 87, 110
   regular 58-61, 87, 90, 94
Simple present 4, 8, 24, 70-71, 75

HOLISTIC ASSESSMENT
Listening / speaking / reading / writing / thinking
   20-21, 42-43, 62-63, 82-83, 102-103

PROCESS WRITING PORTFOLIO PROGRAM: LEVEL C SCOPE AND SEQUENCE

Scope and Sequence: Level C

● ●

THEME		WRITING PROJECT	
1	Friend to Friend	1A	Narrative: A Personal Recollection
		1B	Narrative: A Friendly Letter
2	Families Around the World	2A	Recipe: How to Make Butter
		2B	Dialogue: Play Script
3	Adventures in Space	3A	Nonfiction: Science Report
		3B	Fiction: Comic Strip Adventure Story
4	Across the USA	4A	Poetry: Song Lyrics
		4B	Essay: Autobiography
5	Animals Wild and Tame	5A	Narrative: Instructions
		5B	Poetry: Poem of Address
6	Changing Seasons	6A	Essay: Persuasion
		6B	Poetry: A Haiku Poem

PREWRITING SHEET	PROCESS WRITING SKILLS
Brainstorm: Calendar Notes	Paragraph writing: Main idea/supporting details/summary sentence
Brainstorm: What's New	Standard letter format: Greeting, date, body, closing
Observation List: Making Butter	Sequencing, writing a recipe, note-taking
Brainstorm: Who, What, Why?	Creating plot through dialogue, standard play format
Task Listening: The Solar System	Research skills, paragraph writing, note-taking,
Story Planner: Creative Thinking	Story elements: Character, setting, plot, dialogue
Creative Cloze: My Song	Writing an innovation, writing to an established rhythm
Brainstorm: Now and Then	Paragraph writing
Idea Web: Animal Essentials	Sequencing, note-taking, writing instructions
Quick Write: My Animal	Using poetic devices, writing an innovation
Chart: The Four Seasons	Writing for a specific purpose in a specific voice, paragraph writing
Brainstorm: The Five Senses	Haiku: Using a specific poetic form, writing an innovation

Level C Scope and Sequence

This chart covers skills developed in all components of this level.

	Themes					
	1	**2**	**3**	**4**	**5**	**6**
ORAL LANGUAGE						
Listening Comprehension						
Following TPR directions for tasks and sequence		•	•	•		
Following classroom directions	•	•	•	•	•	•
Listening for specific information	•	•	•	•	•	•
Listening to/discussing a story	•	•	•	•	•	•
Listening to/discussing a poem	•	•	•	•	•	•
Listening to a rhyme or chant	•	•	•	•	•	•
Listening to a song	•			•	•	
Matching spoken words, sentences, and descriptions to pictures	•	•	•	•	•	•
Understanding basic structures, expressions, and vocabulary	•	•	•	•	•	•
Understanding and responding to questions	•	•	•	•	•	•
Understanding and responding to spoken narratives	•	•	•	•	•	•
Oral Communication						
Greeting and identifying people	•					
Asking for and giving information	•	•				•
Asking for and giving directions	•					
Role-playing fixed and free dialogues	•		•		•	•
Giving personal information	•	•	•	•	•	•
Describing/discussing:						
actions, scenes				•		•
air pressure and lift						•
animals					•	
birthdays	•					
characters and setting						•
the circus					•	
climate						•
different kinds of homes		•				
dreams						•
errands			•			
exercise				•		
family relationships		•				
favorite pastimes/weekend activities	•					
food pyramid		•				
food shopping		•				
the future			•			
ice/air			•			
locations		•				
magnets				•		
metaphors						•

	Themes					
	1	2	3	4	5	6
objects	•					
occupations				•		
past actions					•	•
past ongoing actions			•			
pets					•	
plants						•
preferences	•		•			
present ongoing actions		•	•			
quantity, cost		•				
responsibilities						•
saving money					•	
seasons/seasonal activities						•
self				•		
sequence					•	•
solar system			•			
space travel			•			
stamps				•		
story events	•	•	•			
US geography				•		•
ways to communicate	•					
weather						•
Following conversational sequence		•	•	•		•
Expressing:						
feelings	•			•		
obligations						•
opinions 4				•	•	•
ownership			•		•	
personal preference			•			
thanks	•					
wants, needs, requests		•			•	
Identifying:						
baby and adult animals					•	
body parts		•				
coins			•			
days, months, year, seasons	•					•
family members/relationships	•	•				
food		•				
leisure activities				•		
locations			•			
occupations and occupational sites				•		
places in school/home/community	•	•	•			
possessions				•	•	

	Themes					
	1	2	3	4	5	6
rhyming words				•		
Making plans	•					
Talking about self	•	•	•	•	•	•
READING AND WRITING						
Reading Skills						
Following written directions	•	•	•	•	•	•
Participating in shared reading	•	•		•	•	•
Matching written language to pictures	•	•	•	•	•	•
Choral reading	•	•	•	•	•	•
Developing comprehension skills:						
recalling details from a story	•	•	•	•	•	•
identifying and describing a sequence					•	
identifying main idea	•	•	•	•	•	•
retelling a story in own words	•	•			•	
relating fiction/nonfiction to personal experience	•	•		•	•	
Developing basic sight vocabulary	•	•	•	•	•	•
Reading sentences and dialogues	•	•	•	•	•	•
Reading aloud and silently	•	•	•	•	•	•
Reading maps, charts, graphs, schedules	•					•
Reading grammar in context			•			
Scanning					•	
Understanding humor	•	•	•	•	•	•
Writing Skills						
Creative writing	•	•	•	•		•
Descriptive/narrative writing		•		•		
Process writing	•	•	•	•	•	•
Dictating and writing language experience sentences, stories	•	•	•		•	•
Writing poems	•	•	•		•	•
Creating rhymes, chants, song verses				•		
Writing letters	•					
Writing questions					•	
Writing directions					•	
Writing a postcard				•		
Writing sentences, dialogues, stories				•		•
Using charts, graphs, and calendars to record information						•
CRITICAL THINKING						
Brainstorming				•	•	•
Comparing and contrasting	•			•	•	
Classifying	•			•		
Sequencing				•		
Predicting outcomes	•	•	•	•	•	•
Inferring			•	•	•	•

	Themes 1	2	3	4	5	6
Drawing conclusions			•	•	•	•
Distinguishing real from imaginary			•			
Summarizing	•	•	•	•	•	•
Learning Strategies						
Activating prior knowledge	•	•	•	•	•	•
Applying logic to solve problems	•					
Cooperating with classmates	•			•		•
Creating graphic organizers	•				•	•
Doing research				•	•	
Interpreting a map				•		
Problem solving			•			•
Test-taking skills	•	•	•	•	•	•
Using imagery					•	•
Note-taking					•	•
LEARNING THROUGH LITERATURE						
Dramatizing and role-playing	•	•	•	•	•	•
Learning language through poems and songs	•	•	•	•		•
Discussing stories, poems, and nonfiction selections	•	•	•	•	•	•
Developing an appreciation for various forms of literature:						
nonfiction	•			•	•	
fables and tales		•				•
poems		•	•	•		•
song lyrics	•			•	•	
plays		•				
proverbs						•
comic strips			•			
Using repetition, rhyme, and rhythm	•	•	•	•	•	
LEARNING IN THE CONTENT AREAS						
Language Arts						
Learning abbreviations						•
Acquiring vocabulary	•	•	•	•	•	•
Enjoying poems and stories		•	•	•		•
Creating original poems and stories		•	•			
Spelling					•	•
Mathematics						
Adding and subtracting		•				
Counting		•	•			
Making charts/graphs	•				•	
Describing:						
Cost			•			
Quantity		•				
Interpreting graphs/charts	•					•

	Themes					
	1	**2**	**3**	**4**	**5**	**6**
Learning about money					•	
Solving word problems			•		•	
Making a secret number code	•					
Measuring:						
ingredients		•				
weight	•					
with a ruler	•					
Science						
Learning about:						
Butterflies		•				
Electromagnetic fields				•		
Weather						•
Air pressure and lift						•
Animal behavior					•	
Lions					•	
Human body		•				
Plants						•
Seeing eye dogs					•	
Solar system			•			
Space travel			•			
Temperature			•			
Experiments:						
air			•			
counting heartbeats		•				
ice			•			
hands-on projects:						
magnetizing a nail				•		
making an animal habitat chart					•	
making magnetic sailboats				•		
making a rocket launcher			•			
making a scale	•					
making a weather chart						•
using graphic organizers					•	
weather						•
Social Studies						
Planning a trip				•		
Geography				•	•	
Climate						•
Hands-on projects:						
making a Chippewa dream-catcher				•		
making a four-seasons accordion book						•
making fried bananas	•					

	Themes					
	1	2	3	4	5	6
making a kite						•
making a piggy bank					•	
Learning about:						
Anasazi Indians				•		
Chinese calendrs					•	
habitats					•	
Koko the gorilla					•	
meteors			•			
Mount rushmore				•		
occupations					•	
rivers						•
stamps				•		
transportation				•		
Music						
Creating original verses, songs	•			•	•	
Making musical instruments				•		
Singing a song	•			•	•	
Making a graph						•
Art						
Looking at landscapes				•		
Illustrating a poem/story/song		•		•		
Illustrating dreams						•
Drawing		•		•	•	•
Making a collage					•	
Making puppets					•	
Making a mural				•		•
Making kite tails						•
Making a comic strip			•			
Drama	•	•	•	•	•	•
CULTURAL AWARENESS						
Social and Life Skills						
Getting along in school	•					
Getting along in the community	•	•	•	•		
Self-awareness/self-esteem:						
valuing one's own culture/heritage		•				
introducing family customs, activities, food, etc. to classmates		•				
expressing preferences	•		•		•	•
Multicultural Awareness						
Recognizing characteristics of other cultures		•				
Respecting differences in various cultures		•				
Learning about the history and culture of the U.S. and other lands		•		•		•
Learning about the holidays and festivals of many cultures						•

	Themes					
	1	**2**	**3**	**4**	**5**	**6**
Enjoying literature from around the world						•
Appreciating multicultural art						•
LINGUISTIC SKILLS						
Structures						
wh questions	•	•	•	•	•	•
did questions					•	•
do/does questions	•	•	•	•		•
or questions	•	•				
Subject/object pronouns		•	•	•		
Count/non-count nouns		•				
Adjectives:						
comparative, superlative	•					
demonstrative					•	
possessive	•		•	•		
Prepositions of place	•	•				
Verbs						
Simple present tense	•	•		•		
Habitual present tense	•			•		•
Present progressive tense		•	•			•
Future tense with *going to*			•			
Past tense:						
regular			•		•	
irregular				•		•
Past progressive tense			•		•	
Like to + verb	•			•		
Modals:						
can/can't		•	•			
may			•			
Have to/had to + verb						•
Let's + verb	•					
ASSESSMENT						
Holistic assessment	•	•	•	•	•	•
Performance assessment:						
using anecdotal record forms	•	•	•	•	•	•
using assessment portfolios	•	•	•	•	•	•
using oral language checklists	•	•	•	•	•	•
using reading checklists	•	•	•	•	•	•
using writing checklists	•	•	•	•	•	•
Self-assessment	•	•	•	•	•	•
HOME-SCHOOL CONNECTION						
Discussing/writing about home, family, and interests	•	•	•	•	•	•
Sharing school projects with family members	•	•	•	•	•	•

A Publication of the World Language Division

Contributing Writer: Ellen J. Kisslinger

Director of Product Development: Judith Bittinger

Executive Editor: Elinor Chamas

Editorial Development: Angela Castro, Kathleen M. Smith, Karen Howse, Peggy Alper

Text and Cover Design: Taurins Design Associates

Art Direction and Production: Taurins Design Associates

Production/Manufacturing: James W. Gibbons

Permissions: Gina Herlihy, Anita Palmer

Audio Program Producers: Hallary Dworet, Bob Schneider

Audio Engineer and Editor: David Pritchard
Sonic Workshop, Toronto, Canada

Assistant Editor: Greg Corby
Sonic Workshop, Toronto, Canada

Keyboards: John Sheard

Adult Performing Artists: Cindy Cook, Gerry Mendocino, Bob Schneider,

Children: Christina Allsop, Devin Armstrong, Justin Chee, Kerry Dworet, Zachary Florence, Shannon Hunter, Shelley Pope, Erin Robertson, Alan Soberman, Erin Southall, Lauren Tweedie